10.95

The Bloodaxe Book of Modern Australian Poetry

John Tranter was born in Cooma in 1943. He attended country schools and took his BA in 1970 after attending university sporadically. He has published eight volumes of poetry (including a *Selected Poems*, 1982) and edited the controversial anthology *The New Australian Poetry* which featured some of the more experimental work of his own generation. During 1987 and 1988 he was in charge of the ABC Radio National arts program *Radio Helicon*. He lived for some years in Singapore and London and now lives in Sydney.

Philip Mead was born in Brisbane in 1953 and educated in Queensland, the UK and USA. He has been associated with poetry publishing, particularly in little magazines, since 1972. Currently, he is Poetry Editor for *Meanjin* and Lockie Lecturer in Australian writing at the University of Melbourne. He reviews poetry for various magazines and newspapers. His latest volume of poetry is *This River is in the South* (UQP, 1984).

The Bloodaxe Book
of Modern Australian Poetry

Edited by John Tranter and Philip Mead

BLOODAXE BOOKS

ISBN: 1 85224 315 5

This edition first published
in the United Kingdom in 1994 by
Bloodaxe Books Ltd,
P.O. Box 1SN,
Newcastle upon Tyne NE99 1SN.

Original edition first published in 1991 as
The Penguin Book of Modern Australian Poetry
by Penguin Books Australia Ltd,
assisted by the Literature Board
of the Australia Council.

Bloodaxe Books Ltd acknowledges
the financial assistance of Northern Arts.

Printed in Australia by
Australian Print Group, Maryborough, Victoria.

to the memory of Martin Johnston

Contents

Introduction   xxvii

KENNETH SLESSOR (1901–71)

Nuremberg   1
Last Trams   2
Fixed Ideas   3
Out of Time   4
To Myself   5
The All-night Taxi Stand   6
Up in Mabel's Room   7
Choker's Lane   8
William Street   9
Sleep   9
The Night-ride   10
South Country   11
Five Bells   11
Beach Burial   15

A. D. HOPE (b.1907)

Australia   16
Flower Poem   17
Observation Car   18
The Death of the Bird   19
Imperial Adam   20
The Return of Persephone   22
Fafnir   23
Under Sedation   24
Inscription for a War   24
Beyond Phigalia   25

WILLIAM HART-SMITH (1911–90)

Nullarbor   26

JOHN BLIGHT (b.1913)

Down from the Country   30
The Anchor   30
The Landfall   31
Death of a Whale   31
Garfish   32
Into the Ark   33
Sun   33

KENNETH MACKENZIE (1913–55)

Heat   34
The Fool   35
'The door swung open . . .'   36
Searchlights   37
Sick Men Sleeping   37
Ginger-flowers   38
The Children Go   39
Table-birds   40
from: The Hospital – Retrospections
   New Arrival   41

DAVID CAMPBELL (1915–79)

Small-town Gladys   43
Men in Green   44
Here, under Pear-trees   45
Mothers and Daughters   46
Hotel Marine   46
from: Ku-ring-gai Rock Carvings
   The Lovers   47
   Spring   47
   Spiny Ant-eaters   47
   Lizards   47
   Bora Ring   47
   Tench, 1791   47
   Hands   48
   Baiame   48

from: *Starting from Central Station*
  I Starting from Central Station   48
  IX Angina   49
The Anguish of Ants   49
The Man in the Honeysuckle   50

JUDITH WRIGHT (b.1915)

Brother and Sisters   52
Woman to Man   53
The Child   53
Camphor Laurel   54
Night After Bushfire   55
Eli, Eli   55
The Killer   56
Metho Drinker   57
The Old Prison   58
from: *The Blind Man*
  II Country Dance   58
To a Child   60
The Precipice   61
Gum-trees Stripping   62
At Cooloola   62
Pelicans   63
from: *For a Pastoral Family*
  I To my Brothers   64
  V Change   65
River Bend   65
Skins   66

JACK DAVIS (b.1917)

The First-born   67
Warru   67
Desolation   68
One Hundred and Fifty Years   69

JAMES McAULEY (1917–76)

Envoi   71
Gnostic Prelude   71
The Blue Horses   72
Dialogue   75

from: *The Hero and the Hydra*
  IV The Tomb of Heracles   76
Late Winter   76
In a Late Hour   77
Pietà   77
Legendary   78
from: *The Seven Days of Creation*
  The Seventh Day   79
The Cloak   79
Released on Parole   80
One Tuesday in Summer   81
Because   82
Keep the Season   83
Wet Day   84
World on Sunday   84
Nocturne   85
Winter Drive   85

'ERN MALLEY (1918–43)'

Dürer: Innsbruck, 1495   86
Sonnets for the Novachord   86
Sweet William   87
Boult to Marina   88
Sybilline   89
Night Piece   90
Documentary Film   90
Palinode   91
Night-piece (Alternate Version)   92
Baroque Exterior   93
Perspective Lovesong   93
Culture as Exhibit   94
Egyptian Register   95
Young Prince of Tyre   96
Colloquy with John Keats   97
  Coda   98
Petit Testament   99

ROSEMARY DOBSON (b.1920)

The Three Fates   101
Being Called For   101

OODGEROO of the tribe Noonuccal (b.1920)

We are Going   103
No More Boomerang   104
Last of his Tribe   105
Dawn Wail for the Dead   106

GWEN HARWOOD (b.1920)

Clair de Lune   107
In the Park   108
Nightfall   109
Carnal Knowledge I   110
from: Father and Child
    I Barn Owl   111
The Sea Anemones   112
Mid-channel   113
Mother Who Gave Me Life   113

DIMITRIS TSALOUMAS (b.1921)

Note   115
A Progressive Man's Indignation   115
Consolation   116
Old Friend   117
Return of an Ikon   117
Falcon Drinking   118
Autumn Supper   119
The Grudge   119

DOROTHY HEWETT (b.1923)

This Version of Love   121
You Gave Me Hyacinths First a Year Ago   122
Anniversary   123
from: Summer Solstice
    3 ('The sunset flames over the city . . .')   124

VINCENT BUCKLEY (1925–88)

Origins   126
from: Stroke
    I   ('In the faint blue light . . .')   127
    IV   ('Every clod reveals . . .')   128

V   ('Indoors and out . . .')   128
VI   ('The roofs are lit . . .')   129
VII ('At the merest handshake . . .')   130
A Man, a Woman   130
The Child is Revenant to the Man   131

FRANCIS WEBB (1925–73)

A Tip for Saturday   132
The Gunner   133
Port Phillip Night   133
Laid Off
   1 The Bureau, and Later   134
   2 Hard-luck Story   135
Towards the Land of the Composer   135
End of the Picnic   137
A Death at Winson Green   137
Hospital Night   139
from: *Around Costessy*
  from: *7. In Memoriam: Anthony Sandys, 1806–1883*
  IV Art   140
Clouds
   1 Inland   140
   2 The Town   141
   3 Airliner   141
from: *Ward Two*
   1 Pneumo-Encephalograph   142
   2 Harry   143
   3 Old Timer   144
   5 Homosexual   145
   8 Wild Honey   147

BRUCE BEAVER (b.1928)

Angels' Weather   149
from: *Letters to Live Poets*
  I   (Frank O'Hara)   150
  XIX ('I welcome the anonymity . . .')   153

from: *Odes and Days*
   Day 20   154
Déjeuner Sur l'Herbe   155
The Drummer   156
Silo Treading   157
More than 9 Lives   160

PETER PORTER (b.1929)

On This Day I Complete My Fortieth Year   161
Sex and the Over Forties   163
Affair of the Heart   163
'In the New World Happiness is Allowed'   165
The Easiest Room in Hell   166
Talking to You Afterwards   168
And No Help Came   169
What I Have Written I Have Written   170

BRUCE DAWE (b.1930)

Elegy for Drowned Children   172
The Family Man   173
Renewal Notice   173
On the Death of Ronald Ryan   174
Drifters   175
Homecoming   175
Homo Suburbiensis   176
The Copy-writer's Dream   177
Going   177
Morning Becomes Electric   178

FAY ZWICKY (b.1933)

from: *Three Songs of Love & Hate*
   1 The Stone Dolphin   180
   2 Jack Frost   181

JENNIFER STRAUSS (b.1933)

Love Notes   182

CHRIS WALLACE-CRABBE (b.1934)

The Windows   184
The Collective Invention   185
The Mental Traveller's Landfall   185
Abhorring a Vacuum   187
Nub   187
from: The Bits and Pieces
    Opener   188
from: Sonnets to the Left
    IV ('The writer depersonalises . . .')   189
And the World was Calm   190

DAVID MALOUF (b.1934)

The Judas Touch   192
Bicycle   193
For Two Children   194

RANDOLPH STOW (b.1935)

The Calenture   195
Landfall   196
The Singing Bones   197

ANTIGONE KEFALA (b.1935)

Sunday Visit   198
Industrial City   199
The Party   199
Freedom Fighter   200

TOM SHAPCOTT (b.1935)

Shadow of War, 1941   201
The Blue Paisley Shirt   202
Turning Fifty   202
Post Operative   203
The City of Home   204

JUDITH RODRIGUEZ (b.1936)

The Mahogany Ship   206
In-flight Note   207
Nu-plastik Fanfare Red   208
About this Woman: 209
Nasturtium Scanned   210

PHILIP HAMMIAL (b.1937)

Automobiles of the Asylum   211
Petit Guignol   212
Treason's Choice   212
Jane   213
Sadie   213

LES MURRAY (b.1938)

from: The Bulahdelah–Taree Holiday Song Cycle
   1 ('The people are eating . . .')   215
   2 ('It is the season . . .')   215
   6 ('Barbecue smoke is rising . . .')   216
Lament for the Country Soldiers   217
The Broad Bean Sermon   218
The Mitchells   219
from: The Sydney Highrise Variations
   3 The Flight from Manhattan   220
Equanimity   221
Louvres   223
The Drugs of War   224
The Tin Wash Dish   225
Dog Fox Field   226

MUDROOROO (b.1939)

from: The Song Cycle of Jacky
   Song Thirty-Four   228
Hide and Seek   229
Peaches and Cream   229

J. S. HARRY (b.1939)

Walking, when the Lake of the Air is Blue with Spring   231
A Shot of War   232
The Poem Films Itself   234

GEOFFREY LEHMANN (b.1940)

from: *Roses*
   I ('At night, circling . . .')   236
   VI ('There is no absolute rose . . .')   237
   IX ('The harvest moon . . .')   237
from: *Ross's Poems*
   16 ('"What's that bird . . ."')   237
   29 ('Music is unevennesses . . .')   238
   36 ('This house hasn't known . . .')   239
   57 ('Lying on the back . . .')   239
   67 ('A motor-cyclist's head . . .')   240

GEOFF PAGE (b.1940)

Road Show   242
Smalltown Memorials   242
Late Night Radio   244
The Elegist   245
Jerry's Plains, 1848   246

ANDREW TAYLOR (b.1940)

Developing a Wife   248
Clearing Away   249
Fitzroy   249
from: *Travelling to Gleis-Binario*
   X Goethe and Brentano   251

ROGER McDONALD (b.1941)

The Hollow Thesaurus   252
Incident in Transylvania   253

NIGEL ROBERTS (b.1941)

Max Factor Pink   255
The Mona Lisa Tea Towel   255
The Gulls' Flight   256.
A Nigger & Some Poofters   256

RAE DESMOND JONES (b.1941)

Shakti   258
The Front Window   259
James Dean   260

JENNIFER RANKIN (1941–79)

Old Circles   262
Forever the Snake   262
Sea-bundle   264
'A man is following me . . .'   264
Tale   265
Love Affair 36   265
Old Currawong   266

LEE CATALDI (b.1942)

It's Easy   268
We Could Have Met   269
13 November 1983   270
Advice   271

BOBBI SYKES (b.1943)

Cycle   272
One Day   273

JOHN TRANTER (b.1943)

The Moment of Waking   275
from: The Alphabet Murders
    23 ('We could point to the poem . . .')   276
Enzensberger at 'Exiles'   277
The Un-American Women   278
The Great Artist Reconsiders the Homeric Simile   279
Backyard   280

Debbie & Co.   281
Glow-boys   282
Having Completed My Fortieth Year   283
Lufthansa   285

TIM THORNE (b.1944)

Whatever Happened to Conway Twitty?   287
High Country
  1 Homecoming   288
  2 The Hut   288

ROBERT ADAMSON (b.1944)

Action Would Kill It/A Gamble   290
Passing Through Experiences   291
Sibyl   292
from: *Sonnets to be Written from Prison*
  1 ('O to be "in the news" again . . .')   292
  2 ('Once more, almost a joke . . .')   293
  3 ('Yes Your Honour . . .')   293
  6 ('We will take it seriously . . .')   294
My House   294
My Tenth Birthday   295
The Private   296
Rimbaud Having a Bath   296
The Home, The Spare Room   297
Gutting the Salmon   298
Dreaming Up Mother   298
An Elm Tree in Paddington   299

CAROLINE CADDY (b.1944)

Three-Inch Reflector   300

PETER SKRZYNECKI (b.1945)

Hunting Rabbits   302

ROBERT GRAY (b.1945)

Journey: the North Coast   304
Flames and Dangling Wire   305
The Dusk   307

JOANNE BURNS (b.1945)

revisionism   308
marble surfaces   309
reading   310
how   311

KRIS HEMENSLEY (b.1946)

Sulking in the Seventies   312
from: A Mile from Poetry
  1   (for John Thorpe)   313
  2   ('my poem's in the oven . . .')   314
  47 ('look! she said . . .')   314
  48 ('the place was famed . . .')   315

BILLY MARSHALL-STONEKING (b.1947)

Passage   316
Picture Postcard   317
On the Death of Muriel Rukeyser   318

RHYLL McMASTER (b.1947)

Clockface   320
Back Steps Lookout   321

MARTIN JOHNSTON (1947–90)

The Sea-Cucumber   322
In Memoriam   323
from: In Transit: A Sonnet Square
  6   The Café of Situations   326
  12 Drinking Sappho Brand Ouzo   326
Gorey at the Biennale   327

JOHN A. SCOTT (b.1948)

'Changing Room'   328
Plato's Dog   329
Helen Paints a Room (1984)
He Mailed the Letters Himself
  Typing the Letters   332
  Mailing the Letters   333
  Receiving the Letters   334

VICKI VIIDIKAS (b.1948)

Four Poems on a Theme
  Inside of Paradise   336
  A Trunkful of Structures   336
  It's Natural   337
  Going Down. With No Permanence   338
Future   339

ALEX SKOVRON (b.1948)

Election Eve, with Cat   340

ALAN WEARNE (b.1948)

Go on, tell me the season is over   341
from: The Nightmarkets
  from: 5 Terri   342
  from: 8 Elise   344
  from: 9 The Division of O'Dowd   345

MICHAEL DRANSFIELD (1948–73)

Epiderm   348
Portrait of the Artist as an Old Man   348
That which We Call a Rose   349
Visiting Hour (Repatriation Hospital)   350
Day at a Time   351
Endsight   352
The War of the Roses   353
Flying   353
Self-analysis   353
A Strange Bird   354
Memoirs of a Velvet Urinal   354
Minstrel   355

PAMELA BROWN (b.1948)

Leaving   356
I Remember Dexedrine. 1970   356

ANNA COUANI (b.1948)

What a Man, What a Moon   359
The Map of the World   359
The Obvious   360
The Never-dead   360

JENNIFER MAIDEN (b.1949)

Climbing   363
Taste   363
Language   365
Air   366
New   367
In the Gloaming   367
The Foundations   368
Anorexia   369
The Green Side   369

KATE JENNINGS (b.1949)

Just the Two of Us   371
Couples   371

SUSAN HAMPTON (b.1949)

Yugoslav Story   373
The Crafty Butcher   374
Women who Speak with Steak Knives   375
In Andrea's Garden   376

RICHARD KELLY TIPPING (b.1949)

Casino   377
Just after Michael's Death, the Game of Pool   377
Poet at Work   379

ALAN GOULD (b.1949)

Demolisher   380
The Observed Observer   381

LAURIE DUGGAN (b.1949)

from: *Three Found Poems*
  3. Hearts (1983)   383
from: *The Epigrams of Martial*
  I   xxxvii ('You drink from crystal . . .')   383
  III xlvii ('Range Rovers carry . . .')   384
  VIII xx ('Dransfield, who wrote . . .')   384
  X   ii ('Readers, forgive me . . .')   384
from: *The Ash Range*
  1.1 ('In a high wind . . .')   385
  5.1 ('The Ninety-Mile . . .')   387
from: *Dogs*
  South Coast Haiku   388
  Qantas Bags   388
  The Town on the Ten-Dollar Note   388

KEN BOLTON (b.1949)

Nonplussed   389

JOHN JENKINS (b.1949) and KEN BOLTON

In Ferrara   390

JOHN FORBES (b.1950)

T.V.   395
Four Heads & How to Do Them
  The Classical Head   395
  The Romantic Head   396
  The Symbolist Head   396
  The Conceptual Head   397
Love Poem   399
The Age of Plastic   400
Monkey's Pride   400
Speed, a Pastoral   402
Death, an Ode   403

PHILIP SALOM (b.1950)

Walking At Night   404
Ghazal on Signs of Love and Occupation   405

AILEEN CORPUS (b.1950)

blkfern-jungal   407

CHARLES BUCKMASTER (1951–72)

An End to Myth   408
Wilpena Pound   409
Seed   411

ANIA WALWICZ (b.1951)

Little Red Riding Hood   413
Daredevil   413
The Tattoo   414
Big Tease   414
The Abattoir   415
Wonderful   416

ROBERT HARRIS (b.1951)

The Call   419
The Ambition   420
'Literary Excellence'   420
Riding Over Belmore Park   421

PHILIP MEAD (b.1953)

There   422
Melbourne or the Bush   423
Cinema Point   424

KEVIN HART (b.1954)

The Last Day   425
The Story   426

DOROTHY PORTER (b.1954)

Lollies Noir   428
P.M.T.   429

PETER ROSE (b.1955)

Terminus   430
Anglo-Saxon Comedy   431
The Wind Debates Asian Immigration   432

S. K. KELEN (b.1956)

Rabbit Shoeshine   433
The First Circle   433
The Gods Ash Their Cigarettes   434

JUDITH BEVERIDGE (b.1956)

The Domesticity of Giraffes   435
In the Park   436
Dining Out   437

GIG RYAN (b.1956)

In the Purple Bar   438
Cruising   439
If I Had a Gun   439
Ode to My Car   441
Orbit   441
Elegy for 6 So Far   442

ANTHONY LAWRENCE (b.1957)

Robert Penn Warren's Book   444

ARCHIE WELLER (b.1957)

The Story of Frankie . . . My Man   446

LIONEL FOGARTY (b. 1958)

Remember Something Like This   449
No Grudge   451

PHILIP HODGINS (b.1959)

Death Who   453
Shooting the Dogs   454

KATE LILLEY (b.1960)

You Have to Strike Back   456
The Sewing Lesson   456

JOHN KINSELLA (b.1963)

Orpheus   458
Chess Piece Cornered   459
Sick Woman   459

Index   460

Acknowledgements   466

Introduction

This book answers the need for a widely-representative and credible anthology of modern Australian poetry, as seen from the last decade of the twentieth century. The emphasis is on enjoyment. In our experience, poets don't write poems merely to be graded, studied or analysed; they write them, above all, to create for readers the enjoyment of a complex and intense aesthetic experience. In collecting these poems, we've kept that simple fact firmly in mind.

As well as presenting a generous selection of poems, this anthology also offers a guided tour of our modern poetry from around 1930, and by implication it gives tentative answers to some important questions: where does our modern poetry really begin? Of the mass of experimental work written in the 1940s, which poems still have something important to say to us today? What was going on under the surface in the conservative 1950s? What were the really significant discoveries of the late 1960s, and what was just shifting fashion? After the impact of feminism, multicultural writing and postmodern writing and reading strategies, where are we heading as the year 2000 rolls up on the calendar?

Questions like these need to be met with an array of readable poems that can offer some tangible answers. The literary and cultural changes of the last twenty-five years have so altered the ways in which we think about poetry that previous thematic histories and formalist maps of Australian verse are now clearly inadequate. The modern period can no longer be read in any uniform or tidy way. Through its wide display of variety and difference, this collection offers a challenging view of our early modern poetry from 1930 to 1965, and reveals the quarter-century from 1965 to 1990 as a time of growing richness and diversity.

We begin with Kenneth Slessor, because it seems to us that his work best represents the emergence of modern poetry in this country. His last two books of verse were published in 1939 and 1944, and contain poems written in some cases in the early 1920s. There for the first time in Australian poetry is a voice like some of those we hear around us from day to day. It has some of the limitations of its period, but it is talking about material and metaphysical worlds which are still familiar, even though we may no longer inhabit them. The neon-lit urban streets filled with busy traffic and anonymous crowds, the mournful sounds of a city harbour at night – these are the modern landscapes of discontinuity and doubt.

Also in 1944 the figure of the hoax poet 'Ern Malley' appears on the scene – a ghostly presence designed to self-destruct and take Modernism with him into the void. Between these two contradictory urges of lyrical alienation and ironic fabrication, modern poetry sought to clear a space for itself.

What is the 'modern period' since then, and what are the kinds of poetry that are important to its development? Various critical articles and anthologies have tried to construct an answer to that question, but the diversity of poetic activity over the last quarter-century convinced us we should avoid the kind of historical approach that tries to fit all this activity into a formula. A repetitive and combative rhetoric keeps pushing to the front in much comment on modern Australian poetry: modern versus anti-modern, international versus local; closed versus open form; traditional versus postmodern techniques; accessibility versus obscurity; humanist sermonising versus verbal abstraction. These are only some examples from a series of anxiety-laden terms we came across in the (often defensive) introductions to anthologies published over the last decade or so. It seemed to us that most of the argument based on these terms had faded by now into that muted region of past controversy. For one thing, it had been effectively pushed to the side by Susan Hampton and Kate Llewellyn's *Penguin Book of Australian Women Poets* (1986).

In the critical field, Andrew Taylor's *Reading Australian Poetry*, the essays in David Brooks and Brenda Walker's *Poetry and Gender*, Livio Dobrez's *Parnassus Mad Ward* and emergent rereadings of Australian writing under theoretical headings such as 'post-colonial', 'deconstructive' and 'feminist' all urge us to rethink the way we read Australian poetry and to renegotiate the writing of its history. For all the points where we might differ with these perspectives, they offer methods of analysis and understanding for the new poetry that has emerged over the last couple of decades and for what has become, in turn, and perhaps more resiliently, a new combination of poetries. They also reminded us that there are new generations of readers as well as new generations of poets. With the growth in Australian Studies, Australian Cultural Studies and in theoretical approaches to Australian writing generally, these new readers are keen to find fresh ways of looking at poetry, and fresh ways of challenging it and responding to it. This writing also reminded us that, whatever else it may claim to be, an anthology is not just a collection of poems; it is always an act of theory and criticism.

How should we understand the complex collisions and exchanges between contending waves of poetry in the 1960s and 1970s? It isn't enough just to view them as products of the cultural revolution that Australia underwent from the mid 1960s until the Dismissal in 1975, although that was obviously an important starting point. Collections of writings like *Australian Poetry Now* (1970), the 'Preface to the Seventies' special issue of *Poetry Australia* (1970), *Applestealers* (1974), *Mother I'm Rooted* (1975), the 'New Writing in Australia' issue of *Australian Literary Studies* (1977), *The New Australian Poetry* (1979), the papers from the 'American Model' conference at Macquarie University in 1979 and Les Murray's memoir about his involvement with *Poetry Australia* magazine, for example, are important documents in the history of this time. It is now clearer how this writing was variously self-conscious about the processes of history and culture it sought to fashion. But our readings of the past keep changing. It seemed to us that modern Australian poetry needed to be looked at from a perspective that took in not only the issues of the 1960s, but those of the 1940s and the 1980s (and now the 1990s) as well.

If the modern movement has a major theme, it must be the constant questioning of older ways of looking at things. This collection questions previous canons of modern Australian poetry, sometimes sharply. In this sense, it is also a part of the easing of the grip of a previous order, a dismantling begun as early as Rodney Hall and Tom Shapcott's *New Impulses in Australian Poetry* (1968) and Tom Shapcott's *Australian Poetry Now* (1970) and *Contemporary American and Australian Poetry* (1976), and continued more recently by *The New Australian Poetry, The Penguin Book of Australian Women Poets* and Kevin Gilbert's *Inside Black Australia* (1988). Each of these books reflects a different kind of impatience with orthodoxies and with the way writing had been measured and defined by ideas of correctness and tradition. These attacks on convention, and the changes in writing and reading poetry they encouraged, grew out of a culture that was also undergoing change. In our own work here we felt we could take many of the leading directions of these anthologies for granted.

Given that an anthology is about the management of cultural space, we felt we were obliged to make room for new work. As we read and reread traditionally important poems, some of them seemed overrated in the light of later developments. And we kept coming across innovative, skilful and often risky poetic writing which had been relegated to the margins of official poetry or even to the realm of rumour. For example: the very early as well as the later poems of James McAuley, all the poems of 'Ern Malley' (the hoax figure concocted by the young poets Harold Stewart and James McAuley in 1943), the later poems of Judith Wright, poetry by Francis Webb and Kenneth Mackenzie that is repeatedly under-represented, Bruce Beaver's auto-biographical poems, Joanne Burns' and Ania Walwicz's prose-poems, the epigrams of Laurie Duggan, poems by Peter Porter that now don't seem to belong exclusively to an antipodean (British) tradition, Philip Hammial's surrealist poems, Lionel Fogarty's 'guerilla' poetry, collaborative poetry like John Jenkins and Ken Bolton's, the narratives of Archie Weller. This was just some of the diverse and literally *unruly* work we thought needed to be gathered into any live tradition.

The inclusion of all the 'Ern Malley' poems may at first appear a controversial one; the hoax poems of this collaborative persona have never before been anthologised in any substantial way. But it should become apparent how important they are, not as literary curiosities, but as an important work in their own right with an influential role in the poetic ferment of the 1940s, as James McAuley described it, and in the subsequent development of Australian poetry. Written while Roland Barthes was still in his twenties, 'Malley''s poems speak of the death of the Author in a subtle, duplicitous voice and – as McAuley himself prophesied – their enigmas and paradoxes still captivate new generations of young readers in a way that McAuley's or Harold Stewart's other work seems less able to do. 'Ern Malley''s appearance in the Paris magazine *Locus Solus* in 1961, in an issue devoted to collaborative writing, reminds us that these unsettling works of the imagination may be seen as early examples of the postmodernist technique of *bricolage*, of knocking something together from whatever materials are close to hand. Beyond their satirical purpose McAuley and Stewart were tinkering about with textual bits and pieces as part of an experiment that, as with Victor Frankenstein and Dr Jekyll, would get out of their control. The poems they fabricated from many different sources – non-'poetic' ones often – survive as radical, intriguing challenges to traditional ways of writing and reading.

The roles of gender, race and ethnicity are crucial in any act of reading. While this doesn't claim to be a feminist or a multicultural anthology, the selection from recent women's and multicultural poetic writing has a strategic place in our understanding of modernity in Australian poetry. The preponderance of poetry by men overall is largely the product of cultural and educational practices of the 1940s and the 1950s. Judith Wright was one of the few women poets to be published then whose early work occupies an important role in our reading of modern Australian poetry. Poetry by women, though, has claimed a powerful role in postmodern developments in Australian writing over the last two decades, and it does have a strong presence in this anthology. The translation of traditional Aboriginal poetry and song cycles has an important place in the scholarly and anthropological traditions of Australian writing; it has also been part of an influential exchange with white Australian poetry for fifty years. While translations of Aboriginal orature from T.G.H.Strehlow's *Songs of Central Australia* to R.M.W.Dixon and Martin Duwell's *The Honey-ant men's love song* have broadened enormously our awareness of poetic traditions in Australia, we felt an anthology such as this was perhaps not the most appropriate place for this writing. Contemporary Aboriginal poetic voices, though, are some of the most controversial and politically volatile in Australia and representing these various black poetries is important. At least since Vietnam, poetry as protest has had an important life in Australian culture. The existence of Kevin Gilbert's anthology *Inside Black Australia* meant that we needed to be aware in our selection; we didn't wish to appropriate poems from what is, understandably, a separatist poetic movement in some ways. Where we have included poets who also appear in Kevin Gilbert's collection we have tried to represent them differently, but sometimes we have overlapped with his selection.

*

The poets appear in approximate chronological order by year of birth. With some regret, we have decided against including biographical notes. They do little to amplify the poems, they quickly date, and even brief notes would have reduced the number of pages available for poetry. We hope that readers who are keen to follow up a particular writer's work will refer to the acknowledgement pages for individual titles, enquire from a good bookstore, or consult a reference guide such as the *Oxford Companion to Australian Literature*, where detailed information can be found about many of the poets included here.

In compiling this anthology we have been very fortunate in the help, suggestions and guidance that many people have given us. We'd especially like to thank Susan Ryan, who commissioned the project, and also Laurie Duggan, Martin Duwell, Jenny Lee, Jenna Mead, Jock Murphy, Nicholas Pounder, Judith Rodriguez, John Scott, Tom Shapcott, Jennifer Strauss, Lyn Tranter, Albert Tucker, Chris Wallace-Crabbe and Alan Wearne.

*

This selection is a pluralist reading of modernity and postmodernity in Australian poetry. And it is in the *reading* of the poems, rather than any claims of this introduction, that real meanings lie. These poems offer an abundance of textual pleasures; they are evidence of the power of poetic utterance both as seductive language and as disenchantment. These poems also speak of the significance of poetic writing in the formation of our selves, whether inter-personal, political or cultural.

John Tranter
Philip Mead

KENNETH SLESSOR

Nuremberg

So quiet it was in that high, sun-steeped room,
So warm and still, that sometimes with the light
Through the great windows, bright with bottle-panes,
There'd float a chime from clock-jacks out of sight,
    Clapping iron mallets on green copper gongs.

But only in blown music from the town's
Quaint horologe could Time intrude . . . you'd say
Clocks had been bolted out, the flux of years
Defied, and that high chamber sealed away
    From earthly change by some old alchemist.

And, oh, those thousand towers of Nuremberg
Flowering like leaden trees outside the panes:
Those gabled roofs with smoking cowls, and those
Encrusted spires of stone, those golden vanes
    On shining housetops paved with scarlet tiles!

And all day nine wrought-pewter manticores
Blinked from their spouting faucets, not five steps
Across the cobbled street, or, peering through
The rounds of glass, espied that sun-flushed room
    With Dürer graving at intaglios.

O happy nine, spouting your dew all day
In green-scaled rows of metal, whilst the town
Moves peacefully below in quiet joy . . .
O happy gargoyles to be gazing down
    On Albrecht Dürer and his plates of iron!

Last Trams

I

That street washed with violet
Writes like a tablet
Of living here; that pavement
Is the metal embodiment
Of living here; those terraces
Filled with dumb presences
Lobbed over mattresses,
Lusts and repentances,
Ardours and solaces,
Passions and hatreds
And love in brass bedsteads . . .
Lost now in emptiness
Deep now in darkness
Nothing but nakedness,
Rails like a ribbon
And sickness of carbon
Dying in distances.

II

Then, from the skeletons of trams,
Gazing at lighted rooms, you'll find
The black and Röntgen diagrams
Of window-plants across the blind

That print their knuckleduster sticks,
Their buds of gum, against the light
Like negatives of candlesticks
Whose wicks are lit by fluorite;

And shapes look out, or bodies pass,
Between the darkness and the flare,
Between the curtain and the glass,
Of men and women moving there.

So through the moment's needle-eye,
Like phantoms in the window-chink,
Their faces brush you as they fly,
Fixed in the shutters of a blink;

But whose they are, intent on what,
Who knows? They rattle into void,
Stars of a film without a plot,
Snippings of idiot celluloid.

Fixed Ideas

Ranks of electroplated cubes, dwindling to glitters,
Like the other pasture, the trigonometry of marble,
Death's candy-bed. Stone caked on stone,
Dry pyramids and racks of iron balls.
Life is observed, a precipitate of pellets,
Or grammarians freeze it into spar,
Their rhomboids, as for instance, the finest crystal
Fixing a snowfall under glass. Gods are laid out
In alabaster, with horny cartilage
And zinc ribs; or systems of ecstasy
Baked into bricks. There is a gallery of sculpture,
Bleached bones of heroes, Gorgon masks of bushrangers;
But the quarries are of more use than this,
Filled with the rolling of huge granite dice,
Ideas and judgments: vivisection, the Baptist Church,
Good men and bad men, polygamy, birth-control . . .

Frail tinkling rush
Water-hair streaming
Prickles and glitters
Cloudy with bristles
River of thought
Swimming the pebbles –
Undo, loosen your bubbles!

Out of Time

I

I saw Time flowing like the hundred yachts
That fly behind the daylight, foxed with air;
Or piercing, like the quince-bright, bitter slats
Of sun gone thrusting under Harbour's hair.

So Time, the wave, enfolds me in its bed,
Or Time, the bony knife, it runs me through.
'Skulker, take heart,' I thought my own heart said.
'The flood, the blade, go by – Time flows, not you!'

Vilely, continuously, stupidly,
Time takes me, drills me, drives through bone and vein,
So water bends the seaweeds in the sea,
The tide goes over, but the weeds remain.

Time, you must cry farewell, take up the track,
And leave this lovely moment at your back!

II

Time leaves the lovely moment at his back,
Eager to quench and ripen, kiss or kill;
To-morrow begs him, breathless for his lack,
Or beauty dead entreats him to be still.

His fate pursues him; he must open doors,
Or close them, for that pale and faceless host
Without a flag, whose agony implores
Birth, to be flesh, or funeral, to be ghost.

Out of all reckoning, out of dark and light,
Over the edges of dead Nows and Heres,
Blindly and softly, as a mistress might,
He keeps appointments with a million years.

I and the moment laugh, and let him go,
Leaning against his golden undertow.

III

Leaning against the golden undertow,
Backwards, I saw the birds begin to climb
With bodies hailstone-clear, and shadows flow,
Fixed in a sweet meniscus, out of Time,

Out of the torrent, like the fainter land
Lensed in a bubble's ghostly camera,
The lighted beach, the sharp and china sand,
Glitters and waters and peninsula –

The moment's world, it was; and I was part,
Fleshless and ageless, changeless and made free.
'Fool, would you leave this country?' cried my heart,
But I was taken by the suck of sea.

The gulls go down, the body dies and rots,
And Time flows past them like a hundred yachts.

To Myself

After all, you are my rather tedious hero;
It is impossible (damn it!) to avoid
Looking at you through keyholes.
But come! At least you might try to be
Even, let us say, a Graceful Zero
Or an Eminent Molecule, gorgeously employed.

Have you not played Hamlet's father in the wings
Long enough, listening to poets groan,
Seeking a false catharsis
In flesh not yours, through doors ajar
In the houses of dead kings,
In the gods' tombs, in the coffins of cracked stone?

Have you not poured yourself, thin fluid mind,
Down the dried-up canals, the powdering creeks,
Whose waters none remember
Either to praise them or condemn,
Whose fabulous cataracts none can find
Save one who has forgotten what he seeks?

Your uncle, the Great Harry, left after him
The memory of a cravat, a taste in cheese,
And a way of saying 'I am honoured.'
Such things, when men and beasts have gone,
Smell sweetly to the seraphim.
Believe me, fool, there are worse gifts than these.

The All-night Taxi Stand

Behold the brave fellow who sits in his Yellow,
   Attending a ball – or a hearse;
At midnight, like thunder, you'll hear him down under,
   Persuading his cab to reverse.
Like a king in a carriage, he'll drive to a marriage,
   Or drop you at Usher's in style.
From here to Glengariff, it's all the same tariff –
   ONE
   SHILLING
   A MILE.

From midnight to morrow, he sits in dumb sorrow,
   Expecting a constant appeal;
If you peep through your curtain, you'll see him for certain,
   Asleep with his head on the wheel.
Mysterious creatures with shadowy features
   Steal past him, and drown in the night –
Black Jacks in a flutter, and flowers of the gutter,
   They slink out of sight.

In friendly adjacence, with similar patience,
   Through blizzards and earthquakes and fogs,
Another lone toiler broods over a boiler –
   His comrade, the Count of Hot Dogs.
From twelve to four-thirty, on nights dark and dirty,
   They wink at each other a while –
One sells his regard at a
SHILLING
A YARD,

   The other
     ONE
     SHILLING
     A MILE!

Up in Mabel's Room

The stairs are dark, the steps are high –
   Too dark and high for YOU –
Where Mabel's living in the sky
   And feeding on the view;
Five stories down, a fiery hedge,
   The lights of Sydney loom,
But the stars burn on the window-ledge
   Up in Mabel's room.

A burning sword, a blazing spear,
   Go floating down the night,
And flagons of electric beer
   And alphabets of light –
The moon and stars of Choker's Lane,
   Like planets lost in fume,
They roost upon the window-pane
   Up in Mabel's room.

And you with fifty-shilling pride
   Might scorn the top-floor-back,
But, flaming on the walls outside,
   Behold a golden track!

Oh, bed and board you well may hire
    To save the weary hoof,
But not the men of dancing fire
    Up on Mabel's roof.

There Mr Neon's nebulae
    Are constantly on view,
The starlight falls entirely free,
    The moon is always blue,
The clouds are full of shining wings,
    The flowers of carbon bloom –
But you – YOU'LL never see these things
    Up in Mabel's room.

Choker's Lane

In Choker's Lane, the doors appear
    Like black and shining coffin-lids,
Whose fill of flesh, long buried here,
    Familiar visiting forbids.

But sometimes, when their bells are twirled,
    They'll show, like Hades, through the chink,
The green and watery gaslight world
    Where girls have faces white as zinc.

And sometimes thieves go smoothly past,
    Or pad by moonlight home again.
For even thieves come home at last,
    Even the thieves of Choker's Lane.

And sometimes you can feel the breath
    Of beasts decaying in their den –
The soft, unhurrying teeth of Death
    With leather jaws come tasting men.

Then sunlight comes, the tradesmen nod.
    The pavement rings with careless feet,
And Choker's Lane – how very odd! –
    Is just an ordinary street.

William Street

The red globes of light, the liquor-green,
The pulsing arrows and the running fire
Spilt on the stones, go deeper than a stream;
You find this ugly, I find it lovely.

Ghosts' trousers, like the dangle of hung men,
In pawnshop-windows, bumping knee by knee,
But none inside to suffer or condemn;
You find this ugly, I find it lovely.

Smells rich and rasping, smoke and fat and fish
And puffs of paraffin that crimp the nose,
Or grease that blesses onions with a hiss;
You find it ugly, I find it lovely.

The dips and molls, with flip and shiny gaze
(Death at their elbows, hunger at their heels)
Ranging the pavements of their pasturage;
You find it ugly, I find it lovely.

Sleep

Do you give yourself to me utterly,
  Body and no-body, flesh and no-flesh,
Not as a fugitive, blindly or bitterly,
  But as a child might, with no other wish?
Yes, utterly.

Then I shall bear you down my estuary,
Carry you and ferry you to burial mysteriously,
Take you and receive you,
Consume you, engulf you,
In the huge cave, my belly, lave you
With huger waves continually.

And you shall cling and clamber there
And slumber there, in that dumb chamber,
Beat with my blood's beat, hear my heart move
Blindly in bones that ride above you,
Delve in my flesh, dissolved and bedded,
Through viewless valves embodied so –

Till daylight, the expulsion and awakening,
　　The riving and the driving forth,
Life with remorseless forceps beckoning –
　　Pangs and betrayal of harsh birth.

The Night-ride

Gas flaring on the yellow platform; voices running up and down;
Milk-tins in cold dented silver; half-awake I stare,
Pull up the blind, blink out – all sounds are drugged;
The slow blowing of passengers asleep;
Engines yawning; water in heavy drips;
Black, sinister travellers, lumbering up the station,
One moment in the window, hooked over bags;
Hurrying, unknown faces – boxes with strange labels –
All groping clumsily to mysterious ends,
Out of the gaslight, dragged by private Fates.
Their echoes die. The dark train shakes and plunges;
Bells cry out; the night-ride starts again.
Soon I shall look out into nothing but blackness,
Pale, windy fields. The old roar and knock of the rails
Melts in dull fury. Pull down the blind. Sleep. Sleep.
Nothing but grey, rushing rivers of bush outside.
Gaslight and milk-cans. Of Rapptown I recall nothing else.

South Country

After the whey-faced anonymity
Of river-gums and scribbly-gums and bush,
After the rubbing and the hit of brush,
You come to the South Country

As if the argument of trees were done,
The doubts and quarrelling, the plots and pains,
All ended by these clear and gliding planes
Like an abrupt solution.

And over the flat earth of empty farms
The monstrous continent of air floats back
Coloured with rotting sunlight and the black,
Bruised flesh of thunderstorms:

Air arched, enormous, pounding the bony ridge,
Ditches and hutches, with a drench of light,
So huge, from such infinities of height,
You walk on the sky's beach

While even the dwindled hills are small and bare,
As if, rebellious, buried, pitiful,
Something below pushed up a knob of skull,
Feeling its way to air.

Five Bells

Time that is moved by little fidget wheels
Is not my Time, the flood that does not flow.
Between the double and the single bell
Of a ship's hour, between a round of bells
From the dark warship riding there below, ·
I have lived many lives, and this one life
Of Joe, long dead, who lives between five bells.

Deep and dissolving verticals of light
Ferry the falls of moonshine down. Five bells
Coldly rung out in a machine's voice. Night and water
Pour to one rip of darkness, the Harbour floats
In air, the Cross hangs upside-down in water.

Why do I think of you, dead man, why thieve
These profitless lodgings from the flukes of thought
Anchored in Time? You have gone from earth,
Gone even from the meaning of a name;
Yet something's there, yet something forms its lips
And hits and cries against the ports of space,
Beating their sides to make its fury heard.

Are you shouting at me, dead man, squeezing your face
In agonies of speech on speechless panes?
Cry louder, beat the windows, bawl your name!

But I hear nothing, nothing . . . only bells,
Five bells, the bumpkin calculus of Time.
Your echoes die, your voice is dowsed by Life,
There's not a mouth can fly the pygmy strait –
Nothing except the memory of some bones
Long shoved away, and sucked away, in mud;
And unimportant things you might have done,
Or once I thought you did; but you forgot,
And all have now forgotten – looks and words
And slops of beer; your coat with buttons off,
Your gaunt chin and pricked eye, and raging tales
Of Irish kings and English perfidy,
And dirtier perfidy of publicans
Groaning to God from Darlinghurst.

Five bells.

Then I saw the road, I heard the thunder
Tumble, and felt the talons of the rain
The night we came to Moorebank in slab-dark,
So dark you bore no body, had no face,
But a sheer voice that rattled out of air
(As now you'd cry if I could break the glass),
A voice that spoke beside me in the bush,
Loud for a breath or bitten off by wind,
Of Milton, melons, and the Rights of Man,
And blowing flutes, and how Tahitian girls

Are brown and angry-tongued, and Sydney girls
Are white and angry-tongued, or so you'd found.
But all I heard was words that didn't join
So Milton became melons, melons girls,
And fifty mouths, it seemed, were out that night,
And in each tree an Ear was bending down,
Or something had just run, gone behind grass,
When, blank and bone-white, like a maniac's thought,
The naphtha-flash of lightning slit the sky,
Knifing the dark with deathly photographs.
There's not so many with so poor a purse
Or fierce a need, must fare by night like that,
Five miles in darkness on a country track,
But when you do, that's what you think.

Five bells.

In Melbourne, your appetite had gone,
Your angers too; they had been leeched away
By the soft archery of summer rains
And the sponge-paws of wetness, the slow damp
That stuck the leaves of living, snailed the mind,
And showed your bones, that had been sharp with rage,
The sodden ecstasies of rectitude.
I thought of what you'd written in faint ink,
Your journal with the sawn-off lock, that stayed behind
With other things you left, all without use,
All without meaning now, except a sign
That someone had been living who now was dead:
'At Labassa. Room 6 × 8
On top of the tower; because of this, very dark
And cold in winter. Everything has been stowed
Into this room - 500 books all shapes
And colours, dealt across the floor
And over sills and on the laps of chairs;
Guns, photoes of many differant things
And differant curioes that I obtained . . .'

In Sydney, by the spent aquarium-flare
Of penny gaslight on pink wallpaper,
We argued about blowing up the world,
But you were living backward, so each night
You crept a moment closer to the breast,

And they were living, all of them, those frames
And shapes of flesh that had perplexed your youth,
And most your father, the old man gone blind,
With fingers always round a fiddle's neck,
That graveyard mason whose fair monuments
And tablets cut with dreams of piety
Rest on the bosoms of a thousand men
Staked bone by bone, in quiet astonishment
At cargoes they had never thought to bear,
These funeral-cakes of sweet and sculptured stone.

Where have you gone? The tide is over you,
The turn of midnight water's over you,
As Time is over you, and mystery,
And memory, the flood that does not flow.
You have no suburb, like those easier dead
In private berths of dissolution laid –
The tide goes over, the waves ride over you
And let their shadows down like shining hair,
But they are Water; and the sea-pinks bend
Like lilies in your teeth, but they are Weed;
And you are only part of an Idea.
I felt the wet push its black thumb-balls in,
The night you died, I felt your eardrums crack,
And the short agony, the longer dream,
The Nothing that was neither long nor short;
But I was bound, and could not go that way,
But I was blind, and could not feel your hand.
If I could find an answer, could only find
Your meaning, or could say why you were here
Who now are gone, what purpose gave you breath
Or seized it back, might I not hear your voice?

I looked out of my window in the dark
At waves with diamond quills and combs of light
That arched their mackerel-backs and smacked the sand
In the moon's drench, that straight enormous glaze,
And ships far off asleep, and Harbour-buoys

Tossing their fireballs wearily each to each,
And tried to hear your voice, but all I heard
Was a boat's whistle, and the scraping squeal
Of seabirds' voices far away, and bells,
Five bells. Five bells coldly ringing out.

Five bells.

Beach Burial

Softly and humbly to the Gulf of Arabs
The convoys of dead sailors come;
At night they sway and wander in the waters far under,
But morning rolls them in the foam.

Between the sob and clubbing of the gunfire
Someone, it seems, has time for this,
To pluck them from the shallows and bury them in burrows
And tread the sand upon their nakedness;

And each cross, the driven stake of tidewood,
Bears the last signature of men,
Written with such perplexity, with such bewildered pity,
The words choke as they begin –

'Unknown seaman' – the ghostly pencil
Wavers and fades, the purple drips,
The breath of the wet season has washed their inscriptions
As blue as drowned men's lips,

Dead seamen, gone in search of the same landfall,
Whether as enemies they fought,
Or fought with us, or neither; the sand joins them together,
Enlisted on the other front.

El Alamein

15

A. D. HOPE

Australia

A Nation of trees, drab green and desolate grey
In the field uniform of modern wars,
Darkens her hills, those endless, outstretched paws
Of Sphinx demolished or stone lion worn away.

They call her a young country, but they lie:
She is the last of lands, the emptiest,
A woman beyond her change of life, a breast
Still tender but within the womb is dry.

Without songs, architecture, history:
The emotions and superstitions of younger lands,
Her rivers of water drown among inland sands,
The river of her immense stupidity

Floods her monotonous tribes from Cairns to Perth.
In them at last the ultimate men arrive
Whose boast is not: 'we live' but 'we survive',
A type who will inhabit the dying earth.

And her five cities, like five teeming sores,
Each drains her: a vast parasite robber-state
Where second-hand Europeans pullulate
Timidly on the edge of alien shores.

Yet there are some like me turn gladly home
From the lush jungle of modern thought, to find
The Arabian desert of the human mind,
Hoping, if still from the deserts the prophets come,

Such savage and scarlet as no green hills dare
Springs in that waste, some spirit which escapes
The learned doubt, the chatter of cultured apes
Which is called civilization over there.

Flower Poem

Not these cut heads posed in a breathless room,
Their crisp flesh screaming while the cultured eye
Feeds grublike on the double martyrdom:
The insane virgins lusting as they die!
Connoisseurs breathe the rose's agony;
Between their legs the hairy flowers in bloom

Thrill at the amorous comparison.
As the professor snips the richest bud
For his lapel, his scalpel of reason
Lies on the tray; the class yawns for its food –
Only transfusion of a poem's blood
Can save them, bleeding from their civilisation –

Not this cut flower but the entire plant
Achieves its miracle from soil and wind,
Rooted in dung, dirt, dead men's bones; the scent
And glory not in themselves an end; the end:
Fresh seeding in some other dirty mind,
The ache of its mysterious event

As its frail root fractures the subsoil, licks
At the damp stone in passing, drives its life
Deeper to split the ancient bedded rocks
And penetrates the cave beneath, it curls
In horror from that roof. There in its grief
The subterranean river roars, the troll's knife
Winks on his whetstone and the grinning girls
Sit spinning the bright fibre of their sex.

Observation Car

To be put on the train and kissed and given my ticket,
Then the station slid backward, the shops and the neon lighting,
Reeling off in a drunken blur, with a whole pound note in my pocket
And the holiday packed with Perhaps. It used to be very exciting.

The present and past were enough. I did not mind having my back
To the engine. I sat like a spider and spun
Time backward out of my guts - or rather my eyes - and the track
Was a Now dwindling off to oblivion. I thought it was fun:

The telegraph poles slithered up in a sudden crescendo
As we sliced the hill and scattered its grazing sheep;
The days were a wheeling delirium that led without end to
Nights when we plunged into roaring tunnels of sleep.

But now I am tired of the train. I have learned that one tree
Is much like another, one hill the dead spit of the next
I have seen tailing off behind all the various types of country
Like a clock running down. I am bored and a little perplexed;

And weak with the effort of endless evacuation
Of the long monotonous Now, the repetitive, tidy
Officialdom of each siding, of each little station
Labelled Monday, Tuesday - and goodness! what happened to
    Friday?

And the maddening way the other passengers alter:
The schoolgirl who goes to the Ladies' comes back to her seat
A lollipop blonde who leads you on to assault her,
And you've just got her skirts round her waist and her pants round
    her feet

When you find yourself fumbling about the nightmare knees
Of a pink hippopotamus with a permanent wave
Who sends you for sandwiches and a couple of teas,
But by then she has whiskers, no teeth and one foot in the grave.

I have lost my faith that the ticket tells where we are going.
There are rumours the driver is mad - we are all being trucked
To the abattoirs somewhere - the signals are jammed and
    unknowing
We aim through the night full speed at a wrecked viaduct.

But I do not believe them. The future is rumour and drivel;
Only the past is assured. From the observation car
I stand looking back and watching the landscape shrivel,
Wondering where we are going and just where the hell we are,

Remembering how I planned to break the journey, to drive
My own car one day, to have choice in my hands and my foot upon
    power,
To see through the trumpet throat of vertiginous perspective
My urgent Now explode continually into flower,

To be the Eater of Time, a poet and not that sly
Anus of mind the historian. It was so simple and plain
To live by the sole, insatiable influx of the eye.
But something went wrong with the plan: I am still on the train.

The Death of the Bird

For every bird there is this last migration:
Once more the cooling year kindles her heart;
With a warm passage to the summer station
Love pricks the course in lights across the chart.

Year after year a speck on the map, divided
By a whole hemisphere, summons her to come;
Season after season, sure and safely guided,
Going away she is also coming home.

And being home, memory becomes a passion
With which she feeds her brood and straws her nest,
Aware of ghosts that haunt the heart's possession
And exiled love mourning within the breast.

The sands are green with a mirage of valleys;
The palm-tree casts a shadow not its own;
Down the long architrave of temple or palace
Blows a cool air from moorland scarps of stone.

And day by day the whisper of love grows stronger;
That delicate voice, more urgent with despair,
Custom and fear constraining her no longer,
Drives her at last on the waste leagues of air.

A vanishing speck in those inane dominions,
Single and frail, uncertain of her place,
Alone in the bright host of her companions,
Lost in the blue unfriendliness of space,

She feels it close now, the appointed season:
The invisible thread is broken as she flies;
Suddenly, without warning, without reason,
The guiding spark of instinct winks and dies.

Try as she will, the trackless world delivers
No way, the wilderness of light no sign,
The immense and complex map of hills and rivers
Mocks her small wisdom with its vast design.

And darkness rises from the eastern valleys,
And the winds buffet her with their hungry breath,
And the great earth, with neither grief nor malice,
Receives the tiny burden of her death.

Imperial Adam

Imperial Adam, naked in the dew,
Felt his brown flanks and found the rib was gone.
Puzzled he turned and saw where, two and two,
The mighty spoor of Jahweh marked the lawn.

Then he remembered through mysterious sleep
The surgeon fingers probing at the bone,
The voice so far away, so rich and deep:
'It is not good for him to live alone.'

Turning once more he found Man's counterpart
In tender parody breathing at his side.
He knew her at first sight, he knew by heart
Her allegory of sense unsatisfied.

The pawpaw drooped its golden breasts above
Less generous than the honey of her flesh;
The innocent sunlight showed the place of love;
The dew on its dark hairs winked crisp and fresh.

This plump gourd severed from his virile root,
She promised on the turf of Paradise
Delicious pulp of the forbidden fruit;
Sly as the snake she loosed her sinuous thighs,

And waking, smiled up at him from the grass;
Her breasts rose softly and he heard her sigh –
From all the beasts whose pleasant task it was
In Eden to increase and multiply

Adam had learned the jolly deed of kind:
He took her in his arms and there and then,
Like the clean beasts, embracing from behind,
Began in joy to found the breed of men.

Then from the spurt of seed within her broke
Her terrible and triumphant female cry,
Split upward by the sexual lightning stroke.
It was the beasts now who stood watching by:

The gravid elephant, the calving hind,
The breeding bitch, the she-ape big with young
Were the first gentle midwives of mankind;
The teeming lioness rasped her with her tongue;

The proud vicuña nuzzled her as she slept
Lax on the grass; and Adam watching too
Saw how her dumb breasts at their ripening wept,
The great pod of her belly swelled and grew,

And saw its water break, and saw, in fear,
Its quaking muscles in the act of birth,
Between her legs a pigmy face appear,
And the first murderer lay upon the earth.

The Return of Persephone

Gliding through the still air, he made no sound;
Wing-shod and deft, dropped almost at her feet,
And searched the ghostly regiments and found
The living eyes, the tremor of breath, the beat
Of blood in all that bodiless underground.

She left her majesty; she loosed the zone
Of darkness and put by the rod of dread.
Standing, she turned her back upon the throne
Where, well she knew, the Ruler of the Dead,
Lord of her body and being, sat like stone;

Stared with his ravenous eyes to see her shake
The midnight drifting from her loosened hair,
The girl once more in all her actions wake,
The blush of colour in her cheeks appear
Lost with her flowers that day beside the lake.

The summer flowers scattering, the shout,
The black manes plunging down to the black pit –
Memory or dream? She stood awhile in doubt,
Then touched the Traveller God's brown arm and met
His cool, bright glance and heard his words ring out:

'Queen of the Dead and Mistress of the Year!'
– His voice was the ripe ripple of the corn;
The touch of dew, the rush of morning air –
'Remember now the world where you were born;
The month of your return at last is here.'

And still she did not speak, but turned again
Looking for answer, for anger, for command:
The eyes of Dis were shut upon their pain;
Calm as his marble brow, the marble hand
Slept on his knee. Insuperable disdain

Foreknowing all bounds of passion, of power, of art,
Mastered but could not mask his deep despair.
Even as she turned with Hermes to depart,
Looking her last on her grim ravisher
For the first time she loved him from her heart.

Fafnir

Under the stars the great wise Worm lay dead;
But all that night the hero played his part,
Rejoiced the bride and had her maidenhead.
Having tasted for her pleasure Fafnir's heart,
She woke at day-break in the tumbled bed.

In their cool, twilight world the birds began:
She knew their speech; the doom of human kind,
Brimming its banks and babbling as it ran,
Poured through the startled channels of her mind.
In that dim light she watched the sleeping man;

Saw Brynhild waken in the ring of fire,
Saw him with Brynhild in the marriage-bed,
Saw Brynhild wandering crazed with her desire,
The quarrel by the river and Sigurd dead
And Brynhild stretched beside him on the pyre.

Watching the naked man, a wild and grim
And brutal passion kindled in her heart;
She felt no fear; she did not pity him;
But saw with joy his body torn apart,
With love, the blood spout fresh from throat and limb.

The birds talked on, the world grew bright again;
She felt her children born and perish; she knew
Beauty and terror that shape the fates of men;
Her spirit grew hard with wisdom, and withdrew
From memory, and became the dragon's den.

Fierce with desire she watched him wake and stir,
And moved to meet him as he threw her back
And crushed her with his arms and mounted her.
Then Sigurd gazing down saw in the black
Pits of her eyes the endless past recur;

Until once more he met the dragon's stare
Watching him from that dark hole in the ground;
Once more he shuddered as Fafnir left the lair,
And, from the black intestines of the mound,
Came pouring coil on coil into the air.

Under Sedation

Walk warily! Remember, sister, we are
Under sedation of habit, of hope, of lust;
The drug of custom helps us to adjust;
If it did not, how could we possibly bear
Our civilization for a single day?
Although the edges of its knives are wet,
The dripping red is easy to forget.
Your own, or someone else's? Who can say?

Just keep on putting one foot after another;
The horror is blunted, like the ecstasy.
Illusions of normal living serve us, brother,
To keep the heart conditioned not to see
What in his passionate age drove Goya wild:
That old, mad god eating his naked child.

Inscription for a War

> *'Stranger, go tell the Spartans we died
> here obedient to their commands.'*
> *Simonides of Keos*, for the Spartan Dead
> at Thermopylae

Linger not, stranger; shed no tear;
Go back to those who sent us here.

We are the young they drafted out
To wars their folly brought about.

Go tell those old men, safe in bed,
We took their orders and are dead.

Beyond Phigalia

She was a woman obsessed by an old book;
Even its footnotes were occasions of song.
One day she sent to the Oracle, saying: 'Look
Into my case: tell me if I do wrong.

'Should I divorce Pausanias, because
He is enchanted ground; because I fear
I may never return to be the woman I was,
Holding an old stone by a spring more dear?'
The Oracle answered: 'It is already too late.
Go on, go forward: it is all you can do.
She will greet you at nightfall, by a ruined gate,
The woman who waited all these years to be you.'

WILLIAM HART-SMITH

Nullarbor

Here earth and sky are reduced to an ultimate simplicity,
The earth to a completely flat circle,
An ocean-circle of red soil with flecks of white limestone,
Patches of dead brown grass and stiff dead bushes
And tuft-like clumps and knots of dwarf bushes
That look dead,
But really grip their lives tightly away from the sun,
Grip hold of their lives with little hard fists.
The leaves
Are leathery tongues with a small spittle of salt in them.
And the sky is a pure thing,
A flawless cover of glass,
An inverted glass cover upon a table.

When the train stopped I swung my legs over the side,
Jumped down from the roped truck and sat on the dry hot boards of
    the flat-top,
My feet dangling over, idly swinging, my hands behind me,
The palms taking a print from the rough wood
And the cinders and grit,
Making up my mind to take the next jump, the leap to the track,
And curiously examining a reluctance to do so . . .
Sleepers, a slope of cinders and metal, then
The desert, the miraculous, empty, utterly pure desert,
The clean desert and the clean bright wind,
The rim out there
Not abruptly ending, but broken,
An undercutting and a flowing into,
The sky running into the earth and the earth running into the sky,
Long liquid lines of sky, opaque, making inroads into the rim,
The edge of the world,

And long low islands floating . . .
Mirage.
It is the hot air rising,
The air becoming hot and beginning to tremble and throb and
    dance,
Destroys the abruptness, the clean cut-off.

And then you appeared. There you were, suddenly there in the
    desert
Beyond the train, beyond the line of waiting trucks,
As if you had suddenly appeared out of nothing,
With your black body, your brush of sun-bleached hair
And the stick stuck in your belt
Behind you, sticking out like a tail.
You were not looking at us. You were walking away from us when
    you appeared,
Walking away in a queer loping fashion
Going off at an angle with your back to us.
My legs stopped swinging and I stared at you, fascinated,
Looked into your back and wondered what it was you were after,
You, boy . . .
I saw you were a boy.
You stopped then, turned back and ran a little distance,
Then turned again and walked straight towards me,
Closer and closer, till I could see into your eyes,
Closer, without stopping; then you swung yourself up onto the flat-
    top beside me
And sat there looking out over the desert.

How long did we sit there? How long was it we sat there saying
    nothing?
Perhaps an eternity. Sat there saying nothing.
I could hear your breathing. Your body had a familiar strong smell,
An earth smell, a special earth smell;
And I thought of the leaves with the taste of brine in them,
The spicy tang of them, the gnarled old bushes,
Life bunched up in their fists.

I changed. Slowly I changed. I became a grotesque thing.
I became white-skinned, a human being with a white skin . . .
Grotesque!
A thin being with a sharp nose and a strong reek,
Huddled into myself, covered up, cowering away from life,

A distorted thing with my senses only half awake,
My eyes only half opened, my nostrils clogged with a numbing
    deadness,
My ears with a pressure on the drums,
Only partly sensitive.

It was an eternity. I know it was.

Did you break it because of me? Did you speak at last because you
    knew what was happening to me?
Did you do it to save me?
You moved,
You pointed upward with your finger at a bird, a solitary great bird
    with white wings tipped with brown,
Spiralling, making circles, great wide circles and spirals with
    motionless huge wings
High over our heads . . .
'Eaglehawk,' you said. 'Eaglehawk.'

It's funny, but you accepted me then. We used the code of stranger
    approaching stranger.
You came and sat down beyond the limits of my camp,
The camp of my personality and the small fire of my heart,
Waiting with your back to it before my thoughts sent out their
    women
With food and drink, went out and brought you in. We talked.
You asked for a cigarette. I gave you one and lit it for you.
I can see my white hands cupped against the brown skin of your
    face,
The deep ridge of brows as you bent over my hands and sucked in
    the flame; the tuft of beard on your chin.
A boy.
I remarked to myself on the rich body quality of your voice
And unconsciously deepened the tones of my own.
You talked as you smoked, the cigarette looking silly and pathetic in
    your fingers,
Held between ball of thumb and forefinger.

Then my own world broke in. It came
Out of the future, out of the future from a terrible distance,
Roared down on me and shrieked, and pounded fists on my heart.
The clash of jerked couplings shattered something in my head.
You jumped down. I heard above the noise of the soft crunch of
    your feet as they hit the ground

And you looked at me over your shoulder, then turned away,
Turned your back on me and walked away
With that queer loose-swinging lope of yours,
That straight-backed, loose-limbed walk full from the hips.
You walked away and never looked back.

I sat there as the train moved
And the ground began to slide sideways under my feet,
Sideways under my boots,
Until the blur made me giddy and sick.
And when I looked up you had gone.
I looked back, but you had gone.
The desert was flowing away to the left
Bringing the clean wind strong on the right side of my head;
And the stones and low bushes were flowing away, faster and faster,
Faster. Only the desert remained itself, remained unchanged,
Flowing away from itself,
Yet continually renewing itself from right to left, faster, faster,
And the wind a gale,

And under me a grind and clatter of wheels.

JOHN BLIGHT

Down from the Country

When we came down from the country, we were strangers to the sea.
The rise and fall of waters without rain,
the lunglike breathing of the estuary
caused our amazement; and the white stain
of salt on the rocks, when the tide receded,
where we were used to dark mud that a flood leaves behind,
held us enthralled; and we needed
some mental adjustment which people noticed. When the mind
is confronted by such magnitudes of sight and sound
there is no mask for refuge in frown or grimace;
but the face looks blank, as if it were dragged up, drowned.

How much loneliness is there in a different place,
out of one's shell, out of all knowledge, to be caught
out of the dullness of self by such alien thought?

The Anchor

Know then, the only joy of an anchor – to be strong,
have iron arms, and be long
immersed holding by cable a ship
like an iron kite in the blue, deep
waters of a port. Know then, the anguish
of its cross – to lie as stone, while fish
hover and flutter like leaves, and love
bites, in a barnacle, a red groove

into its flukes. To be the 'pick'
in common talk, thrown over through slick
to the dirty bottom with bottles and tins;
an anchor in all its servitude, its sins
flaking off in rust like a scurvy:
yet straining to hold a city in heaven – cause topsy-turvy.

The Landfall

There was a tide-mark on the jetty which
marked this side of ocean, and so the leagues
seemed meaningless after our landfall – pitch
and toss of the long weeks when sea-legs
ferried us, numbed us ashore. Nobody
down the long, strong jetty spoke a word.
No wave to carry us, but the shoddy
bus on the beach, and a screaming sea bird
handkerchief-white, a gesture of
departure, once over the sea wall's eyelid
closed – with the sea out of view and the stuff
of our sea trip grubby around our feet. 'Rid
of that damned, dirty weather at last!' someone said,
while names like spiders crawled all over our waiting-shed.

Death of a Whale

When the mouse died, there was a sort of pity:
the tiny, delicate creature made for grief.
Yesterday, instead, the dead whale on the reef
drew an excited multitude to the jetty.
How must a whale die to wring a tear?

Lugubrious death of a whale: the big
feast for the gulls and sharks; the tug
of the tide simulating life still there,
until the air, polluted, swings this way
like a door ajar from a slaughterhouse.
Pooh! pooh! spare us, give us the death of a mouse
by its tiny hole; not this in our lovely bay.
– Sorry we are, too, when a child dies;
but at the immolation of a race who cries?

Garfish

Creatures that live in a wave, glass-housed,
luxury-living garfish, yellow-lipped
and pretty as flat-women. Slim-hipped,
bubble-sipping surface-livers, espoused
by the sun. Garfish that are not fish
but meteors, in the eyes of the star-gazer
– star-dripping meteors that the dozer
on the mud bottom would trap in a wish.
Sinker-sodden star-gazer, sick and sorry fish:
while the flappers are storeys up – gars
in the planetarium drinking bubbling spas;
off-this-planet plankton, trifling, for a dish;
and catching a breaker now and then –
it, a late tram crammed with white-shirted men.

Into the Ark

The clean otter, I have not seen other
than in this young man, this sailor and his brother,
the old sea-bear, potter about in the lee time
waiting on shipping to take to sea in time,
before they grapple together and, between them,
the white ghost of their seafaring is forgotten;
knifed, in a shore-ditch for a bawd who's rotten
with some disease the elder can't shake off.

Before they come to this, there's mateship. Break off
the ties of the brothel. Let them lumber the wharf
for a sea-bound vessel and be seen aboard,
again living lives that limber them for their Lord.

It's lucky and good for the young man, this land's cloud
is behind them. Like a giant stain, it has cleared
from their blue sky, the sea – a heaven revered
by its worshippers, the sailors, in the Ark stowed;
fortunately, without a dove in their ship, and faint hope
of landfall or leaf beyond the last cape.

Sun

Sometimes too personal, sun, you
slap my face with sunburn until
used to your straight blows on the beach
I tan like leather, and the weight
of your crushing light gleams as
a shining cream poured over
my body in warm ease, ray-white
as a living froth of blossoms'
spray which springs from the forest-
green of the breakers. Your profuse
ardour livens our game of hide-
and-seek in the water. We are like
bride and groom; but I've told
you, sun, you are too personal.

KENNETH MACKENZIE

Heat

'Well, this is where I go down to the river,'
the traveller with me said, and turned aside
out of the burnt road, through the black trees
spiking the slope, and went down, and never
came back into the heat from water's ease
in which he swooned, in cool joy, and died.

Often since then, in brutal days of summer
I have remembered him, with envy too;
thought of him sinking down above his knees
in a cold torrent, senseless of the rumour
of death gone down behind him through the trees,
through the dead grass and bushes he shoved through.

He must have tasted water after walking
miles and miles along that stream of road,
gulping and drooling it out of his mouth
that had for one day been too dry for talking
as we went on through drought into the south
shouldering leaden heat for double load.

Plainly he couldn't bear it any longer.
Like the hand of a bored devil placed
mercilessly upon a man's head,
it maddened him. I was a little stronger
and knew the river, rich with many dead,
lustrous and very cold, but two-faced

like some cold, vigorous, enticing woman
quite at the mercy of her remote source
and past springs. I could not warn him now –
not if he were here now. I could warn no man
while these red winds and summer lightnings blow
frantic with heat across my dogged course

into the south, beside the narrow river
which has that traveller's flesh and bones, and more.
Often I see him walking down that slope
thirsty and mad, never to return, never
quenched quite of his thirst, or of his hope
that heat would be arrested on its shore.

The Fool

Now in an hour you have me, tight, and loose me.
I am your sacred fool: you squeeze out over
my haggard head your wine-skin that undoes me,
and turn about to proclaim me your lover.

You laugh upon my laughter. In my night
of folly made more foolish by your jest
I see your breasts show out as wickedly white
as if to ask, Choose which of us is best.

I see your unkind eyes shine in the dark,
while round my ears a thousand devils say,
'She is made up of shell and stone and bark.
Her blood is icy, and her flesh is clay.'

Why then do I come back and ask for more?
Why do I want it? Should I not desire
such women as the Spartan mothers bore –
the strong, the violent and quick of fire?

No! I want you – a hundred times a day
I want your conscious coldness and your scorn.
I want you cruel, barren, icily gay.
I am your fool, and for you I was born!

The door swung open . . .

The door swung open.
           'Stranger,' I said, 'come in,'
  and in walked Death, well wrapped from foot to head
in a great cloak of moonlight-coloured green.
  He stared at me.
           'I'm sorry, friend,' I said.

He turned and locked the door. His tread was light
  in my floor's dust; his smile was broad and kind.
He had no eyes, but did not need their sight,
  nor had he speech, nor soul, nor heart, nor mind

to interrupt our silent re-uniting,
  for I, his god-child and his secret friend,
had long since told him how his brood were fighting
  to bring his weary duty to its end.

He stretched upon my bed, in his great cloak,
  and pointed at the ceiling with his toes.
No breath came to or from him. No one spoke
  till almost dawn, when I, who, as he knows,

have not his patience nor his skill, stood up
  and asked him to be gone before daylight,
but to return and bring with him his cup
  soon, to charm me off to his private night

where I could rest as he has rested here
  stretched out and well beyond the rim of life,
careless of tombstones, freed of fire and fear,
  we two together, husband to each, and wife.

He went. The door swung after him. The room
  resumed its shape, and in the window's square
there blossomed, like a rose within the gloom
  of Death's departure, Dawn with yellow hair.

Searchlights

When I see the searchlights splitting the moonlight,
coldly caressing each other deep in the zenith
of almost-midnight, loving one another
like chill blue hoses of fireless flame gone amorous,
it's you, not them, I think of. During summer
when no one knew, we shared the big bed lazily,
and there your warm brown legs were the splayed beams,
the sultry heat of the room was night, fluid
and smooth against the searching limbs like milk,
while out beyond the open windows the lights
sought for a winged enemy. Inside,
you sought and fought that way, too, and you won
now and again. The beams burst in my eyes,
the glassy air of night exploded softly,
multiplications of your voice confused me
with moon-like gentleness; and yet I watched
over your mountainous shoulder the cold searchlights
solemnly flaying night, their streaming ribbons
tying the stars to earth in wavering folly,
touching each other madly, with no purpose,
while I touched you in their reflected light
and afterwards lay down and loved my rest.

They sprayed the night long afterwards. I saw them
once, when I turned my head in waking.

Sick Men Sleeping

Some one calls out, and some one else
answers from seven beds away
as if to say that dream was false
which shook his brain to spill the cry.

The dusky silence lapping sleep
ripples with memory, and rocks
each listener down its swooning slope:
the ropes are snapped, the rings, the racks

are smashed aside, the fire is gone
to ash, the stake is split at last,
but still one hears the banging gun;
one knows his tortured courage best;

one feels the bayonet in his heart;
one treads a trail and cannot rest,
and one whose body was not hurt
knows in his brain the gnawing rust

of death outlived while youth is green –
he speaks for all, but cannot grieve
beyond the speechless sleeping groan
of men alive who feel the grave
press down upon their screaming lips.

Ginger-flowers

The perfume of the ginger-flowers
fumes through the empty house tonight,
in by the summer windows flowing;
a tide, a spell, enchantment and delight
set on by darkness, coming and going.

Those bold priapic blossoms, sunlit and chrome
flare through the gloom. In every one
is an hermaphroditic lust, shameless
because the bees crave it – it alone –
or so the leaping phallus of the stigma,
man-womanly and moist, seems
in putting to you its profound enigma
to mean you to believe.

So they invade the house, which dreams
of poisoned tropics, where the orchids leave
staleness on the dark air
and lilies, like the ginger-flower,
breathe on the night's warm hair
of breath of amorous and inhuman potency –
beyond compare.

The Children Go

The children go.
They go for a year, with delight:
the boy with his cap just so – just right
on his hair that is mine (or is it?), and his brow
that is no one's in this family.
The girl – well, she
has a brow that is mine, I think,
though the boy has my eyes . . . So –
the children go.

They are gone now, and now
the whole house settles to sleep
with a sigh that changes to a snore,
as though it had nothing to keep any more –
not even the toy worlds smashed and scattered on the floor;
its brisk blood suddenly stilled,
its dear life suddenly cheap, so cheap
that the spiders hidden away
come out and weave up day
to the deadly beauty of a net,
quickly – lest they forget
how often and why they have killed
what they have killed.
They are here, and so, too, are we –
parents of the two children, saying
Thank God they always go like that – happily
away from us to their school home
$\qquad\qquad\qquad\qquad$ but saying

Who are we?
Knowing that in our death was their beginning;
and knowing, with a knowledge that must be borne,
that, from the moment they were got and born,
the children go.

They go out like flowers, from the seed to the sun,
having at first not much purpose
until some thing they have done,
some good deed or bad deed,
shows them the way: *before you walk you must run,*
and must fall down. But they pay no heed.
                                        Let us
pretend to love one another
over a strangely silent meal at last
after so long: I am the father, you the mother
– or so we say; but the meal is a fast,
and the house is asleep already, the spiders' work half-done
and the children gone.

Table-birds

The match-bark of the younger dog sets fire to
an indignation of turkeys under the olives.
Scurf-wigged like senescent judges, drum-puffing desire,
they bloat their wattles, and the chorus gives
a purple biased judgment on the pup:
Trouble enough, pup, bloody trouble enough!

So much for morning and the sun's generous
flattery of the metal of their feathers.
Noon makes them somnolent, dusty, glad to drowse
the fly-slurred hours of midday August weather
in scooped hollows under the ripe trees
whose fruit sweetens them for the Christmas season.

The tilted sun, the craw's shrunk emptiness
wake them to stir their lice and strut again,
head back, tail spread, and dangling crest
and greedy, angered eye . . . The spinsterly hen
blinks the lewd fan and frets among the grains,
knife-grey and sleek, hungrier, less restrained

by stifling turkey pride beneath the red
slap of the leering comb. But they submit.
The fan snaps to; head doubles over head –
and day's escape delineates them fitfully
like darkness clotted into nervous shapes
under the olives, in whose night they sleep.

from: *The Hospital – Retrospections*

New Arrival

Burgess was drunk when he was admitted
    not with alcohol – with pain.
The wailing ambulance that brought him
    grumbled and growled away again.

Pain was the brilliant light the smell
    of nurse and surgeon the strange faces
swimming in bluish air then gone:
    but he had been in stranger places –

but never strangeness and pain together
    never the incurious wish to die
that squeezed his mind like the white fingers
    probing his pelvis ribs and thigh.

Transported, drunk with so much anguish,
    Burgess observed the ceiling part
to show him heaven and hell united
    ready to fall upon his heart.

Each of his wounds cried out against it
    voiceless and twisted mouths of blood.
Clasped in a cruel consciousness
    he closed his lips on the sacred flood

of revelation that welled up in him.

    The needle lying within the vein
sobered and then annihilated
    Burgess the faces the light the pain.

DAVID CAMPBELL

Small-town Gladys

There are rows of bottles against the glass;
I look between and my hair's blonde grass,
My lips are berries and my skin is cream
And I fill my frock to the very brim
And twirl a curl when the sportsmen pass –
And I'm a good girl, I am.

They call me Glad and say I'm a queen.
I look in the glass and my eyes are green
And they talk to men though they make no sound
For it's love that makes the world go round;
But go too far and I say, 'Go on;
I am a good girl, I am.'

In every novel I'm Lady Jane,
I use the book as a wicked fan,
And I sit on a stool and my fingers knit
A web to snare a sportsman's wit;
And they look at me as they look for rain,
But I'm a good girl, I am.

Under the willows, under the night,
Where schoolboys spy and the parson might,
I am the moon that rules the tides
Of men. And I shake and hold my sides
And I say, 'My make-up's an awful sight –
And I'm a good girl, I am.'

Men in Green

There were fifteen men in green,
Each with a tommy-gun,
Who leapt into my plane at dawn;
We rose to meet the sun.

Our course lay to the east. We climbed
Into the break of day,
Until the jungle far beneath
Like a giant fossil lay.

We climbed towards the distant range
Where two white paws of cloud
Clutched at the shoulders of the pass.
The green men laughed aloud.

They did not fear the ape-like cloud
That climbed the mountain crest
And rode the currents of the air
And hid the pass in mist.

They did not fear the summer's sun
In whose hot centre lie
A hundred hissing cannon shells
For the unwatchful eye.

And when at Dobadura we
Set down, each turned to raise
His thumb towards the open sky
In mockery and praise.

But fifteen men in jungle green
Rose from the kunai grass
To come aboard, and my green men
In silence watched them pass:
It seemed they looked upon themselves
In a prophetic glass.

There were some leaned on a stick
And some on stretchers lay,
But few walked on their own two feet
In the early green of day.

They had not feared the ape-like cloud
That climbed the mountain crest;
They had not feared the summer's sun
With bullets for their breast.

Their eyes were bright, their looks were dull,
Their skin had turned to clay.
Nature had met them in the night
And stalked them in the day.

And I think still of men in green
On the Soputa track
With fifteen spitting tommy-guns
To keep a jungle back.

Here, under Pear-trees

Here, under pear-trees, on the broad verandahs,
Children like sleeping gods play games;
Surprised, awake in picture-frames,
Leaving a stuffed grouse, debts, and ten thousand acres,

An ancestral trick of speech or way of standing.
Their ponies with skinned-back lips devour
The blackboys, stolen in an hour
Time slept through, drugged by birds in the summer garden.

Horses and stolen roses, fine-woolled rams;
Frail youthful grandmothers who say
That things were different in their day,
Hearing the jets smash windows over the township.

Between the grey lake and the lyrebird peak,
A fleece of haze. Now tractors move.
By careless roads of hate and love,
They go to serious parties, gay committees.

Mothers and Daughters

The cruel girls we loved
Are over forty,
Their subtle daughters
Have stolen their beauty;

And with a blue stare
Of cool surprise,
They mock their anxious mothers
With their mothers' eyes.

Hotel Marine

Lost in glass gullies, searching for a suitcase:
The white sun shatters in ten thousand windows,
And splinters scatter, colouring the crowd
Looking for the Hotel Marine.

Our books are there, small treasures, a transistor
And all our marvellous clothes. I guess that's why
We wander naked through the rush-hour traffic
Looking for the Hotel Marine.

We use our hands as shields but no one sees us
In this steel garden with its paper leaves.
Their eyes are twenty blocks or hours before them
Looking for the Hotel Marine.

We keep together, eyes wide for a policeman,
But no one cares. Perhaps they are not here
But somewhere in the past or in the future
Looking for the Hotel Marine.

Maybe it's round the corner, sunlit, floating;
The doorman smiles and cats are on the sofas –
How should it vanish, leaving us with nothing,
Looking for the Hotel Marine?

from: *Ku-ring-gai Rock Carvings*

The Lovers

Making love for ten thousand years on a rockledge:
    The boronia springs up purple
  From the stone, and we lay together briefly
  For as long as those two lovers.

Spring

The Chase is mad with sex. Flowered trees sustain
    The act of love a season;
  While from stone loins wild orchids spring
  Whose pleasure is in intercourse with beetles.

Spiny Ant-eaters

Spring comes in gold and purple, and the stone echidnas
    Dawdle across the rockface:
  It may be a prickly business
  But their desire goes on forever.

Lizards

Lizards are kin and can return to stone
    At will. Transfixing a shield
  Like a spear a lizard froze in the sun, a thing
  Of bronze, yet quick. See the dart of his tongue!

Bora Ring

The kangaroo has a spear in his side. It was here
    Young men were initiated,
  Tied to a burning tree. Today
  Where are such cooling pools of water?

Tench, 1791

Flesh carvings: for theft, before the assembled tribes,
    A convict was flogged. Daringa,
  Her nets forgotten, wept: while Barangaroo
  Threatened the lasher. A feckless if tender people.

Hands

An artist blew ruddy ochre to outline his hand
    In a cave the water glazed.
You can shake hands with this dead man.
It teases the mind like John Keats' hand.

Baiame

Baiame, the All-father, is a big fellow with a big dong
    And the rayed crown of a god.
He looks at his Sunday children who snigger and drive
Home to their home-units. The god is not surprised.

from: *Starting from Central Station*

I Starting from Central Station

A moon hangs in the air,
Its hands at ten past ten:
My father leaps alive
And I shrink to his son.

My father strides ahead
And stops to have a word
With men in caps who laugh.
He slips them a reward.

The trolley rolls behind
With boxes stacked like bricks:
Smoke and a whistle blow
And I am fifty-six.

Houses move through the parks,
Streets run with greens and reds:
Night conjures up the same
Old promises and dreads.

The train is on its way
And daylight gets to work,
Puts father in a box
And shoves him in the dark.

IX Angina

He feared angina from his thirtieth year:
A doctor, he knew what to fear.
On the stair I saw him stop,
Take his pulse and climb the mountain top.

Drought, boredom, loneliness, could bring it on,
And his unlikely son:
Deeper than Eros' dart
Care struck my father's heart.

On Kismet, his roan mare,
He cut out cow and steer;
Then chained up his blue heeler, and
For fear of germs, scrubbed hand on hand.

I do the same myself now. But in Scot
He said at our last row, 'You'll nae forget,'
And climbed to fix a mill. At seventy-three
Was it angina or did he die of me?

The Anguish of Ants

Meat ants, meat-coloured, greet each other
On the hard roads between their gravel cities,
Granite red;
Cross antennae, bow and turn about
On serious unintelligible business
Of state: maybe a whale stranded

In a dry gully; and they lift it like bulldozers,
Bear it off in a bucket,
A bug three times their weight:
Iron ants make light work of it.

How many sets of feet
Beat this highway, carrying merchandise, news,
Between metropolis and lichened farms?
And should a grazing horse stray
Planting a hoof in the market place,
Or boys in short pants stir up New York with a stick,
Their alarm system is the scent of resin,
A stink of pine, a siren
Shrieking in the sense of smell. Archaic
Armies manoeuvre, nurseries are evacuated,
Horatio fronts a tractor blade alone.

But the trees fall: blackbutt and candlebark,
Archipelagos of the huge,
Stacked up in rows by dozers much like ants;
And the autumn burn bloodies the sun. Over nude
Ridges men stride planting out pine:
Conifers march in green ranks over
The meat ants' thin red lines, each tree
Destined for paper mill, the morning news;
While tense in the scent of resin,
Whole cities perish of anxiety.

The Man in the Honeysuckle

There is a face in the honeysuckle – eyes
Like the nests of funnel-web spiders
Intent in the brown crossed-sticks of the face
And sinister with the sky breaking through
If it weren't for the crown of new leaves.
You can see such faces in flood-debris,
In the bullock skull in the heifer field

Leafed with a fine lichen – a bicycle-seat,
The parts scattered.
                              Who rides here
Tempting something to happen,
The match of the new year?
                              Flick
And the man in the honeysuckle
Crackles like pork, young leaves of flame
Clambering over the black framework.
We didn't mean it, didn't mean . . .
The farmers say it will be a good season.

JUDITH WRIGHT

Brother and Sisters

The road turned out to be a cul-de-sac;
stopped like a lost intention at the gate
and never crossed the mountains to the coast.
But they stayed on. Years grew like grass and leaves
across the half-erased and dubious track
until one day they knew the plans were lost,
the blue-print for the bridge was out of date,
and now their orchards never would be planted.
The saplings sprouted slyly; day by day
the bush moved one step nearer, wondering when.
The polished parlour grew distrait and haunted
where Millie, Lucy, John each night at ten
wound the gilt clock that leaked the year away.

The pianola – oh, listen to the mocking-bird –
wavers on Sundays and has lost a note.
The wrinkled ewes snatch pansies through the fence
and stare with shallow eyes into the garden
where Lucy shrivels waiting for a word,
and Millie's cameos loosen round her throat.
The bush comes near, the ranges grow immense.

Feeding the lambs deserted in early spring
Lucy looked up and saw the stockman's eye
telling her she was cracked and old.
                                   The wall
groans in the night and settles more awry.
O how they lie awake. Their thoughts go fluttering
from room to room like moths: 'Millie, are you awake?'
'Oh John, I have been dreaming.' 'Lucy, do you cry?'
 – meet tentative as moths. Antennae stroke a wing.
'There is nothing to be afraid of. Nothing at all.'

Woman to Man

The eyeless labourer in the night,
the selfless, shapeless seed I hold,
builds for its resurrection day –
silent and swift and deep from sight
foresees the unimagined light.

This is no child with a child's face;
this has no name to name it by:
yet you and I have known it well.
This is our hunter and our chase,
the third who lay in our embrace.

This is the strength that your arm knows,
the arc of flesh that is my breast,
the precise crystals of our eyes.
This is the blood's wild tree that grows
the intricate and folded rose.

This is the maker and the made;
this is the question and reply;
the blind head butting at the dark,
the blaze of light along the blade.
Oh hold me, for I am afraid.

The Child

To be alone in a strange place in spring
shakes the heart. The others are somewhere else;
the shouting, the running, the eating, the drinking –
never alone and thinking,
never remembering the Dream or finding the Thing,
always striving with your breath hardly above the water.
But to go away, to be quiet and go away,
to be alone in a strange place in spring
shakes the heart.

To hide in a thrust of green leaves
with the blood's leap and retreat
warm in you;
burning, going and returning
like a thrust of green leaves
out of your eyes, out of your hands and your feet –
like a noise of bees, growing, increasing;
to turn and to look up,
to find above you the enfolding, the exulting
may-tree
shakes the heart.

Spring is always the red tower of the may-tree,
alive, shaken with bees, smelling of wild honey,
and the blood a moving tree of may;
like a symbol for a meaning; like time's recurrent morning
that breaks and beckons, changes and eludes,
that is gone away;
that is never gone away.

Camphor Laurel

Here in the slack of night
the tree breathes honey and moonlight.
Here in the blackened yard
smoke and time and use have marred,
leaning from that fantan gloom
the bent tree is heavy in bloom.

The dark house creaks and sways;
'Not like the old days.'
Tim and Sam and ragbag Nell,
Wong who keeps the Chinese hell,
the half-caste lovers, the humpbacked boy,
sleep for sorrow or wake for joy.
Under the house the roots go deep,
down, down, while the sleepers sleep;

splitting the rock where the house is set,
cracking the paved and broken street.
Old Tim turns and old Sam groans,
'God be good to my breaking bones';
and in the slack of tideless night
the tree breathes honey and moonlight.

Night After Bushfire

There is no more silence on the plains of the moon
and time is no more alien there, than here.
Sun thrust his warm hand down at the high noon,
but all that stirred was the faint dust of fear.

Charred death upon the rock leans his charred bone
and stares at death from sockets black with flame.
Man, if he come to brave that glance alone,
must leave behind his human home and name.

Carry like a threatened thing your soul away,
and do not look too long to left or right,
for he whose soul wears the strict chains of day
will lose it in this landscape of charcoal and moonlight.

Eli, Eli

To see them go by drowning in the river –
soldiers and elders drowning in the river,
the pitiful women drowning in the river,
the children's faces staring from the river –
that was his cross, and not the cross they gave him.
To hold the invisible wand, and not to save them –

to know them turned to death, and yet not save them;
only to cry to them and not to save them,
knowing that no one but themselves could save them –
this was the wound, more than the wound they dealt him.

To hold out love and know they would not take it,
to hold out faith and know they dared not take it –
the invisible wand, and none would see or take it,
all he could give, and there was none to take it –
thus they betrayed him, not with the tongue's betrayal.

He watched, and they were drowning in the river;
faces like sodden flowers in the river –
faces of children moving in the river;
and all the while, he knew there was no river.

The Killer

The day was clear as fire,
the birds sang frail as glass,
when thirsty I came to the creek
and fell by its side in the grass.

My breast on the bright moss
and shower-embroidered weeds,
my lips to the live water
I saw him turn in the reeds.

Black horror sprang from the dark
in a violent birth,
and through its cloth of grass
I felt the clutch of earth.

O beat him into the ground.
O strike him till he dies,
or else your life itself
drains through those colourless eyes.

I struck again and again.
Slender in black and red
he lies, and his icy glance
turns outward, clear and dead.

But nimble my enemy
as water is, or wind.
He has slipped from his death aside
and vanished into my mind.

He has vanished whence he came,
my nimble enemy;
and the ants come out to the snake
and drink at his shallow eye.

Metho Drinker

Under the death of winter's leaves he lies
who cried to Nothing and the terrible night
to be his home and bread. 'O take from me
the weight and waterfall of ceaseless Time
that batters down my weakness; the knives of light
whose thrust I cannot turn; the cruelty
of human eyes that dare not touch nor pity.'
Under the worn leaves of the winter city
safe in the house of Nothing now he lies.

His white and burning girl, his woman of fire,
creeps to his heart and sets a candle there
to melt away the flesh that hides the bone,
to eat the nerve that tethers him in Time.
He will lie warm until the bone is bare
and on a dead dark moon he wakes alone.
It was for Death he took her; death is but this
and yet he is uneasy under her kiss
and winces from that acid of her desire.

The Old Prison

The rows of cells are unroofed,
a flute for the wind's mouth,
who comes with a breath of ice
from the blue caves of the south.

O dark and fierce day:
the wind like an angry bee
hunts for the black honey
in the pits of the hollow sea.

Waves of shadow wash
the empty shell bone-bare,
and like a bone it sings
a bitter song of air.

Who built and laboured here?
The wind and the sea say
– Their cold nest is broken
and they are blown away.

They did not breed nor love.
Each in his cell alone
cried as the wind now cries
through this flute of stone.

from: *The Blind Man*

II Country Dance

The dance in the township hall is nearly over.
Hours ago the stiff-handed wood-cheeked women
got up from the benches round the walls
and took home their aching eyes and weary children.
Mrs McLarty with twenty cows to milk
before dawn, went with the music stinging
like sixty wasps under her best dress.

Eva Callaghan whose boy died in the army
sat under the streamers like a house to let
and went alone, a black pot brimming with tears.
'Once my body was a white cedar, my breasts the buds on the
    quince-tree,
that now are fallen and grey like logs on a cleared hill.
Then why is my blood not quiet? what is the good
of the whips of music stinging along my blood?'

The dance in the township hall is nearly over.
Outside in the yard the fire like a great red city
eats back into the log, its noisy flames fallen.
Jimmy Dunn has forgotten his camp in the hills
and sleeps like a heap of rags beside a bottle.
The young boys sit and stare at the heart of the city
thinking of the neon lights and the girls at the corners
with lips like coals and thighs as silver as florins.
Jock Hamilton thinks of the bally cow gone sick
and the cockatoos in the corn and the corn ready to pick
and the wires in the thirty-acre broken.
Oh, what rats nibble at the cords of our nerves?
When will the wires break, the ploughed paddocks lie open,
the bow of the fiddle saw through the breast-bone,
the dream be done, and we waken?

Streamers and boughs are falling, the dance grows faster.
Only the lovers and the young are dancing
now at the end of the dance, in a trance of singing.
Say the lovers locked together and crowned with coloured paper:
'The bit of black glass I picked up out of the campfire
is the light that the moon puts on your hair.'
'The green pool I swam in under the willows
is the drowning depth, the summer night of your eyes.'
'You are the death I move to.' 'O burning weapon,
you are the pain I long for.'

Stars, leaves and streamers fall in the dark dust
and the blind man lies alone in his sphere of night.

Oh, I,
red centre of a dark and burning sky,
fit my words to music, my crippled words to music,
and sing to the fire with the voice of the fire.
Go sleep with your grief, go sleep with your desire,

go deep into the core of night and silence.
But I hold all of it, your hate and sorrow,
your passion and your fear; I am the breath
that holds you from your death.
I am the voice of music and the ended dance.

To a Child

When I was a child I saw
a burning bird in a tree.
I see became *I am,*
I am became *I see.*

In winter dawns of frost
the lamp swung in my hand.
The battered moon on the slope
lay like a dune of sand;

and in the trap at my feet
the rabbit leapt and prayed,
weeping blood, and crouched
when the light shone on the blade.

The sudden sun lit up
the webs from wire to wire;
the white webs, the white dew,
blazed with a holy fire.

Flame of light in the dew,
flame of blood on the bush
answered the whirling sun
and the voice of the early thrush.

I think of this for you.
I would not have you believe
the world is empty of truth
or that men must grieve,

but hear the song of the martyrs
out of a bush of fire –
'All is consumed with love;
all is renewed with desire.'

The Precipice

At last it came into her mind, the answer.
She dressed the children, went out and hailed the driver.
There she sat holding them; looking through the window;
behaving like any woman, but she was no longer living.

To blame her would mean little; she had her logic,
the contained argument of the bomb, not even tragic,
to which each day had made its small addition
ending at last in this, which was completion.

There was no moon but she had brought her torch
and the dark of the mountain forest opened like flesh
before her purpose; possessed and intent as any lover
she fled along the path, the children with her.

So reaching the edge at last and no less certain
she took the children in her arms because she loved them
and jumped, parting the leaves and the night's curtain.

Now, and for years to come, that path is seared
by the blazing headlong torrent of their direction;
and we must hold our weathercock minds from turning
into its downward gale, towards destruction.

Gum-trees Stripping

Say the need's born within the tree,
and waits a trigger set for light;
say sap is tidal like the sea,
and rises with the solstice-heat –
but wisdom shells the words away
to watch this fountain slowed in air
where sun joins earth – to watch the place
at which these silent rituals are.

Words are not meanings for a tree.
So it is truer not to say,
'These rags look like humility,
or this year's wreck of last year's love,
or wounds ripped by the summer's claw.'
If it is possible to be wise
here, wisdom lies outside the word
in the earlier answer of the eyes.

Wisdom can see the red, the rose,
the stained and sculptured curve of grey,
the charcoal scars of fire, and see
around that living tower of tree
the hermit tatters of old bark
split down and strip to end the season;
and can be quiet and not look
for reasons past the edge of reason.

At Cooloola

The blue crane fishing in Cooloola's twilight
has fished there longer than our centuries.
He is the certain heir of lake and evening,
and he will wear their colour till he dies,

but I'm a stranger, come of a conquering people.
I cannot share his calm, who watch his lake,
being unloved by all my eyes delight in,
and made uneasy, for an old murder's sake.

Those dark-skinned people who once named Cooloola
knew that no land is lost or won by wars,
for earth is spirit: the invader's feet will tangle
in nets there and his blood be thinned by fears.

Riding at noon and ninety years ago,
my grandfather was beckoned by a ghost –
a black accoutred warrior armed for fighting,
who sank into bare plain, as now into time past.

White shores of sand, plumed reed and paperbark,
clear heavenly levels frequented by crane and swan –
I know that we are justified only by love,
but oppressed by arrogant guilt, have room for none.

And walking on clean sand among the prints
of bird and animal, I am challenged by a driftwood spear
thrust from the water; and, like my grandfather,
must quiet a heart accused by its own fear.

Pelicans

Funnel-web spider, snake and octopus,
pitcher-plant and vampire-bat and shark –
these are cold water on an easy faith.
Look at them, but don't linger.
If we stare too long, something looks back at us;
something gazes through from underneath;
something crooks a very dreadful finger
down there in an unforgotten dark.

Turn away then, and look up at the sky.
There sails that old clever Noah's Ark,
the well-turned, well-carved pelican
with his wise comic eye;
he turns and wheels down, kind as an ambulance-driver,
to join his fleet. Pelicans rock together,
solemn as clowns in white on a circus-river,
meaning: this world holds every sort of weather.

from: *For a Pastoral Family*

I To my Brothers

Over the years, horses have changed to Land-Rovers.
Grown old, you travel your thousands of acres
deploring change and the wickedness of cities
and the cities' politics; hoping to pass to your sons
a kind of life you inherited in your generation.
Some actions of those you vote for stick in your throats.
There are corruptions one cannot quite endorse;
but if they are in our interests, then of course . . .

Well, there are luxuries still,
including pastoral silence, miles of slope and hill,
the cautious politeness of bankers. These are owed
to the forerunners, men and women
who took over as if by right a century and a half
in an ancient difficult bush. And after all
the previous owners put up little fight,
did not believe in ownership, and so were scarcely human.

Our people who gnawed at the fringe
of the edible leaf of this country
left you a margin of action, a rural security,
and left to me
what serves as a base for poetry,
a doubtful song that has a dying fall.

V Change

At best, the men of our clan
have been, or might have been,
like Yeats' fisherman.
A small stream, narrow but clean,

running apart from the world.
Those hills might keep them so,
granite, gentle and cold.
But hills erode, streams go

through settlement and town
darkened by chemical silt.
Dams hold and slow them down,
trade thickens them like guilt.

All men grow evil with trade
as all roads lead to the city.
Willie Yeats would have said,
perhaps, the more the pity.

But how can we be sure?
Wasn't his chosen man
as ignorant as pure?
Keep out? Stay clean? Who can?

River Bend

What killed that kangaroo-doe, slender skeleton
tumbled above the water with her long shanks
cleaned white as moonlight?
Pad-tracks in sand where something drank fresh blood.

Last night a dog howled somewhere,
a hungry ghost in need of sacrifice.

Down by that bend, they say, the last old woman,
thin, black and muttering grief,
foraged for mussels, all her people gone.

The swollen winter river
curves over stone, a wild perpetual voice.

Skins

This pair of skin gloves is sixty-six years old,
mended in places, worn thin across the knuckles.

Snakes get rid of their coverings all at once.
Even those empty cuticles trouble the passer-by.

Counting in seven-year rhythms I've lost nine skins
though their gradual flaking isn't so spectacular.

Holding a book or a pen I can't help seeing
how age crazes surfaces. Well, and interiors?

You ask me to read those poems I wrote in my thirties?
They dropped off several incarnations back.

JACK DAVIS

The First-born

Where are my first-born, said the brown land, sighing;
They came out of my womb long, long ago.
They were formed of my dust – why, why are they crying
And the light of their being barely aglow?

I strain my ears for the sound of their laughter.
Where are the laws and the legends I gave?
Tell me what happened, you whom I bore after.
Now only their spirits dwell in the caves.

You are silent, you cringe from replying.
A question is there, like a blow on the face.
The answer is there when I look at the dying,
At the death and neglect of my dark proud race.

Warru

Fast asleep on the wooden bench,
Arms bent under the weary head,
There in the dusk and the back-street stench
He lay with the look of the dead.

I looked at him, then back through the years,
Then knew what I had to remember –
A young man, straight as wattle spears,
And a kangaroo hunt in September.

We caught the scent of the 'roos on the rise
Where the gums grew on the Moore;
They leaped away in loud surprise,
But Warru was fast and sure.

He threw me the fire-stick, oh what a thrill!
With a leap he sprang to a run.
He met the doe on the top of the hill,
And he looked like a king in the sun.

The wattle spear flashed in the evening light,
The kangaroo fell at his feet.
How I danced and I yelled with all my might
As I thought of the warm red meat.

We camped that night on a bed of reeds
With a million stars a-gleaming.
He told me tales of Noong-ah* deeds
When the world first woke from dreaming.

He sang me a song, I clapped my hands,
He fashioned a needle of bone.
He drew designs in the river sands,
He sharpened his spear on a stone.

I will let you dream – dream on, old friend –
Of a boy and a man in September,
Of hills and stars and the river's bend –
Alas, that is all to remember.

* Noong-ah – Aboriginal tribe of the south-west of Western Australia

 ## Desolation

You have turned our land into a desolate place.
We stumble along with a half-white mind.
Where are we?
What are we?
Not a recognized race . . .
There is desert ahead and desert behind.

The tribes are all gone,
The boundaries are broken:
Once we had bread here,
You gave us stone.

We are tired of the benches, our beds in the park,
We welcome the sundown that heralds the dark.
White Lady Methylate!
Keep us warm and from crying.
Hold back the hate
And hasten the dying.

The tribes are all gone,
The spears are all broken:
Once we had bread here,
You gave us stone.

One Hundred and Fifty Years

Written in protest at the non-inclusion of Aborigines in the celebrations of
150 years of European settlement in Western Australia, 1829–1979

I walked slowly along the river.
Old iron, broken concrete, rusted cans
scattered stark along the shore,
plastic strewn by man and tide
littered loudly mute on sparse growth
struggling to survive.
A flock of gulls quarrelled over debris,
a lone shag looked hopefully down at turgid water
and juggernauts of steel and stone made jigsaw
patterns against the city sky.

So now that the banners have fluttered,
the eulogies ended and the tattoos have rendered
the rattle of spears,
look back and remember the end of December
and one hundred and fifty years.

Three boys crackled past on trailbikes
long blond hair waving in the wind,
speedboats erupted power
while lesser craft surged along behind.
The breeze rustled a patch of bull-oak
reminding me of swan, bittern, wild duck winging –
now all alien to the river.
Sir John Forrest stood tall in stone
in St George's Terrace,
gun across shoulder,
symbolic of what had removed
the river's first children.

And that other river, the Murray,
where Western Australia's
first mass murderer Captain Stirling,
trappings flashing, rode gaily
at the head of twenty-four men.
For an hour they fired
and bodies black, mutilated,
floated down the blood-stained stream.

So now that the banners have fluttered,
the eulogies ended and the tattoos have rendered
the rattle of spears,
look back and remember the end of December
and one hundred and fifty years.

JAMES McAULEY

Envoi

There the blue-green gums are a fringe of remote disorder
And the brown sheep poke at my dreams along the hillsides;
And there in the soil, in the season, in the shifting airs,
Comes the faint sterility that disheartens and derides.

Where once was a sea is now a salty sunken desert,
A futile heart within a fair periphery;
The people are hard-eyed, kindly, with nothing inside them,
The men are independent but you could not call them free.

And I am fitted to that land as the soul is to the body,
I know its contractions, waste, and sprawling indolence;
They are in me and its triumphs are my own,
Hard-won in the thin and bitter years without pretence.

Beauty is order and good chance in the artesian heart
And does not wholly fail, though we impede;
Though the reluctant and uneasy land resent
The gush of waters, the lean plough, the fretful seed.

Gnostic Prelude

The light was out; the sky was down;
Night walked in a black-bellied gown
Where for a season I found room,
A discontent within a shade
A clot of treason that betrayed
The dark instinctive gnosis of the womb.

I rose up in my infant might
And blinked upon the monstrous light
Repenting the lost fluid gloom:
The dawn was red and streaked with pain,
Dark Eden would not come again
In sleep or lover's tantrums or the tomb.

In midnight hours when quiet breath
Catches upon some rib of death
Some polished bone of memory;
When nightmare breathes upon the mind
As on a glass and peers behind
With mad and watchful eyes, malevolently;

When in the sexual night descended
The spirit quivers undefended
At the quick of human mystery;
When a woman's hair is a bush of pain
And the heart is a blind man in the rain
That nightlong sings of what it cannot see:

How then the blood in sightless grope
Seeks vainly for that Eden slope
And far declivity of doom;
Nor ever now is felt or heard
The murmur of sweet bones interred
The distant heart-beat pumping in the gloom.

The Blue Horses

I

What loud wave-motioned hooves awaken
Our dream-fast members from the cramp of sleep?
The tribal images are shaken
And crash upon their guardians. The skies
Are shivered like a pane of glass.

Progeny of winds, sea-forms, earth-bestriders,
From the blue quarries of their natal hills
Terribly emerging to their riders,
Blue Horses lift their neighing trumpets to the moon!
They stamp among the spiritual mills
That weave a universe from our decay:
The specious outline crumbles at the shock
Of visionary hooves, and in dismay
Men hide among the tumbled images.

The silver trumpets strike the moon!
O grasp the mane with virgin hand:
Beneath the knocking of the magic hoof
New spaces open and expand.

For in the world are spaces infinite
And each point is a mighty room
Where flowers with strange faces bloom
In the amazing light;
And every little crystal minute
Has many aeons locked within it
Within whose crystal depths we see
Times upon times eternally.

II

The whittled moon
Lies on the steep incline of night
Flanked by a stair of fading stars.
The hooves are silent.
Chimney-stacks
Pour their first smoke-trail across
The lightening cloud-bars.
The first wheel clacks
On grinding gears,
The pulley whirrs upon its boss.
Naked you lie and your own silence keep;
The arms of love are laid aside in sleep.
Soon it will be day like other days:
I cannot hold this hour in my hand
Nor press

Its image on a substance beyond time.
Possess!
But we are never in possession
And nothing stays at our command.
Possess!

Yet day comes on.
The delicate steel cranes manoeuvre
Like giant birds above their load;
The high song of the tyres is heard
Along the whitening road.
Possess!
All things escape us, as we too escape.
We have owned nothing and have no address
Save in the poor constriction
Of a legal or poetic fiction.
He that possesses is possessed
And falsifies perception lest
The visionary hooves break through
The simple seeming world he knew.

The harbour derricks swing their load upon the shore.
The sacred turbines hum, the factories
Set up their hallowed roar.
Men must awake betimes and work betimes
To furnish the supplies of war.
For some shall work and some possess
And all shall read the morning papers
And in the world's ripped entrails there displayed
Haruspicate for trends of love and trade.

Sleep no more, for while you sleep
Our love is stolen by the cheating sun
And angry frightened men destroy
Our peace with diktat, pact, and gun.
The old men of the tribe go mad
And guard with malice, fraud and guile
The sacred enzymes of a world gone bad.
The hoof-beats thunder in my ears.
Leave to the councillors the garbage-plot,
The refuse and the greasy tins
Of this slum-culture – these are not
The area where love begins.

The brutal and the vile are set
As watchers at the gate,
But the Blue Horses scream aloud:
A sudden movement shakes the crowd
Stampeded on the hooves of fate.

Dialogue

There was a pattering in the rafters, mother,
My dreams were troubled by the sounds above.

– That is just a young man's fancy, son,
Lightly turning now to thoughts of love.

I heard things moving in the cellar, mother,
And once I thought that something touched my side.

– Your father used to hear those noises, son,
About the time that I became a bride.

And when I woke up in the cold dawn, mother,
The rats had come and eaten my face away.

– Never mind, my son, you'll get another,
Your father he had several in his day.

from: *The Hero and the Hydra*

IV The Tomb of Heracles

A dry tree with an empty honeycomb
Stands as a broken column by the tomb:
The classic anguish of a rigid fate,
The loveless will, superb and desolate.

This is the end of stoic pride and state:
Blind light, dry rock, a tree that does not bear.

Look, cranes still know their path through empty air;
For them their world is neither soon nor late;
But ours is eaten hollow with despair.

Late Winter

The pallid cuckoo
Sent up in frail
Microtones
His tiny scale

On the cold air.
What joy I found
Mounting that tiny
Stair of sound.

In a Late Hour

Though all men should desert you
My faith shall not grow less,
But keep that single virtue
Of simple thankfulness.

Pursuit had closed around me,
Terrors had pressed me low;
You sought me, and you found me,
And I will not let you go.

The hearts of men grow colder,
The final things draw near,
Forms vanish, kingdoms moulder,
The Antirealm is here;

Whose order is derangement:
Close-driven, yet alone,
Men reach the last estrangement –
The sense of nature gone.

Though the stars run distracted,
And from wounds deep rancours flow,
While the mystery is enacted
I will not let you go.

Pietà

A year ago you came
Early into the light.
You lived a day and night,
Then died; no one to blame.

Once only, with one hand,
Your mother in farewell
Touched you. I cannot tell,
I cannot understand

A thing so dark and deep,
So physical a loss:
One touch, and that was all

She had of you to keep.
Clean wounds, but terrible,
Are those made with the Cross.

Legendary

You are the fish that hides
In the dangerous sea-cave
Or darts in the breaking wave.
Mine the thread that slides

From the evening star above.
Your greedy mouth once caught
You jerk the nylon taut
With the silver body of love.

And played before you are landed,
Fighting upon the hook,
For all the time you took

At length you lie gasping, stranded.
For us the legends waken,
This fish meant to be taken.

from: *The Seven Days of Creation*

The Seventh Day

Stillness is highest act,
Therefore be still and know
The pattern in the flow,
The reason in the fact.

Sabbath of the mind:
The beaked implacable
Tearing of the will
Arrested and defined.

Not to need either
To kill or to possess
Is a day's clear weather.

The grinding stops; we untether
The abused beast, and confess
We've heard of happiness.

The Cloak

With fifty years not lived but gone, we find
Death the Magician, his dark cloak crimson-lined,
    Performing to the crowd we've known.
    No volunteer? But the cloak is thrown

Over this or that one, and they disappear,
Leaving in us an astonished void, a fear,
    A decent numbness, or raw grief,
    And sometimes that obscene relief

We feel when one we've wronged, or who knew our shame,
Is not there to cast a shadow of blame –
    He may have forgotten, or forgiven:
    We wish him very well in heaven.

The cloak's lining, is that red for pain,
Or promise? Death doesn't comment or explain.
  Caped in darkness, do they fly
  Into the land of symmetry,

To the jade mountain veined with crystal streams,
Or whatever else they saw in dreams?
  We don't know. The house is packed;
  He doesn't need to change the act.

Released on Parole

Out walking in July
I see wind, cloud and light
Weave pictures in the sky.
Blest by so clear a sight,
I never want to look
At shadows in a book.

Light snow there on bare rock;
A hawk balanced in air;
And over his cirrus flock
The sun's silver stare
Saying, look what *I* give:
Won't you consent to live?

Well, I consent; I'll try.
I've done twenty years hard –
A life term, God knows why,
With exercise in the yard.
And alas, to have done time
Becomes itself a crime.

One Tuesday in Summer

That sultry afternoon the world went strange.
Under a violet and leaden bruise
The air was filled with sinister yellow light;
Trees, houses, grass took on unnatural hues.

Thunder rolled near. The intensity grew and grew
Like doom itself with lightnings on its face.
And Mr Pitt, the grocer's order-man,
Who made his call on Tuesdays at our place,

Said to my mother, looking at the sky,
'You'd think the ending of the world had come.'
A leathern little man, with bicycle-clips
Around his ankles, doing our weekly sum,

He too looked strange in that uncanny light;
As in the Bible ordinary men
Turn out to be angelic messengers,
Pronouncing the Lord's judgments why and when.

I watched the scurry of the small black ants
That sensed the storm. What Mr Pitt had said
I didn't quite believe, or disbelieve;
But still the words had got into my head,

For nothing less seemed worthy of the scene.
The darkening imminence hung on and on,
Till suddenly, with lightning-stroke and rain,
Apocalypse exploded, and was gone.

By nightfall things had their familiar look.
But I had seen the world stand in dismay
Under the aspect of another meaning
That rain or time would hardly wash away.

Because

My father and my mother never quarrelled.
They were united in a kind of love
As daily as the *Sydney Morning Herald*,
Rather than like the eagle or the dove.

I never saw them casually touch,
Or show a moment's joy in one another.
Why should this matter to me now so much?
I think it bore more hardly on my mother,

Who had more generous feelings to express.
My father had dammed up his Irish blood
Against all drinking praying fecklessness,
And stiffened into stone and creaking wood.

His lips would make a switching sound, as though
Spontaneous impulse must be kept at bay.
That it was mainly weakness I see now,
But then my feelings curled back in dismay.

Small things can pit the memory like a cyst:
Having seen other fathers greet their sons,
I put my childish face up to be kissed
After an absence. The rebuff still stuns

My blood. The poor man's curt embarrassment
At such a delicate proffer of affection
Cut like a saw. But home the lesson went:
My tenderness thenceforth escaped detection.

My mother sang *Because*, and *Annie Laurie*,
White Wings, and other songs; her voice was sweet.
I never gave enough, and I am sorry;
But we were all closed in the same defeat.

People do what they can; they were good people,
They cared for us and loved us. Once they stood
Tall in my childhood as the school, the steeple.
How can I judge without ingratitude?

Judgment is simply trying to reject
A part of what we are because it hurts.
The living cannot call the dead collect:
They won't accept the charge, and it reverts.

It's my own judgment day that I draw near,
Descending in the past, without a clue,
Down to that central deadness: the despair
Older than any hope I ever knew.

Keep the Season

Keep the season: let the hive
Rob the day to pay the dark;
Pollen-scented thieves deprive
Leatherwood and ironbark,
Then in telltale dance expound
Where the sweetness can be found.

Keep the season: birds repeat
In the plainchant we have lost
Melismatic turns so sweet
As to hide what love can cost:
Let their Latin fill the air
With devotion, with despair.

Keep the season: let the heart
Work its mystery one more time,
Fabricating, sick with art,
Virtue crazed and stained like crime.
If we knew enough to give
We might find a way to live.

Wet Day

Rain sweeps in as the gale begins to blow,
The water is glaucous-green and mauve and grey.
A pelican takes refuge on the bay;
Snow-white and black it rides the complex flow.

A child stands in a yellow mackintosh.
Gulls lift away and circle round about.
Cans, bottles, and junk appear as the tide runs out.
Wind cannot sweep away nor water wash

The dreck of our vulgarity. I think
The world has never been redeemed; at least
The marks it bears are mostly of the Beast –
The broken trust, the litter, and the stink.

World on Sunday

Brown lilac, roses filled with rain;
Hayfever streaming off mown grass.
Traffic roars down the underpass
Like water swallowed by a drain.

Disordered beds where we have lain;
Life and death offered at Mass;
Our thoughts are giddy, weak, and crass.
It isn't easy to explain.

Dusk brings wanderers out again,
Kept moving by a sense of loss.
The lights change; cars and people cross.

I turn back from the sunset stain.
A huge moon yellow like dull brass
Lengthens my shadow down the lane.

Nocturne

A gull flies low across the darkening bay.
Along the shore the casuarinas sigh.
Resentful plovers give their ratcheting cry
From the mown field scattered with bales of hay.

The world sinks out of sight. The moon congealed
In cloud seems motionless. The air is still.
A cry goes out from the exhausted will.
Nightmares and angels roam the empty field.

Winter Drive

Fallow fields, dark pewter sky,
Steely light on the wet plain,
Evening falls in freezing rain
With a promise and a lie.

Promise in the leaden sky,
In the leaden fields' bleak shine,
In the slate vats full of wine,
In the knowledge that we die.

But the lie is in the soul,
And it rots the world we have
Till there's nothing left to save.

Dying world and deadened sky,
Traffic roars beyond control.
What is left to make us try?

'ERN MALLEY'

Dürer: Innsbruck, 1495

I had often, cowled in the slumberous heavy air,
Closed my inanimate lids to find it real,
As I knew it would be, the colourful spires
And painted roofs, the high snows glimpsed at the back
All reversed in the quiet reflecting waters –
Not knowing then that Dürer perceived it too.
Now I find that once more I have shrunk
To an interloper, robber of dead men's dream,
I had read in books that art is not easy
But no one warned that the mind repeats
In its ignorance the vision of others. I am still
the black swan of trespass on alien waters.

Sonnets for the Novachord

I

Rise from the wrist, o kestrel
Mind, to a clear expanse.
Perform your high dance
On the clouds of ancestral
Duty. Hawk at the wraith
Of remembered emotions.
Vindicate our high notions
Of a new and pitiless faith.
It is not without risk!

In a lofty attempt
The fool makes a brisk
Tumble. Rightly contempt
Rewards the cloud-foot unwary
Who falls to the prairie.

II

Poetry: the loaves and fishes,
Or no less miracle;
For in this deft pentacle
We imprison our wishes.

Though stilled to alabaster
This Ichthys shall swim
From the mind's disaster
On the volatile hymn.

If this be the norm
Of our serious frolic
There's no remorse:

Our magical force
Cleaves the ignorant storm
On the hyperbolic.

Sweet William

I have avoided your wide English eyes:
But now I am whirled in their vortex.
My blood becomes a Damaged Man
Most like your Albion;
And I must go with stone feet
Down the staircase of flesh
To where in a shuddering embrace
My toppling opposites commit
The obscene, the unforgivable rape.

One moment of daylight let me have
Like a white arm thrust
Out of the dark and self-denying wave
And in the one moment I
Shall irremediably attest
How (though with sobs, and torn cries bleeding)
My white swan of quietness lies
Sanctified on my black swan's breast.

Boult to Marina

Only a part of me shall triumph in this
(I am not Pericles)
Though I have your silken eyes to kiss
And maiden-knees
Part of me remains, wench, Boult-upright
The rest of me drops off into the night.

What would you have me do? Go to the wars?
There's damned deceit
In these wounds, thrusts, shell-holes, of the cause
And I'm no cheat.
So blowing this lily as trumpet with my lips
I assert my original glory in the dark eclipse.

Sainted and schismatic would you be?
Four frowning bedposts
Will be the cliffs of your wind-thrummelled sea
Lady of these coasts,
Blown lily, surplice and stole of Mytilene,
You shall rest snug to-night and know what I mean.

Sybilline

That rabbit's foot I carried in my left pocket
Has worn a haemorrhage in the lining
The bunch of keys I carry with it
Jingles like fate in my omophagic ear
And when I stepped clear of the solid basalt
The introverted obelisk of night
I seized upon this Traumdeutung as a sword
To hew a passage to my love.

And now out of life, permanent revenant
I assert: the caterpillar feet
Of these predictions lead nowhere,
It is necessary to understand
That a poet may not exist, that his writings
Are the incomplete circle and straight drop
Of a question mark
And yet I know I shall be raised up
On the vertical banners of praise.

The rabbit's foot of fur and claw
Taps on the drain-pipe. In the alley
The children throw a ball against
Their future walls. The evening
Settles down like a brooding bird
Over streets that divide our life like a trauma
Would it be strange now to meet
The figure that strode hell swinging
His head by the hair
On Princess Street?

Night Piece

The swung torch scatters seeds
In the umbelliferous dark
And a frog makes guttural comment
On the naked and trespassing
Nymph of the lake.

The symbols were evident,
Though on park-gates
The iron birds looked disapproval
With rusty invidious beaks.

Among the water-lilies
A splash - white foam in the dark!
And you lay sobbing then
Upon my trembling intuitive arm.

Documentary Film

Innumerable the images
The register of birth and dying
Under a carved rococo porch
The Tigris - Venice - Melbourne - The Ch'en Plain -
And the sound track like a trail of saliva.
Dürer:
'Samson killing the Lion' 1498
Thumbs twisting the great snarl of the beast's mouth
Tail thrashing the air of disturbed swallows
That fly to the castle on the abraded hill
London:
Samson that great city, his anatomy on fire
Grasping with gnarled hands at the mad wasps
Yet while his bearded rage survives contriving
An entelechy of clouds and trumpets.
There have been interpolations, false syndromes
Like a rivet through the hand

Such deliberate suppressions of crisis as
Footscray:
The slant sun now descending
Upon the montage of the desecrate womb
Opened like a drain.
The young men aspire
Like departing souls from leaking roofs
And fractured imploring windows to
(All must be synchronized, the jagged
Quartz of vision with the asphalt of human speech)
Java:
The elephant motifs contorted on admonitory walls,
The subtle nagas that raise the cobra hood
And hiss in the white masterful face.
What are these mirk channels of the flesh
That now sweep me from
The blood-dripping hirsute maw of night's other temple
Down through the helpless row of bonzes
Till peace suddenly comes:
Adonai:
The solemn symphony of angels lighting
My steps with music, o consolations!
Palms!
O far shore, target and shield that I now
Desire beyond these terrestrial commitments.

Palinode

There are ribald interventions
Like spurious seals upon
A Chinese landscape-roll
Or tangents to the rainbow.
We have known these declensions,
Have winked when Hyperion
Was transmuted to a troll.
We dubbed it a sideshow.

Now we find, too late
That these distractions were clues
To a transposed version
Of our too rigid state.
It is an ancient forgotten ruse
And a natural diversion.
Wiser now, but dissident,

I snap off your wrist
Like a stalk that entangles
And make my adieu.
Remember, in any event,
I was a haphazard amorist
Caught on the unlikely angles
Of an awkward arrangement. Weren't you?

Night-piece

(Alternate Version)

The intemperate torch grazed
With fire the umbel of the dark.
The pond-lilies could not stifle
The green descant of frogs.

We had not heeded the warning
That the iron birds creaked.
As we swung the park-gates
Their beaks glinted with dew.

A splash – the silver nymph
Was a foam flake in the night.
But though the careful winds
Visited our trembling flesh
They carried no echo.

Baroque Exterior

When the hysterical vision strikes
The facade of an era it manifests
Its insidious relations.
The windowed eyes gleam with terror
The twin balconies are breasts
And at the efflux of a period's error
Is a carved malicious portico.
Everyman arrests
His motives in these anthropoid erections.

Momentarily we awake –
Even as lately through wide eyes I saw
The promise of a new architecture
Of more sensitive pride, and I cursed
For the first time my own obliteration.
What Inigo had built I perceived
In a dream of recognition,
And for nights afterwards struggled
Helpless against the choking
Sands of time in my throat.

Perspective Lovesong

It was a night when the planets
Were wreathed in dying garlands.
It seemed we had substituted
The abattoirs for the guillotine.
I shall not forget how you invented
Then, the conventions of faithfulness.

It seemed that we were submerged
Under a reef of coral to tantalize
The wise-grinning shark. The waters flashed
With Blue Angels and Moorish Idols.
And if I mistook your dark hair for weed
Was it not floating upon my tides?

I have remembered the chiaroscuro
Of your naked breasts and loins.
For you were wholly an admonition
That said: 'From bright to dark
Is a brief longing. To hasten is now
To delay.' But I could not obey.

Princess, you lived in Princess St.,
Where the urchins pick their nose in the sun
With the left hand. You thought
That paying the price would give you admission
To the sad autumn of my Valhalla.
But I, too, invented faithfulness.

Culture as Exhibit

'Swamps, marshes, borrow-pits and other
Areas of stagnant water serve
As breeding-grounds . . .' Now
Have I found you, my Anopheles!
(There is a meaning for the circumspect)
Come, we will dance sedate quadrilles,
A pallid polka or a yelping shimmy
Over these sunken sodden breeding-grounds!
We will be wraiths and wreaths of tissue-paper
To clog the Town Council in their plans.
Culture forsooth! Albert, get my gun.

I have been noted in the reading-rooms
As a borer of calf-bound volumes
Full of scandals at the Court. (Milord
Had his hand upon that snowy globe
Milady Lucy's sinister breast . . .) Attendants
Have peered me over while I chewed
Back-numbers of Florentine gazettes
(Knowst not, my Lucia, that he
Who has caparisoned a nun dies

With his twankydillo at the ready? . . .)
But in all of this I got no culture till
I read a little pamphlet on my thighs
Entitled: 'Friction as a Social Process.'
What?
Look, my Anopheles,
See how the floor of Heav'n is thick
Inlaid with patines of etcetera . . .
Sting them, sting them, my Anopheles.

Egyptian Register

The hand burns resinous in the evening sky
Which is a lake of roses, perfumes, idylls
Breathed from the wastes of the Tartarean heart.
The skull gathers darkness, like an inept mountain
That broods on its aeons of self-injury.
The spine, barbed and venomous, pierces
The one unmodulated cumulus of cloud
And brings the gush of evanescent waters.
The lungs are Ra's divine aquaria
Where the striped fish move at will
Towards a purpose darker than a dawn.
The body's a hillside, darling, moist
With bitter dews of regret.
The genitals (o lures of starveling faiths!)
Make an immense index to my cold remorse.

Magic in the vegetable universe
Marks us at birth upon the forehead
With the ancient ankh. Nature
Has her own green centuries which move
Through our thin convex time. Aeons
Of that purpose slowly riot
In the decimals of our deceiving age.
It may be for nothing that we are:
But what we are continues

In larger patterns than the frontal stone
That taunts the living life.
O those dawn-waders, cold-sea-gazers,
The long-shanked ibises that on the Nile
Told one hushed peasant of rebirth
Move in a calm immortal frieze
On the mausoleum of my incestuous
And self-fructifying death.

Young Prince of Tyre

> 'Thy ear is liable, thy food is such
> As hath been belch'd on by infected lungs'
> Pericles

Inattentive, suborned, betrayed, and shiftless,
You have hawked in your throat and spat
Outrage upon the velocipede of thriftless
Mechanical men posting themselves that
Built you a gibbet in the vile morass
Which now you must dangle on, alas.

The eyeless worm threads the bone, the living
Stand upright by habitual insouciance
Else they would fall. But how unforgiving
Are they to nonce-men that falter in the dance!
Their words are clews that clutched you on the post
And you were hung up, dry, a fidgety ghost.

The magpie's carol has dried upon his tongue
To a flaky spittle of contempt. The loyalists
Clank their armour. We are no longer young,
And our rusty coat fares badly in the lists.
Poor Thaisa has a red wound in the groin
That ill advises our concupiscence to foin.

Yet there is one that stands i' the gaps to teach us
The stages of our story. He the dark hero
Moistens his finger in iguana's blood to beseech us
(Siegfried-like) to renew the language. Nero
And the botched tribe of imperial poets burn
Like the rafters. The new men are cool as spreading fern.

Now get you out, as you can, makeshift singers:
'Sail seas in cockles, have an wish for't.'
New sign-posts stretch out the road that lingers
Yet on the spool. New images distort
Our creeping disjunct minds to incredible patterns,
Else thwarting the wayward seas to fetch home the slatterns,

Take it for a sign, insolent and superb
That at nightfall the woman who scarcely would
Now opens her cunning thighs to reveal the herb
Of content. The valiant man who withstood
Rage, envy and malignant love, is no more
The wrecked Prince he was on the latter shore.

Colloquy with John Keats

> 'And the Lord destroyeth the imagination of all them
> that had not the truth with them.'
>
> Odes of Solomon 24.8

I have been bitter with you, my brother,
Remembering that saying of Lenin when the shadow
Was already on his face: 'The emotions are not skilled workers.'
Yet we are as the double almond concealed in one shell.
I have mistrusted your apodictic strength
Saying always: Yet why did you not finish Hyperion?
But now I have learned not to curtail
What was in you the valency of speech
The bond of molecular utterance.

I have arranged the interstellar zodiac
With flowers on the Goat's horn, and curious
Markings on the back of the Crab. I have lain
With the Lion, not with the Virgin, and become
He that discovers meanings.

Now in your honour Keats, I spin
The loaded Zodiac with my left hand
As the man at the fair revolves
His coloured deceitful board. Together
We lean over that whirl of
Beasts flowers images and men
Until it stops . . . Look! my number is up!
Like you I sought at first for Beauty
And then, in disgust, returned
As did you to the locus of sensation
And not till then did my voice build crenellated towers
Of an enteric substance in the air.
Then first I learned to speak clear; then through my turrets
Pealed that Great Bourdon which men have ignored.

Coda

We have lived as ectoplasm
The hand that would clutch
Our substance finds that his rude touch
Runs through him a frightful spasm
And hurls him back against the opposite wall.

Petit Testament

In the twenty-fifth year of my age
I find myself to be a dromedary
That has run short of water between
One oasis and the next mirage
And having despaired of ever
Making my obsessions intelligible
I am content at last to be
The sole clerk of my metamorphoses.
Begin here:

In the year 1943
I resigned to the living all collateral images
Reserving to myself a man's
Inalienable right to be sad
At his own funeral.
(Here the peacock blinks the eyes
of his multipennate tail.)
In the same year
I said to my love (who is living)
Dear we shall never be that verb
Perched on the sole Arabian Tree
Not having learnt in our green age to forget
The sins that flow between the hands and feet
(Here the Tree weep gum tears
Which are also real: I tell you
These things are real)
So I forced a parting
Scrubbing my few dingy words to brightness.

Where I have lived
The bed-bug sleeps in the seam, the cockroach
Inhabits the crack and the careful spider
Spins his aphorisms in the corner.
I have heard them shout in the streets
The chiliasms of the Socialist Reich
And in the magazines I have read
The Popular Front-to-Back.

But where I have lived
Spain weeps in the gutters of Footscray
Guernica is the ticking of the clock
The nightmare has become real, not as belief
But in the scrub-typhus of Mubo.

It is something to be at last speaking
Though in this No-Man's-language appropriate
Only to No-Man's-Land.
Set this down too:
I have pursued rhyme, image, and metre,
Known all the clefts in which the foot may stick,
Stumbled often, stammered,
But in time the fading voice grows wise
And seizing the co-ordinates of all existence
Traces the inevitable graph
And in conclusion:
There is a moment when the pelvis
Explodes like a grenade. I
Who have lived in the shadow that each act
Casts on the next act now emerge
As loyal as the thistle that in session
Puffs its full seed upon the indicative air.
I have split the infinitive. Beyond is anything.

ROSEMARY DOBSON

The Three Fates

At the instant of drowning he invoked the three sisters.
It was a mistake, an aberration, to cry out for
Life everlasting.

He came up like a cork and back to the river-bank,
Put on his clothes in reverse order,
Returned to the house.

He suffered the enormous agonies of passion
Writing poems from the end backwards,
Brushing away tears that had not yet fallen.

Loving her wildly as the day regressed towards morning
He watched her swinging in the garden, growing younger,
Bare-foot, straw-hatted.

And when she was gone and the house and the swing and daylight
There was an instant's pause before it began all over,
The reel unrolling towards the river.

Being Called For

Come in at the low-silled window,
Enter by the door through the vine-leaves
Growing over the lintel. I have hung bells at the
Window to be stirred by the breath of your
Coming, which may be at any season.

In winter the snow throws
Light on the ceiling. If you come in winter
There will be a blue shadow before you
Cast on the threshold.

In summer an eddying of white dust
And a brightness falling between the leaves.

When you come I am ready: only, uncertain –
Shall we be leaving at once on another journey?
I would like first to write it all down and leave the pages
On the table weighted with a stone,
Nevertheless I have put in a basket
The coins for the ferry.

OODGEROO OF THE TRIBE NOONUCCAL

We are Going

for Grannie Coolwell

They came in to the little town
A semi-naked band subdued and silent,
All that remained of their tribe.
They came here to the place of their old bora ground
Where now the many white men hurry about like ants.
Notice of estate agent reads: 'Rubbish May Be Tipped Here'.
Now it half covers the traces of the old bora ring.
They sit and are confused, they cannot say their thoughts:
'We are as strangers here now, but the white tribe are the strangers.
We belong here, we are of the old ways.
We are the corroboree and the bora ground,
We are the old sacred ceremonies, the laws of the elders.
We are the wonder tales of Dream Time, the tribal legends told.
We are the past, the hunts and the laughing games, the wandering
    camp fires.
We are the lighning-bolt over Gaphembah Hill
Quick and terrible,
And the Thunderer after him, that loud fellow.
We are the quiet daybreak paling the dark lagoon.
We are the shadow-ghosts creeping back as the camp fires burn low.
We are nature and the past, all the old ways
Gone now and scattered.
The scrubs are gone, the hunting and the laughter.
The eagle is gone, the emu and the kangaroo are gone from this
    place.
The bora ring is gone.
The corroboree is gone.
And we are going.'

No More Boomerang

No more boomerang
No more spear;
Now all civilized –
Colour bar and beer.

No more corroboree,
Gay dance and din.
Now we got movies,
And pay to go in.

No more sharing
What the hunter brings.
Now we work for money,
Then pay it back for things.

Now we track bosses
To catch a few bob,
Now we go walkabout
On bus to the job.

One time naked,
Who never knew shame;
Now we put clothes on
To hide whatsaname.

No more gunya,
Now bungalow,
Paid by higher purchase
In twenty year or so.

Lay down the stone axe,
Take up the steel,
And work like a nigger
For a white man meal.

No more firesticks
That made the whites scoff.
Now all electric,
And no better off.

Bunyip he finish,
Now got instead
White fella Bunyip,
Call him Red.

Abstract picture now –
What they coming at?
Cripes, in our caves we
Did better than that.

Black hunted wallaby,
White hunt dollar;
White fella witch-doctor
Wear dog-collar.

No more message-stick;
Lubras and lads
Got television now,
Mostly ads.

Lay down the woomera,
Lay down the waddy.
Now we got atom-bomb,
End *every*body.

Last of His Tribe

Change is the law. The new must oust the old.
I look at you and am back in the long ago,
Old pinnaroo lonely and lost here,
Last of your clan.
Left only with your memories, you sit
And think of the gay throng, the happy people,
The voices and the laughter
All gone, all gone,
And you remain alone.

I asked and you let me hear
The soft vowelly tongue to be heard now
No more for ever.
For me
You enact old scenes, old ways, you who have used
Boomerang and spear.
You singer of ancient tribal songs,
You leader once in the corroboree,
You twice in fierce tribal fights
With wild enemy blacks from over the river,
All gone, all gone. And I feel
The sudden sting of tears, Willie Mackenzie
In the Salvation Army Home.
Displaced person in your own country,
Lonely in teeming city crowds,
Last of your tribe.

Dawn Wail for the Dead

Dim light of daybreak now
Faintly over the sleeping camp.
Old lubra first to wake remembers:
First thing every dawn
Remember the dead, cry for them.
Softly at first her wail begins,
One by one as they wake and hear
Join in the cry, and the whole camp
Wails for the dead, the poor dead
Gone from here to the Dark Place:
They are remembered.
Then it is over, life now,
Fires lit, laughter now,
And a new day calling.

GWEN HARWOOD

Clair de Lune

Poet to Bluestocking

Let us walk with this cone of light
lying seaward. It points where earth's ashen
impoverished fragment importunes
all oceans and lovers and poets,
whose waxing has made and whose waning
unmade you, whose wall-scaling tinsel
has captured your vizored city.

On our right lie flickering houses
but seaward emptiness filters through
your inhaling nostrils. You nibble at space,
blot a starfield out with a starfish hand,
while streaking and scraping the moonlit shore
your image deformed scrawls a body
impenetrable by this light.

As tensile as spider webbing
is your nightshade self, is your weightless
unliving siege in this scandalous town.
In Amazon forests the Indians
empty the stomachs of captured apes
and parrots that feed in unscalable trees,
then feed on the half-digested fruits.

So towering spirits caught
by your prick-eared wit are opened
and an after-image of rapture, a fragment of passion
savoured and sucked.

                              Ah, nature
is wasteful, the wild thrust of lovers
is careless, the flux of this swarming sea
is endless. The artist alone

is sparing. In light from a single source,
with calm and indolent judgement,
with the tip of a pen, with a paintbrush,
he will seal and transfigure the changing face
of truth, which is living, and moving with us as we walk,
and stays with the lovers who lie in creation's act;
like this cone of light on the sea.

In the Park

She sits in the park. Her clothes are out of date.
Two children whine and bicker, tug her skirt.
A third draws aimless patterns in the dirt.
Someone she loved once passes by - too late

to feign indifference to that casual nod.
'How nice,' et cetera. 'Time holds great surprises.'
From his neat head unquestionably rises
a small balloon . . . 'but for the grace of God . . .'

They stand a while in flickering light, rehearsing
the children's names and birthdays. 'It's so sweet
to hear their chatter, watch them grow and thrive,'
she says to his departing smile. Then, nursing
the youngest child, sits staring at her feet.
To the wind she says, 'They have eaten me alive.'

Nightfall

One evening when a genial air
ruffled the jacaranda trees
Professor Kröte spread his square
musician's hands on his plump knees,
and, sighing, sat alone amongst the uncaring
derelict drunks, and lovers, while the flaring

coat of the river glowed and flamed
with sunset, and declined to drab
monotony, and smokestacks framed
in saffron light rose up to stab
his breast with memories: a yellow sky;
cypress, jet-black; a boy plays 'Islamei'

with arrogant skill; his teacher claws
a fine gilt chair with nervous pride –
and then the turbulent applause;
rococo gods and cherubs ride
his winds of promise, and their gilded scrolls
shine in that glittering hall; the Danube rolls

past those high windows in its skin
of sunset.
              'Who would know me now,
a second-rate musician in
an ignorant town? Or tell me how
discords of fading light find and restore
the colours of a day that comes no more?'

So Kröte mused, as if his lost
hope darkened on the water's face.
The poor drunks slept beneath a host
of falling flowers. In light embrace
awaiting night, young lovers moved their tender
hands with instinctive gestures of surrender.

Sleep with its textureless draperies
curtained him. His lean spirit stayed
watchful among the shaken trees
drinking God's peace, and humbly prayed
for daily bread, for one hour when he might
rejoice, that his should be not required that night.

Kröte, waking from troubled rest,
tossing with his wild musician's hair,
feeling the torment leave his breast
and vanish in the gentle air,
knew he must find, in his soul's night, alone,
what more the city held than brick and stone.

Carnal Knowledge I

Roll back, you fabulous animal
be human, sleep. I'll call you up
from water's dazzle, wheat-blond hills,
clear light and open-hearted roses,
this day's extravagance of blue
stored like a pulsebeat in the skull.

Content to be your love, your fool,
your creature tender and obscene
I'll bite sleep's innocence away
and wake the flesh my fingers cup
to build a world from what's to hand,
new energies of light and space

wings for blue distance, fins to sweep
the obscure caverns of your heart,
a tongue to lift your sweetness close
leaf-speech against the window-glass
a memory of chaos weeping
mute forces hammering for shape

sea-strip and sky-strip held apart
for earth to form its hills and roses
its landscape from our blind caresses,
blue air, horizon, water-flow,
bone to my bone I grasp the world.
But what you are I do not know.

from: *Father and Child*

I Barn Owl

Daybreak: the household slept.
I rose, blessed by the sun.
A horny fiend, I crept
out with my father's gun.
Let him dream of a child
obedient, angel-mild –

old No-Sayer, robbed of power
by sleep. I knew my prize
who swooped home at this hour
with daylight-riddled eyes
to his place on a high beam
in our old stables, to dream

light's useless time away.
I stood, holding my breath,
in urine-scented hay,
master of life and death,
a wisp-haired judge whose law
would punish beak and claw.

My first shot struck. He swayed,
ruined, beating his only
wing, as I watched, afraid
by the fallen gun, a lonely
child who believed death clean
and final, not this obscene

bundle of stuff that dropped,
and dribbled through loose straw
tangling in bowels, and hopped
blindly closer. I saw
those eyes that did not see
mirror my cruelty

while the wrecked thing that could
not bear the light nor hide
hobbled in its own blood.
My father reached my side,
gave me the fallen gun.
'End what you have begun.'

I fired. The blank eyes shone
once into mine, and slept.
I leaned my head upon
my father's arm, and wept,
owl-blind in early sun
for what I had begun.

The Sea Anemones

Grey mountains, sea and sky. Even the misty
seawind is grey. I walk on lichened rock
in a kind of late assessment, call it peace.
Then the anemones, scarlet, gouts of blood.
There is a word I need, and earth was speaking.
I cannot hear. These seaflowers are too bright.
Kneeling on rock, I touch them through cold water.
My fingers meet some hungering gentleness.
A newborn child's lips moved so at my breast.
I woke, once, with my palm across your mouth.
   The word is: *ever*. Why add salt to salt?
   Blood drop by drop among the rocks they shine.
   Anemos, wind. The spirit, where it will.
Not flowers, no, animals that must eat or die.

Mid-Channel

*'The days shall come upon you, that he will take you away
with hooks, and your posterity with fishhooks.'*

Amos IV, 2

Cod inert as an old boot,
tangling dance of the little shark,
perch nibble, flathead jerk –
blindfold I'd know them on my line.

Fugitive gleam on scale and fin,
lustrous eye, opalescent belly
dry and die in the undesired
element. A day will come,

matter-of-fact as knife and plate,
with death's hook in my jaw, and language
unspeakable, the line full out.
I'll tire you with my choking weight

old monster anchored in the void.
My God, you'll wonder what you've caught.
Land me in hell itself at last
I'll stab and swell your wounds with poison.

Not here, not now. Water's my kingdom
tonight, my line makes starspecks tremble.
The dinghy's decked with golden eyes
and still the cod boil round my bait.

Mother Who Gave Me Life

Mother who gave me life
I think of women bearing
women. Forgive me the wisdom
I would not learn from you.

It is not for my children I walk
on earth in the light of the living.
It is for you, for the wild
daughters becoming women,

anguish of seasons burning
backward in time to those other
bodies, your mother, and hers
and beyond, speech growing stranger

on thresholds of ice, rock, fire,
bones changing, heads inclining
to monkey bosom, lemur breast,
guileless milk of the word.

I prayed you would live to see
Halley's Comet a second time.
The Sister said, When she died
she was folding a little towel.

You left the world so, having lived
nearly thirty thousand days:
a fabric of marvels folded
down to a little space.

At our last meeting I closed
the ward door of heavy glass
between us, and saw your face
crumple, fine threadbare linen

worn, still good to the last,
then, somehow, smooth to a smile
so I should not see your tears.
Anguish: remembered hours:

a lamp on embroidered linen,
my supper set out, your voice
calling me in as darkness
falls on my father's house.

DIMITRIS TSALOUMAS

Note

The day took such a time to pass
   where have you been
in your courtyard it was fine but now
   the air strikes chill
and I must leave before the evening comes.
   Three times I knocked
there seemed to be someone at the door
   bitter unwelcome thought
so I must leave now it makes no matter
   if I can I'll come again.

A Progressive Man's Indignation

Why the hell do you grumble and blame tourism
for everything? What's wrong with it in any case?
Would you prefer hovels still and market-gardens
so you can ride between them on donkey-back and scratch
your knees on the withies? Or to creep around
hugging the wall of old Kalafatas's property, jumping
like a hare lest the wave should catch you and
you squelch to work as though you'd pissed yourself?
For sure, you folk would rather have the people
slaving for a crust of bread, so you could hear
the gentle evening clack of wheel-wells, tinkling bells
at dawn, and have the beach all to yourselves at noon.
If I had a property in the spot that yours is in,

115

I'd raise a fifty-room hotel, I'd . . .
That's how my fellow-countrymen go on, and truly
they've never yet had whiter bread to eat,
nor portlier corporations,
nor a glossier sheen on their bald heads.

Consolation

Yesterday's conversation has been on my mind all day
    and it annoys me now that I succumbed
to the pressure of your despondency. I know it's hard
    to tell of your loss among the empty chairs
that string the island beach at summer's end,
    as twilight falls like a tear
and you have the whole winter ahead of you
    with the four walls of your house
for company. But what's to be done, old friend?
    Did you think of me in your days of glory
when you set birds to sing in my sleep
    lest the brightness of your days should fade?
Or do you think, seeing that I'm used to it, that loss
    and deprivation cannot hurt the poor?
Maybe. Yet to have held something in your hands
    is worth the bitterness of losing it.

Old Friend

I came, you know, but your gate was locked
and barbed wire topped the walls. Beyond the foliage
sun-dappled shadow on a distant wall:
the house was not where the old one stood.
I heard news of you in the coffee-house,
what struggles you'd had, what victories; it seems
my youthful dreams have been fulfilled in you.
Don't complain if I leave without seeing you.
These days there's nothing left for us to share.

Return of an Ikon

I placed my hand cupped
over your eyes
and snuffed the fearsome sun.
A playful gesture merely,
neither symbol nor metaphor
in the clangorous blazonry of surf
noontide and youthful flesh.

Pushing through years unmemorable
this image now returns
candle-bright in wakeful passion.
Your eyelashes flutter
against my palm like moths
trapped in the chilly dome
of some crepuscular cathedral.

Falcon Drinking

Awakened to this other bleakness
I sit to read my daily portion

of the wall. Sometimes it's voices:
women disputing a place at the head

of public fountains in years of drought,
Orpheus pleading in the basement,

the anguished bidding at the 'Change.
Sometimes it's touch:

shuddering flesh and silken skin,
the clammy passage of darkness

in the night corridors, forgotten scars
and varnishes on old violins.

Today is seeing time. Knife-sharp,
a cruel blade of light cuts through

the brain's greyness, sweeps over mists
and hints at ridges, distantly.

Close in, at the stone-trough
hard by the spring of language where

the cypress stands, a falcon drinks.
The cypress ripples in shattered water

nights of many moons and nightingales.
The bird stoops shivering to sip

then tilts its head back skywards,
stammers its beak and trills

the narrow tongue. Spilt drops
hang bright in midair, hard as tears.

Autumn Supper

Only this table by the draughty window
bare since the beginning of time:

a knife, black olives, a hunk of bread.
The bottle glows dark in the late

autumn light, and in the glass,
against the wind and the raging seas,

the one rose of the difficult year.
All my life long I've hankered

after simplicity. When night falls
don't come to light the candles and pour

the wine. There's not enough for two;
I cannot share my hunger.

The Grudge

Strange that your image should occur to me
as I beat the grass for snakes in this

forsaken patch. It doesn't seem right to me.
I have always thought your manner somewhat

too correct, but your business dealings
are of good report. Or is it the woman

who shares my bed? She burns in the flesh
of many a man and I find it galling, I confess,

that you should never look at her that way.
It kind of blunts the sting of my pleasure.

Nor does the splendour of my house and fame
move you much. Yet there you are, my friend,

flushed out of grass by the scouting stick
amid the knotted vines, pleasant as ever,

tall in the haze a cut above the likes of me.
It bothers me. This is my brother's vineyard.

DOROTHY HEWETT

This Version of Love

I have seen her, wonderful!
A waterfall of hair, body like glass,
Wading through the goldfish pools in winter,
Her white shark-skin dress dark-wet above her thighs,
The very shape and effigy of love:
Or turbanned, earringed, lying on the lawn
Among the clover burrs, her bangles clacking,
                        reading Ern Malley.
Oh! her nipples under her black lace bras
And flimsy blouses, her gold hair pins
Strewn in the car upholstery.

In the bar of the O.B.H. the crème de menthe
Slopped in the green squid bottles on the shelf,
The rain beat in great waves, running down
                    the plate glass windows.
On V.E. day a Yank gob somersaulted through
A jagged icy cut-out in the air,
Crusted with drops of blood.
'Shall I marry?
        Who shall I marry?
        Shall I die now
Swallowing lysol one glittering afternoon
Before my breasts fall and my womb tilts?'
Salt and water, the stomach pump
Coils like an evil creeper, wraps her round,
Choking and arching in the public ward.
In the queues outside the abortionist's
The white statues of cupids tumble at her feet.

The police-woman stands righteous beside her bed.
'Next time you try it you won't get away with it.'
'Obliterate me, save me, I go down
Hanging by my hair into the great avenues
                       of dust and leaves.'

Fugitive as morning light she moves
In a thin rain out and across the river
                  leaving no footprints.

You Gave Me Hyacinths First a Year Ago

The world's a stranger's room, we meet to part,
I stand, transfixed, an arrow through my heart.

My ageing Cupid, careful of his aim,
plucks out the shaft, and causes twice the pain.
My awkward arms are full of brandy, sin,
helpless I watch our promenade begin.

Hands touch, eyes falter, tremble, fix and cling,
the heart leaps up, the blood beneath the skin
tingles like frost, then all disguise is shed,
until he husks me naked in my bed.

My hyacinths are nettles, the cold breath
of the Toad Prince is in my ear like death.
'What will become of us?' 'We'll live to die,'
and in that restless void, disfigured, lie
forever, and forever answer, 'No.'
Contending on heaven's plain we'll weep and go.

So without choice, and convinced of doom,
I go to meet you in the stranger's room.

Anniversary

Death is in the air –

today is the anniversary of his death in October
(he would have been thirty-one)
I went home to High Street
& couldn't feed the new baby
my milk had dried up
so I sat holding him numbly
looking for the soft spot on the top of his head
while they fed me three more librium
you're only crying for yourself he said
but I kept on saying *It's the waste I can't bear.*

All that winter we lived
in the longest street in the world
he used to walk to work in the dark
on the opposite side of the street
somebody always walked with him but they never met
he could only hear the boots
& when he stopped they stopped.

The new baby swayed in a canvas cot lacing his fingers
I worried in case he got curvature of the spine
Truby King said a baby needed firm support
he was a very big bright baby
the cleaner at the Queen Vic. said every morning
you mark my words that kid's been here before.

The house was bare and cold with a false gable
we had no furniture only a double mattress
on the floor a big table and two deal chairs
every morning I dressed the baby in a shrunken jacket
and caught the bus home to my mother's to nurse the child
who was dying   the house had bay windows
hidden under fir trees smothered in yellow roses
the child sat dwarfed at the end of the polished table
pale as death in the light of his four candles
singing *Little Boy Blue.*

I pushed the pram to the telephone box
I'm losing my milk I told her *I want to bring him
home to die   Home* she said *you left
home a long time ago to go with that man.*

I pushed them both through the park
over the dropped leaves (his legs were crippled)
a magpie swooped down black out of the sky
and pecked his forehead   a drop of blood splashed on
his wrist   he started to cry

It took five months and everybody was angry
because the new baby was alive and cried for attention
pollen sprinkled his cheeks under the yellow roses.

When he died it was like everybody else
in the public ward with the screens around him
the big bruise spreading on his skin
his hand came up out of the sheets *don't cry*
he said   *don't be sad*

I sat there overnight in my Woolworths dress
not telling anybody in case they kept him alive
with another transfusion –

        Afterwards I sat by the gas fire
in my old dressing gown turning over the photographs
wondering why I'd drunk all that stout
& massaged my breasts every morning to be
        a good mother.

from: *Summer Solstice*

        3

The sunset flames over the city
I wanted to be your adorable mistress
with midnight 'phone calls
loveletters burning the pillarbox

but we forget the secret nouns of our bodies
I ring once a month write the occasional letter
Oh! you Jeremiah the summer has come
and is passing   but we are not saved . . .

the air cools
with the first blast
the fire burns
with the first rains
a change in the weather
now we can write poetry
and share the past
there is no present
never *living together*
I can't imagine what you do
with your days
but dedicating these volumes
we gently blow up the blaze . . .

Autumn returns again
all my life waiting
as I come down the stairs
you are reading Rimbaud
behind you the wind sweeps in
through the rose window   the camphor laurel
shaking a headful of rain
my husband makes up the fire
my blonde daughter puts on
her wistful clothes
sometimes happiness catches me unawares
I have learnt not to expect you
life is so frail   unpredictable   come
quickly before it is too late.

VINCENT BUCKLEY

Origins

Down the irrationally humped
and winding back road, he would carry
the week's supplies: whiskey,
bread, tea, jam,
the bushels of feed, the picture calendar,
maybe something to read
for the children: not the mother: not himself.

Through the two gates, with their old rusty
tin plaques, he was cut off
as in a highrock wilderness.

He kept no line to us; he never left
his name written; he rode, or walked,
the brown hills like a severed body.

So let your mind ease back
to the closed soft place, its must
of dark orderings, and dried rot
like a bloodstain on the floorboards,
a separate silt in the tankwater.
There, from there, by peculiar effort,
you might see, in the background,
not in history
at all, the clear air-shape of mountains.

Home   where your father gulped
the water and sugar
of a mother's love, and the whole house
kept its nap of smell
against the cold winds
and the earth-centred heat.

Rustle of sacks, the straw-ends
crushed in, the seasoned leather,
mice, spittle, bread, dung, oats,
whiskey, old papers, the sunsmell beating down
onto the halfdoor, from between round hills,
till it took a mushroom or a tuberous
density; smell of sapling in the ash.
In these smells we were begotten.

from: *Stroke*

I

In the faint blue light
We are both strangers; so I'm forced to note
His stare that comes moulded from deep bone,
The full mouth pinched in too far, one hand
Climbing an aluminium bar.
Put, as though for the first time,
In a cot from which only a hand escapes,
He grasps at opposites, knowing
This room's a caricature of childhood.
'I'm done for.'

'They're treating you all right?'
We talk from the corners of our mouths
Like old lags, while his body strains
To notice me, before he goes on watching
At the bed's foot
His flickering familiars,
Skehan, Wilson, Ellis, dead men, faces,
Bodies, paused in the aluminium light,
Submits his answer to his memories,
'Yes, I'm all right. But still it's terrible.'

Words like a fever bring
The pillar of cloud, pillar of fire
Travelling the desert of the mind and face.

The deep-set, momentarily cunning eyes
Keep trying for a way to come
Through the bed's bars to his first home.
And almost find it. Going out I hear
Voices calling requiem, where the cars
Search out the fog and gritty snow,
Hushing its breathing under steady wheels.
Night shakes the seasonable ground.

IV

Every clod reveals an ancestor.
They, the spirit hot in their bodies,
Burned to ash in their own thoughts; could not
Find enough water; rode in a straight line
Twenty miles across country
For hatred jumping every wire fence;
With uillean pipes taunted the air
Ferociously that taunted them;
Spoke with rancour, but with double meanings;
Proud of muscle, hated the bone beneath;
Married to gain forty acres
And a family of bond servants; died bound.
I, their grandson, do not love straight lines,
And talk with a measured voice – in double meanings –
Remembering always, when I think of death,
The grandfather, small, loveless, sinister,
  ('The most terrible man I ever seen,'
  Said Joe, who died thin as rice paper)
Horse-breaker, heart breaker, whose foot scorches,
Fifty years after, the green earth of Kilmore.
It's his heat that lifts my father's frame
Crazily from the wheel-chair, fumbles knots,
Twists in the bed at night,
Considers every help a cruelty.

V

Indoors and out, weather and winds keep up
Time's passion: paddocks white for burning.
As usual, by his bed, I spend my time
Not in talk, but restless noticing:

If pain dulls, grief coarsens.
Each night we come and, voyeurs of decay,
Stare for minutes over the bed's foot,
Imagining, if we think at all,
The body turning ash, the near insane
Knowledge when, in the small hours,
Alone under the cold ceiling, above
The floor where the heating system keeps its pulse,
He grows accustomed to his own sweat
And sweats with helplessness, remembering
How, every day, at eight o'clock
The Polish nurse kisses him goodnight.
His arms are bent like twigs; his eyes
Are blown to the door after her; his tears
Are squeezed out not even for himself.
Where is the green that swells against the blade
Or sways in sap to the high boughs? To the root
He is dry wood, and in his sideways
Falling brings down lights. Our breath
Mingles,
Stirs the green air of the laurel tree.

VI

The roofs are lit with rain.
Winter. In that dark glow,
Now, as three months ago,
I pray that he'll die sane.

On tiles or concrete path
The old wheeling the old,
For whom, in this last world,
Hope is an aftermath.

And the damp trees extend
Branch and thorn. We live
As much as we believe.
All things covet an end.

Once, on the Kerrie road,
I drove with him through fire.
Now, in the burnt cold year,
He drains off piss and blood,

His wounded face tube-fed,
His arm strapped to a bed.

VII

At the merest handshake I feel his blood
Move with the ebb-tide chill. Who can revive
A body settled in its final mood?
To whom, on what tide, can we move, and live?

Later I wheel him out to see the trees:
Willows and oaks, the small plants he mistakes
For rose bushes; and there
In the front, looming, light green, cypresses.
His pulse no stronger than the pulse of air.

Dying, he grows more tender, learns to teach
Himself the mysteries I am left to trace.
As I bend to say 'Till next time', I search
For signs of resurrection in his face.

A Man, a Woman

A man, a woman, straighten up from where
they have been dragged by a kerosene tin
they cooked and did their washing in. Their shoulders
are bent and lifted by it. Now, on the fire,
it makes a yellowish steam spitting around
its rim and sides: the cauldron of the poor.

Yet they burned good fuel, pinecones,
mallee roots, messmate and resin wood.
They raked twigs and stalks to catch the fire.
They sat round telling Depression jokes

of pannikin bosses, flash clobber, and winning Tatts.
Memory is unreliable and self-serving,
as the critic said. But I recall the flame-core,
the cores of all the flames, as vivid yellow
turning to vivid orange, like cordial in the water,
like the new gush of petrol in the old puddle,
like meaning in a quarrel. I won't forget that.

The Child is Revenant to the Man

In the frayed apple leaves a grin of copper.
The figtree tied its arms together;
just as you were learning to be one thing
you were forced to become another;

you saw the horizons change size,
you gritted your mind and mourned
their grey, crimson, their sisterly blue.
Many dreams were rolled into those fringes.

Before your lust started you could see
there would be no one to receive it fully:
you, the anonymous you
of modern poems, to whom daythings happen,

you are in your proper time, it is I,
the I so filled with dread
I almost welcome nightmares, who have
slipped out of it

and see time as that endless past in which
I am getting ready, I am almost ready
to play my part in the colourful, nuanced
contradictions of figtree and sky.

FRANCIS WEBB

A Tip for Saturday

I met Jack on a Friday night,
Headway was medium, in spite
Of lurching walls in the spinning town,
Taxis that sought to mow him down,
Strange girls that dashed into his arms,
Then cursed him in no uncertain terms.
The air was still, the sky was grey.
I thought of tips for Saturday.

The navigator's task affords
Small safety from a spate of words.
He pointed me to starry skies
On stilts of queer philosophies,
While oaths made rapid cubic gain,
Like roly-poly on the plain.

I quote one mighty thought on wars:
There'd be some friction if the stars
Were like us, macrocosms jammed
Edgeways like sardines on this damned
Insignificant little planet:
Figuratively, literally, he spat on it.

Meekly surrendering to the shocks
Of war, religion, politics,
My voice could not attempt a breach.
Jack filled the road with noisy speech,
With gusto, verve, and animation
From Windsor pub to Town Hall station.

The air was still, the sky was grey.
Reluctantly I turned away
Without a tip for Saturday.

The Gunner

When the gunner spoke in his sleep the hut was still,
Uneasily strapped to the reckless wheel of his will;
Silence, humble, directionless as fog,
Lifted, and minutes were rhythmical on the log;

While slipstream plucked at a wafer of glass and steel,
Engines sliced and scooped at the air's thin wall,
And those dim spars dislodged from the moon became
Red thongs of tracer whipping boards aflame.

Listening, you crouched in the turret, watchful and taut
 – *Bogey two thousand, skipper, corkscrew to port* –
Marvellous, the voice: driving electric fires
Through the panel of sleep, the black plugs, trailing wires.

The world spoke through its dream, being deaf and blind,
Its words were those of the dream, yet you might find
Forgotten genius, control, alive in this deep
Instinctive resistance to the perils of sleep.

Port Phillip Night

Lights. Not the histrionic reds and golds
Of the manufacturer's name upon six o'clock air,
Nor the shine where stagey Public Safety unfolds
His haul of tinsel headlights with every care.
Lights. Not the street-lamps along the waterfront road;
Nor neon tapping his fork while the Passions bow down
To the jazz from the jetty, dits and dahs of a code.
Lights are aboard in our sealed and delivered town.

White liner from Bergen: is it a style of grief,
Your hull bound to the dock at an easy slope?
You are only disciplined voltage and stilled thunder,
Laid up, peaceful if it is peace to be under
The freezing old deposition of the rope
While all the beacons are hollering, *here's a reef.*

Lights. Lights. Lights. Because there are two:
This man and this woman, hackneyed and fearless, spying
Wharfward in a lucky shadow. Over to you.
They set the clock running and the aneroid eyeing
The Cool Change; they cusp the dismantled wave.
And for you, Berganger, their hands on the wheel are steady:
Freedom, the pilot, comes to the mesmerised slave –
Arterial flag-dip, crouch of motors at the ready.

Lights. Not of the bullock-fed infantry
Howling in their sleep-of-Ares among the tents.
These are the spying lights, the undertone.
And the more deeply and the more finally known,
The more deeply, finally foreign these elements
Of the Fingal's Cave revelation of moon on sea.

Laid Off

I. The Bureau, and Later

Outside the Bureau all the trams and trains
Prattled securely, with us out of air
To ply like bits of refuse among drains
Nudging each other nastily when it rains.

Only the suck or slap of rubber sole
At marble was our case and hearing. Spare
Butts, down to earth, drafted one smoky scroll
For factory, office, wharf, and police patrol.

I pitied the man behind the counter, who'd
Hear us be cruelly serious, hear us swear,
Be funny, No-speak-English – see us bowed
Under the weight of tools to make him God.

Later: – this swine with platitudinous
Squeaks of his oily leather-bottomed chair
Makes up his mouth to tell me less and less
And plays at being Satan, with more success.

To the most dangerous driver, righteous heat,
Our traffic-lights are neither here nor there.
I stare at the pock-marked baby while I eat,
And walk past the blind mouth-organist on the street.

2 Hard-luck Story

'Yes, this is the stop for Central. Yes, right here.
Cold weather? Right, I'll try a tailor-made' –
Breaking the ice is moving mountains, sheer
Bravado if there's no time for a prayer.

Frayed eyelids button on to me; this thin
Lip of the cold snap will not have me wade
Or even pet my carefully nourished skin
To reassure it before plunging in.

Taxes and breadless children swim or drown
Without mercy inside his overcoat. Afraid?
So I am – but citizens pay to see again
A great dramatist's aquarium of pain.

His bony, dickering, artist's hands attach
Years to my ears; from their ice-box of shade
Castles crane forward, puff themselves up, and watch
For the foolhardy twinkle of my match.

Towards the Land of the Composer

Rain tries the one small foot and at length the other
On the tin roof.
Valves of my cheap set
Manage your name after some notes on the weather.

And we must all be moving, with all our baggage:
Icon of knobby tree,
Kouros of long-tailed animal,

Lepidoptera,
River Yarra,
Harbour Bridge,
Four-letter words, and tons of more personal luggage.

And the best fire of 'em all, made of mallee-roots,
Must stop this breezy nonsense,
Pull itself together
To run red and straight, after the swagman's boots.

And fair in the heel of the hunt our cloud-formations,
Our sun,
Our flocks,
Our tribespeople,
Grease of desert,
Blazing skewer of harvest,
The statues of Colonel Light, and the railway-stations.

And the heaven-bent squatters lash to their holy backs
Acre and acre,
Rifle and rifle,
The Family Tree,
The Family Bible,
At a sign from deadbeaters who carry only their packs.

And never a word nor a squeak from us when we meet
All the new islands,
All the old temples,
All the strange accents:
For the Leader has just this moment taken his seat.

And the latecoming bearded fish, and the smack and her crew,
Man-eating headlands,
Crystal women,
Sagas of ice,
Front-seat fjords,
Whirling noiselessly in to be close to you.

End of the Picnic

When that humble-headed elder, the sea, gave his wide
Strenuous arm to a blasphemy, hauling the girth
And the sail and the black yard
Of unknown *Endeavour* towards this holy beach,
Heaven would be watching. And the two men. And the earth,
Immaculate, illuminant, out of reach.

It must break – on sacred water this swindle of a wave.
Thick canvas flogged the sticks. Hell lay hove-to.
Heaven did not move.
Two men stood safe: even when the prying, peering
Longboat, the devil's totem, cast off and grew,
No god shifted an inch to take a bearing.

It was Heaven-and-earth's jolting out of them shook the men.
It was uninitiate scurf and bone that fled.
Cook's column holds here.
Our ferry is homesick, whistling again and again;
But still I see how the myth of a daylight bled
Standing in ribbons, over our heads, for an hour.

A Death at Winson Green

There is a green spell stolen from Birmingham;
Your peering omnibus overlooks the fence,
Or the grey, bobbing lifelines of a tram.
Here, through the small hours, sings our innocence.
Joists, apathetic pillars plot this ward,
Tired timbers wheeze and settle into dust,
We labour, labour: for the treacherous lord
Of time, the dazed historic sunlight, must
Be wheeled in a seizure towards one gaping bed,
Quake like foam on the lip, or lie still as the dead.

Visitors' Day: the graven perpetual smile,
String-bags agape, and pity's laundered glove.
The last of the heathens shuffles down the aisle,
Dark glass to a beauty which we hate and love.
Our empires rouse against this ancient fear,
Longsufferings, anecdotes, levelled at our doom;
Mine-tracks of old allegiance, prying here,
Perplex the sick man raving in his room.
Outside, a shunting engine hales from bed
The reminiscent feast-day, long since dead.

Noon reddens, trader birds deal cannily
With Winson Green, and the slouch-hatted sun
Gapes at windows netted in wire, and we
Like early kings with book and word cast down
Realities from our squared electric shore.
Two orderlies are whistling-in the spring;
Doors slam; and a man is dying at the core
Of triumph won. As a tattered, powerful wing
The screen bears out his face against the bed,
Silver, derelict, rapt, and almost dead.

Evening gropes out of colour; yet we work
To cleanse our shore from limpet histories;
Traffic and factory-whistle turn berserk;
Inviolate, faithful as a saint he lies.
Twilight itself breaks up, the venal ship,
Upon the silver integrity of his face.
No bread shall tempt that fine, tormented lip.
Let shadow switch to light – he holds his place.
Unmarked, unmoving, from the gaping bed
Towards birth he labours, honour, almost dead.

The wiry cricket moiling at his loom
Debates a themeless project with dour night,
The sick man raves beside me in his room;
I sleep as a child, rouse up as a child might.
I cannot pray; that fine lip prays for me
With every gasp at breath; his burden grows
Heavier as all earth lightens, and all sea.
Time crouches, watching, near his face of snows.
He is all life, thrown on the gaping bed,
Blind, silent, in a trance, and shortly, dead.

Hospital Night
(Second Version)

The side-room has sweated years and patience, rolls its one eye
Skyward, nightward; hours beyond sleep I lie;
And the fists of some ardent Plimsoll have laboured this wall
Clear of its plaster beside my chosen head.
Someone murmurs a little, dithers in bed.
Against that frail call
Are imminent the siege-works of a huge nightfall.

Trees, drawn up, rustle forward in the steep time of gloaming;
Crude green labours, gathers itself to a darkness, dreaming
Of perished ice-world summers, birds few, unwieldy, tame.
Darkness is astir, pondering, touching
Kinship with the first Dark in a trunk's crouching.
Darkness lays claim
To that vague breath-labour of a century, my name.

Someone calls again in his sleep, and my thought is pain,
Pain, till chanticleer will carol truce again
To the faceless joustings of green and green by an old cell,
With time roundabout, and labouring shapes of sin;
To the knotted fist of lightning, or tilting rain;
To the wind's lapse and swell
 – Old die-hards of whom the birds shiver to tell.

Sleep is a labour amid the dilatory elder light;
But now a star is uttered in the long night,
Pitched beyond altercations of tree and storm;
For these, isled upon time, are murmuring, murmuring ever
Of good or evil becoming a darkness; but never
Darkens that star,
Housed in a glory, yet always a wanderer.

It is pain, truth, it is you, my father, beloved friend,
Come to me in the guile and darkness of a day's end,
As a frail intense blue burning, near nor far.
Old hands were stripped from the keyboard of time, they favour
White notes nor black, but they glitter and glitter of a lover,
As out of war
I labour, breathing deeply, and tremble towards your star.

from: *Around Costessey*
from: 7. *In Memoriam: Anthony Sandys, 1806–1883*

IV Art

I see him in a sense as strapped to his chair,
Bloodstained with erudition, unafraid;
Into the studio earth comes floundering
Under swag of gifts to embrace the senses, sting,
Or do both often. So he sups keenest air,
Coughs into laundered silk, with windows wide.

And I see the Broads at sunset, skimming past:
Shadows on water, sun, and natural blue
Moving as one at supernatural speed.
To engage those Broads of the spirit is their need.
Beauty, be tongue of fire, of the Holy Ghost,
For the mill and the haggard Cross are moving too.

And I see, downstairs and teased by cockroaches,
Cool crayon, oil, and glittering watercolour:
A courage unmans me, a ritual generous teaching
Forsaken for a spell but overreaching
Staircase and cockroach and forgetfulness,
While machines of burning mumble in the cellar.

Clouds

I Inland

The rich surplus of consciousness rots at the wharves.
That one big bird will not preen his shallow shoulder
Nor peer at his ghost in water – there is none.
For the stooping gaffer daylight only serves
To bear in his muggy dungarees the moulder
Of mare's-tail (or teacake) and that old boiled lolly the sun.

All assignations of brooding grain with earth,
All childhood, manhood among diehard trees
As litter of string, paper, and leather are wound
In the hot palms of the wind, sent thrumming forth
To whirl above shoaling plains and memories
And drum you, tissue of waters, out of mind.

2 The Town

The entrance to the Hall
Is two splayed marble calves
Propping a lap of stone.
Plumb in the centre of all
Itinerant hatreds, loves,
Is this mentor, but all alone.
Woolworths and Lyonses lean
All askew at twelve
(Time for a beer or tea)
And watch the flittering scene
Of scamper and gabble, delve
Into known asymmetry
For their children to buy and buy
Colours and tinny stars;
They are going too fast it seems.
No one looks at the sky
With all its department stores
Auctioning thuds and gleams
And greasy meccano cloud.
Oaths rattle in heaven,
Big fists clear away:
No one has heard a word,
No signals, omens even
In the town this day.

3 Airliner

I am become a shell of delicate alleys
Stored with the bruit of the motors, resolute thunders
And unflagging dance of the nerves.
Beneath me the sad giant frescoes of the clouds:

Towerings and defiles through intense grey valleys,
Huge faces of kings, queens, castles – travelling cinders,
And monuments, and shrouds.
A fortress crammed with engines of warfare swerves

As we bank into it, and all the giant sad past
Clutches at me swimming through it: here
Is faith crumbling – here the engines of war
In sleek word and sad fresco of print,
Landscapes broken apart; and here at last
Is home all undulant, banners hanging drear
Or collapsing into chaos, burnt.
And now we are through, and now a barbarous shore

Grimaces in welcome, showing all its teeth
And now the elder sea all wrinkled with love
Sways tipsily up to us, and now the swing
Of the bridge; houses, islands, and many blue bushlands come.
Confine me in Pinchgut, bury me beneath
The bones of the old lag, analyse me above
The city lest I drunkenly sing
Of wattles, wars, childhoods, being at last home.

from: *Ward Two*

1 Pneumo-encephalograph

Tight scrimmage of blankets in the dark;
Nerve-fluxions, flints coupling for the spark;
Today's guilt and tomorrow's blent;
Passion and peace trussed together, impotent;
Dilute potage of light
Dripping through glass to the desk where you sit and write;
Hour stalking lame hour . . .
May my every bone and vessel confess the power
To loathe suffering in you
As in myself, that arcane simmering brew.

Only come to this cabin of art:
Crack hardy, take off clothes, and play your part.
Contraband enters your brain;
Puckered guerilla faces patrol the vein;
The spore of oxygen passes
Skidding over old inclines and crevasses,
Hunting an ancient sore,
Foxhole of impulse in a minute cosmic war.
Concordat of nature and desire
Was revoked in you; but fire clashes with fire.

Let me ask, while you are still,
What in you marshalled this improbable will:
Instruments supple as the flute,
Vigilant eyes, mouths that are almost mute,
X-rays scintillant as a flower,
Tossed in a corner the plumes of falsehood, power?
Only your suffering.
Of pain's amalgam with gold let some man sing
While, pale and fluent and rare
As the Holy Spirit, travels the bubble of air.

   2 Harry

It's the day for writing that letter, if one is able,
And so the striped institutional shirt is wedged
Between this holy holy chair and table.
He has purloined paper, he has begged and cadged
The bent institutional pen,
The ink. And our droll old men
Are darting constantly where he weaves his sacrament.

Sacrifice? Propitiation? All are blent
In the moron's painstaking fingers – so painstaking.
His vestments our giddy yarns of the firmament,
Women, gods, electric trains, and our remaking
Of all known worlds – but not yet
Has our giddy alphabet
Perplexed his priestcraft and spilled the cruet of innocence.

We have been plucked from the world of commonsense,
Fondling between our hands some shining loot,
Wife, mother, beach, fisticuffs, eloquence,

As the lank tree cherishes every distorted shoot.
What queer shards we could steal
Shaped him, realer than the Real:
But it is no goddess of ours guiding the fingers and the thumb.

She cries: *Ab aeterno ordinata sum.*
He writes to the woman, this lad who will never marry.
One vowel and the thousand laborious serifs will come
To this pudgy Christ, and the old shape of Mary.
Before seasonal pelts and the thin
Soft tactile underskin
Of air were stretched across earth, they have sported and are one.

Was it then at this altar-stone the mind was begun?
The image besieges our Troy. Consider the sick
Convulsions of movement, and the featureless baldy sun
Insensible – sparing that compulsive nervous tic.
Before life, the fantastic succession,
An imbecile makes his confession,
Is filled with the Word unwritten, has almost genuflected.

Because the wise world has for ever and ever rejected
Him and because your children would scream at the sight
Of his mongol mouth stained with food, he has resurrected
The spontaneous though retarded and infantile light.
Transfigured with him we stand
Among walls of the no-man's-land
While he licks the soiled envelope with lover's caress

Directing it to the House of no known address.

3 Old Timer

I have observed even among us the virus
Eating its way, lipping, complaining
In a multitude of cozening wheedling voices:
O Being is tender and succulent and porous:
Erect your four paternal walls of stone
(Gauleiters with burnished window-badges, no faces):
Checkmate the sun, the cloud, the burning, the raining,
Let deferential stars peep in one by one:
Sit, feed, sleep, have done.

Isolate the Identity, clasp its dwindling head.
Your birth was again the birth of the All,
The Enemy: he treads roads, lumbers through pastures,
Musters the squeaking horde of the countless dead.
To guard your spark borrow the jungle art
Of this hospital yard, stamp calico vestures
For H.M. Government, for your funeral;
And in this moment of beads let nothing start
Old rages leaping in the dying heart.

So we become daily more noncommittal:
This small grey mendicant man must lean
Against his block of wall, old eyes rehearsing time
Whose hanged face he is. I take my fatal vital
Steps to the meal, the toilet, in worse than derision
Of his pipe craving a fill, of his monologue and rhyme:
Children who loved him, Bathurst, Orange, of green
Neighbourlinesses, of the silken and stony vision:
His faith-healing, his compassion.

But some little while ago it was all appalling.
He knew my footstep, even the pipe
Between blackened teeth hissed in its comeliness
As an exotic snake poising itself for the falling
Of heart's blood, tobacco; an ancient iron of unrest
Melted before his hopeful word of address.
Christ, how I melted! for healing and faith were ripe
As Bathurst opening the gigantic West
Or Orange golden as the breast.

   5 Homosexual

To watch may be deadly. There is no judgment, compulsion,
And the object becomes ourselves. That is the terror:
We have simply ceased, are not dead, and have been
And are; only movement – our movement – is relegated,
Only thought, being – our thought, being – are given
Over; and pray God it be simply given.
So, at this man's ending, which is all a watching,
Let us disentangle the disgust and indifference,

Be all a thin hurried magnanimity:
For that is movement, our movement. Let us study
Popular magazines, digests, psychoanalysts:
For that is thought, being, our thought, our being.

I shall only watch. He is born, seized by joy,
I shall not speak of that joy, seeing it only
As the lighted house, the security, the Beginning.
Unselfconscious as the loveliest of flowers
He grows – and here we enter: the house stands yet,
But the joists winge under our footsteps. Now the God,
The Beginning, the joy, give way to boots and footmarks.
Pale glass faces contorted in hate or merriment
Embody him; and words and arbitrary laws.
He is embodied, he weeps – and all mankind,
Which is the face, the glass even, weeps with him.

The first window broken. Something nameless as yet
Resists embodiment. Something, the perennial rebel,
Will not rest. And this, his grandest element,
Becomes his terror, because of the footsteps, us.

I shall not consider sin beginning, our sin,
The images, furtive actions. All is a secret
But to us all is known as on the day of our birth.
He will differ, must differ among all the pale glass faces,
The single face contorted in hate or merriment.

Comes the day when his mother realizes all.
Few questions, and a chaos of silence. Her thin eyes
Are emptied. Doors rattle in the house,
Foundations stagger. The Beginning becomes us;
And he is mulcted of words, remain to him only
The words of sin, escape, which is becoming all of life.
Easier, the talk with his father, rowdy, brief
Thank God, and only the language of the gutter.
He watches the moth pondering the gaslight, love-death,
Offers a wager as to her love or death or both.
His father stops speaking, fingers some papers on the desk.

And now he is here. We had him conveyed to this place
Because our pale glass faces contorted in hate or merriment
Left only sin as flesh, the concrete, the demanded.
He does not speak or hear – perhaps the pox.

But all his compatriots in sin or in other illness
Are flesh, the demanded, silent, watching, not hearing:
It is all he ever sought. Again I am tempted, with the Great,
To see in ugliness and agony a way to God:
Worse, I am tempted to say he has found God
Because we cannot contort our faces in merriment,
And we are one of the Twelve Tribes – he our king.
He has dictated silence, a kind of peace
To all within these four unambiguous walls,
Almost I can say with no answering scuffle of rejection,
He is loving us now, he is loving all.

8 Wild Honey

Saboteur autumn has riddled the pampered folds
Of the sun; gum and willow whisper seditious things;
Servile leaves now kick and toss in revolution,
Wave bunting, die in operatic reds and golds;
And we, the drones, fated for the hundred stings,
Grope among chilly combs of self-contemplation
While the sun, on sufferance, from his palanquin
Offers creation one niggling lukewarm grin.

But today is Sports Day, not a shadow of doubt:
Scampering at the actual frosty feet
Of winter, under shavings of the pensioned blue,
We are the Spring. True, rain is about:
You mark old diggings along the arterial street
Of the temples, the stuttering eyeball, the residue
Of days spent nursing some drugged comatose pain,
Summer, autumn, winter the single sheet of rain.

And the sun is carted off; and a sudden shower:
Lines of lightning patrol the temples of the skies;
Drum, thunder, silence sing as one this day;
Our faces return to the one face of the flower
Sodden and harried by diehard disconsolate flies.
All seasons are crammed into pockets of the grey.
Joy, pain, desire, a moment ago set free,
Sag in pavilions of the grey finality.

Under rain, in atrophy, dare I watch this girl
Combing her hair before the grey broken mirror,
The golden sweetness trickling? Her eyes show
Awareness of my grey stare beyond the swirl
Of golden fronds: it is her due. And terror,
Rainlike, is all involved in the golden glow,
Playing diminuendo its dwarfish rôle
Between self-conscious fingers of the naked soul.

Down with the mind a moment, and let Eden
Be fullness without the prompted unnatural hunger,
Without the doomed shapely ersatz thought: see faith
As all such essential gestures, unforbidden,
Persisting through Fall and landslip; and see, stranger,
The overcoated concierge of death
As a toy for her gesture. See her hands like bees
Store golden combs among certified hollow trees.

Have the gates of death scrape open. Shall we meet
(Beyond the platoons of rainfall) a loftier hill
Hung with such delicate husbandries? Shall ascent
Be a travelling homeward, past the blue frosty feet
Of winter, past childhood, past the grey snake, the will?
Are gestures stars in sacred dishevelment,
The tiny, the pitiable, meaningless and rare
As a girl beleaguered by rain, and her yellow hair?

BRUCE BEAVER

Angels' Weather

Watching Rushcutters' bright bayful of masts and coloured keels,
Half-sensing Dufy's muse walking on that gull, sail
And cobalt sky reflecting surface,
I open my senses to the gift of it and hear
The yacht club telecommunication paging
A Mr Fairweather over the water;
Watch gulls wheeling one after the other
After another with sustenance in its beak.
Frantic as white sharks they thresh the blue waters of the air.
Perched on a dory a shag replete
Flaps dry and stretches out its black umbrella wings.
On the mud-flat's rank solarium
A few grounded parent birds are teaching their young
To walk tip-web-toe,
Heads pointed up at the sun-mote
Swarms of gnat-fry,
Fishing the citron-scented shallows of noon.

Passing are pattern stockinged girls
With old dogs and strollers full of family.
Prim seated or grass floored the sun imbibers,
Some still hung from last night's
Vinegary round of dark: the White Lady presiding
Somewhere near the tolling two o'clock till,
Honing her crescent. Now only
The grass poking its tongues out at our fears;
The coral trees' crimson beaks of bloom pecking the blue.
Above the doughy park's arena of tiger-striped
And cougar-charcoaled athletes
A murmuration of applause for no one in particular
From the immense and yellow foliaged
Fig leafing through the wind;

Spectator of the sportive weather.
Olympiads of effort are stored, restored
Within that echo-memory of clapping leaf.
Now we are all sun lovers, steaming in tweeds and combinations.
Be it upon our own heads
This blessed incontinent surrendering
To the open handed noon broadcasting silence
And the bright winged seeds of peace which find their nest
In an evening of visionary trees.

from: *Letters to Live Poets*

I (Frank O'Hara)

God knows what was done to you.
I may never find out fully.
The truth reaches us slowly here,
is delayed in the mail continually
or censored in the tabloids. The war
now into its third year
remains undeclared.
The number of infants, among others, blistered
and skinned alive by napalm
has been exaggerated
by both sides we are told,
and the gas does not seriously harm;
does not kill but is merely
unbearably nauseating.
Apparently none of this
is happening to us.

I meant to write to you more than a year
ago. Then there was as much to hear,
as much to tell.
There was the black plastic monster
prefiguring hell
displayed on the roof

of the shark aquarium at the wharf.
At Surfers' Paradise were Meter Maids
glabrous in gold bikinis.
It was before your country's
president came among us like a formidable
virus. Even afterwards –
after I heard (unbelievingly)
you had been run down on a beach
by a machine
apparently while sunning yourself;
that things were terminal again –
even then I might have written.

But enough of that. I could tell by the tone
of your verses there were times
when you had ranged around you,
looking for a lift from the gift horse,
your kingdom for a Pegasus.
But to be trampled by the machine
beyond protest . . .

I don't have to praise you; at least
I can say I had ears for your voice
but none of that really matters now.
Crushed though. Crushed on the littered sands.
Given the *coup de grâce* of an empty beer can,
out of sight of the 'lordly and isolate satyrs'.
Could it have happened anywhere else
than in your country, keyed to obsolescence?

I make these words perform for you
knowing though you are dead, that you 'historically
belong to the enormous bliss of American death',
that your talkative poems remain
among the living things
of the sad, embattled beach-head.

Say that I am, as ever, the young-
old fictor of communications.
It's not that I wish to avoid
talking to myself or singing
the one-sided song.
It's simply that I've come to be
more conscious of the community

world-wide, of live, mortal poets.
Moving about the circumference
I pause each day
and speak to you and you.
I haven't many answers, few
enough; fewer questions left.
Even when I'm challenged 'Who
goes there?' I give ambiguous
replies as though the self linking
heart and mind had become a gap.

You see, we have that much in common
already. It's only when I stop
thinking of you living I remember
nearby our home there's an aquarium
that people pay admission to,
watching sharks at feeding time:
the white, jagged rictus in the grey
sliding anonymity,
faint blur of red through green,
the continually spreading stain.

I have to live near this, if not quite with it.
I realize there's an equivalent
in every town and city in the world.
Writing to you keeps the local, intent
shark-watchers at bay
(who if they thought at all
would think *me* some kind of ghoul);
rings a bell for the gilded coin-slots
at the Gold Coast;
sends the president parliament's head on a platter;
writes Vietnam like a huge four-letter
word in blood and faeces on the walls
of government; reminds me when
the intricate machine stalls
there's a poet still living at this address.

XIX

I welcome the anonymity of the middle years, years of the spreading
girth and conversational prolixity, when the whole being loosens
the stays of the thirties and lengthens out into paragraphs of
    perceptiveness
where once had bristled the pointed phrase. And the other aspect,
    the merely boring
raconteur, the redundant conversationalist; the not young
not old, twice told tale teller; the paunched, bejowelled double-chinned
bumbler. These I welcome, also the watcher unperceived on corners
from verandahs of youth, voyeuristic, grateful beyond the tang of sour
grapes to be no longer privy to the ingrowing secret, the deathly
held breaths of years, the cold and burning self-trials. The quaintly
acquainted with the antique masques of childhood, the mummies
    and daddies,
the nurses and doctors, the pantomimic routines of getting the hang
    of
living and dying young. No, childhood's well and truly categorised
and pigeon-holed somewhere within that depot of lapsed tenders,
    the unconscious. It's the witnessing
of the adolescent saga that sometimes chills me to my still vulnerable
marrow, burns me down to the fire of being and sifts me into a
    vacuum
of loveless nine to five nightmares on wretched wages, the between
    grown
and ungrown, the lonely braggart loping like a werewolf past the
unattainable beauties on the peeling posters, past the burning
girls that, plain as sisters, would, and onto the illimitable
utmost, absolute and factual plateau of the self's serfdom
to solitude, the sad king in the bone castle, the bitter end
of beginnings and the beginning of fiddling appetites and the
    myriad
arbitrations of early manhood (in my case, alas, a prolongation
of mad simulated adolescence). Only now the hypertensive
head and lazy bowels, with a heart as whole as a tin of dog's meat
may I pause between poems of letters to you, my alter egos, and
    pronounce

peace be occasionally with you all and, at no matter what cost,
  with me here,
no longer (I pray) completely at odds with self and world,
  accommodating
room by room like a shabby genteel boarding house, age.

from: *Odes and Days*

Day 20

The green gossip of the maidenhair
fern potted upon the table
above my book interposed
itself between the vibrant noon
silence and sonorities of
Henry James. I note its modest
jubilance of leaf, a generous
crowding of neat petals. They
overhang without overshadowing
the sad history of Isabel Archer's
Roman journey. From a spiny
tenacity of brown stems to a
transparency of green tendrils
they quiver and caress in air
the faint spring warmth in the
moon-wan and milky light.
The lace cloth beneath my angled
pen-holding hand imprints its
knotted pattern. Between the moist
maidenhair and the dry lace
the century-old and mellowed tones
of the expatriate master draw me back to
the ever-so civilized hell of the human condition.

Déjeuner Sur l'Herbe

Everywhere I look in the garden
I see old cutlery –
Old knives, forks, spoons,
Greened-over silver and worn down
Handles of bone.
It is as though my mother
Has made a meal of her gardening.
I knew she drew sustenance from it
But never quite equated the garden
With a banquet of multitudinous courses,
From escargots on the half shell
To crème de Carnation;
From mud pies to chives and chokos.
She has laid her table and spread upon it
A green cloth of couch.
Not quite a cordon bleu
Of a garden nor yet a cafeteria.
Uninvited guests abound:
The minute gluttonous sparrow;
The picking pernickety dove;
The gourmet peewit
And the gate-crashing cat
Who's all for gobbling guests.
Morning and noon she dines
Jabbing and spooning at half-baked soil.
Of an evening she stands and hoses
Drinking in the quenched garden.
At night in moon or star shine
Or no shine at all
I count the clicking glinting cutlery
Like a servant of the house
Making light of my task
In the knowledge of belonging.

The Drummer

I have been a privileged spectator at innumerable acts of vandalism;
Have stood swaying in the shaded second class compartments
As knives sliced the hymeneal leather, ballpoints defaced
The clever hairless advertisements, initialed crapulous
Graffiti in the sweet and sour of countless city urinals
I have watched from nonentity, invisible as a cement
Column under a fly-over, a lamp-post on a sepia lit
Highway; have seen, fusing at intervals the grey and blind-white coil
   of traffic,
Acts as bare and violent as the spasming of a lightning bolt.

No need to ask where this one or that one went. They were about
For a while. Some even etched a pattern on
The retinas of others, lasting maybe as long as the flowering
Of a neon-lit fountain, the sun flash at noon from a twentieth-storey
Window. One you remember ran berserk in the city day
Beating on the incredibly thick window of a ground-floor office
With a rolled umbrella, fell and was comforted by frightened
Clerks and a World War Two veteran lift-driver. Another
Simply went out in the quiet evening to stroll and was found
Still on the calvary of a flight of steps.

                  Some of course
Carried it with them wherever they went, nursing it huddled
On hard chairs in gas smelling kitchens or pushed it
In front of them shuffling in side-streets half awake with early
   morning
Light: the little wonder death kit guaranteed to appeal
To the vandal in all of us. I'm on a premium
This winter only to spread the word around –
   You'll note my nails
Are black, my eyes are reddened with the icy heat of
Winds, my voice is gruff but gentler than most salesmen's. Note also
The rock-like rigour of the line that runs
From leathered shoulder down the tightened denim to the
Non-fleecy-lined black legend of the boot. It moves.
Kicks down and lifts bracing to the old

Roar of a thousand conchs, a thousand thousand
Battles.

       Don't forget the night-dark anonymity of goggles,
The white receding blur of skull and bones.

Silo Treading

At silo filling time the air was similarly wet
between the dense-packed, leaf-clustered corn rows, in the little
shed that housed the howling, belting, stalk-chopping silage-
making machine and in the empty silo, treading under
a rain of moist fragments the corn leaves, corn stalks, stray cobs
into a green pudding that would cook itself, beginning
the thermic process even while we trod that upright vintage.
But the whole process depended on corn. And corn is a truly magic
thing. As much a gift from the gods as the grape. It shares with the
grape religious rites and its history is linked with the dismembering
and rebirth of a god. I was nearly partially dismembered myself
one season, hacking at heavy stalks and zipping swiftly upwards
with a saw-bladed reaping hook. It slipped from my grasp in my
    sweat-slippery hand
and I mechanically hauled at it stuck in the base of a stalk and tore
a half inch gash in my second finger, nearly lifting off
the top of it, only the bone and the nail held things together until
about forty-eight hours had passed and my relatives said they
    needed more help.
But sometimes there was the picking of the fruit of the corn. I dimly
remember as a child it must have been picked in its husk because
there would be at the appropriate time get-togethers of neighbouring
    families
after tea and late into the night for little boys and girls.
After the fiendish games of pursuing the nesting mice to their deaths
from the barn's cornerfuls of unhusked corn we would at first
with enthusiasm gradually turned into lethargy run the finger
taloned with leatherheld three inch nail down the harsh cocoon
of the husk to disclose the gold, the betel-red, the milk-white grains,

157

until someone would carry us snoozing into a shadowy corner on
top of more corn (and mice) and fulsome sacks of sweet and foul
   smelling mixtures
of things that only adults understood the use of. But in
the later years my uncle husked the cobs on the standing stalk
and fed them to the cattle as an additive or prelude
to the plum-pudding silage that the cows went crazy over, screaming
like overweight adolescent girls to get at it as though
it were some edible pop-performer, another dismembered god
and would roll their eyes and bony hips and bump the stalls and
belch and shit while gorging. Cows are unmentionably crass and
canny at the same time. Bulls are bulls – that is, you keep out of their
way in and out of serving times. Sometimes they sing in Brahmsian
monotones, sometimes they shriek and kick up clods, sometimes
they even rupture their pizzles masturbating into a grassy
mound. But only cows really care for them. And only
they really care for cows as cows despite the farmer's habitual
endearments and namings. But corn – or the stalks thereof – and the
   sandpaper raspy
leaves. And the thick, wet air between the neverending rows.
One humid day after several hours of hacking, humping and dumping
those full green six feet and more stalks I fell down dead asleep
in a chocolate furrow and did not dream of anything for the first
and last time in my life. When I awoke an hour later
my disgusted cousin was half a dozen rows on having left mine
like gapped teeth in between. However, my uncle even stopped letting
the cobs grow on the green stalks and soon it was cut and hack
and stack on the sled and chop and stamp down, and that was it.
The neighbour's son upheld the Attis myth in the form of adding
three severed fingers to the silage pudding. Those machines
were gluttonous for everything choppable. But while there was
the neighbour's mutilated son, there were also the neighbour's
daughters to help stamp down the silage and in between loads there
were sessions of mutual inspection. Then, one sad afternoon
the good share-farmer's better daughter, sweet Laura of the warm,
wide face and narrow hips and feet like pizza plates came shyly
up to me as I stamped on and on under a shower of fragrant,
tickling chips and looked at me from the ladder top and spoke
with eyes as large as curiosity, and I nodded, thinking
she was offering maximum assistance with her remarkably functional
feet, not knowing both of us may have been blessedly released
from virginity's yoke. So we glumly trod. And I kept wondering why

she looked and looked with sadder and sadder, if not wiser, blue
eyes towards me. And as I'd shrug heaps of the wet green chips from
   my shoulders she'd briefly
smile, and then there was a welcome pause and as I rolled
a cigarette with far from trembling hands she slowly crossed
without a word to the ladder, leaving as silently as she came.
And that no doubt is why her eldest child is one or two years
younger than it might have been. Then the roar and green rush
of relentless ensilage in the making all but drowned by donkey-
at-the-water-wheel treading, till I prayed like some mad catherine-
   wheeling
anchorite those masochistic prayers of pious-randy
youth, and trod and trod the green wheel of the neverending
 hours, stained green and yellow, smelling like a sweaty stalk,
talking and singing songs of food and drink and love to myself
in the most innocuous words ever disassembled, the cowboy tunes
of the Thirties and Forties: 'San Antonio Rose', 'You are my Sun-
   shine',
'Be Honest With Me', 'I'm Walkin the Floor Over You', 'Goodbye
   Little Darlin',
'Old Shep', 'Cool Water' – delirious with weariness and love
unsatisfied while the Niagara of shredded stalks descended
upon my cropped head, down my neck, inside my khaki shirt,
even into my underpants. Deluged with god, the blood
and semen of the cornstalk deity, I trod and chanted,
always ascending like an apprentice shaman towards that last
hole in the concrete roof from whence I'd issue on leaf-green wings
and tread upon the air up to the glazed galactophil-
ideal heaven of Khamaduk, the celestial bovine with ever-
flowing teats and other accommodations – for bulls. Back to
the heavy-footed, the Frankensteinian monster's tread, Boris's
bandy, soulful plod. In several months we'd shovel off
the top muck and the chooks would gobble it, a solid cross
between Drambuie and mud, and lurch and flap drunkenly for
a few days. Then the silage would be ready. And ploughing begin.

More than 9 Lives

Memo: you have only 16 lifetimes
more to live – as a general,
as a tycoon, as a biter-off of rats' heads
in village pubs, as a sterile
advocate of women's rights, as a lesbian
mother, as a blind maker of violins,
as a tone-deaf music critic,
as a whisky priest with no other vocation,
as a party member with no member,
as a three foot Amazon witchdoctor,
as a student of Aztec rope language
who gets knotted, as a werewolf
and a fey professor at the same time,
as a mixer of Pepsi Cola in a South Pacific depot,
as another poet, a race commentator,
and a bigamous, legless chicken sexer
not all at once.

PETER PORTER

On This Day I Complete My Fortieth Year

Although art is autonomous
somebody has to live in the poet's body
and get the stuff out through his head,
    someone has to suffer

especially the boring sociology of it
and the boring history, the class war
and worst of all the matter of good luck,
    that is to say bad luck –

for in the end it is his fault, i.e. your fault
not to be born Lord Byron and saying
there has already been a Lord Byron is no excuse –
    he found it no excuse –

to have a weatherboard house and a white
paling fence and poinsettias and palm nuts
instead of Newstead Abbey and owls and graves
    and not even a club foot;

above all to miss the European gloom
in the endless eleven o'clock heat among
the lightweight suits and warped verandahs,
    an apprenticeship, not a pilgrimage –

the girl down the road vomiting dimity
incisored peanuts, the bristly boss speaking
with a captain's certainty to the clerk,
    'we run a neat ship here':

well, at forty, the grievances lie around
like terminal moraine and they mean
nothing unless you pay a man in Frognal
    to categorize them for you

161

but there are two sorts of detritus, one a pile
of moon-ore, the workings of the astonished
mole who breathes through your journalism
   'the air of another planet',

his silver castings are cherished in books and papers
and you're grateful for what he can grub up
though you know it's little enough beside
   the sea of tranquillity –

the second sort is a catalogue of bitterness,
just samples of death and fat worlds of pain
that sail like airships through bed-sit posters
   and never burst or deflate;

far more real than a screaming letter,
more embarrassing than an unopened statement
from the bank, more memorable than a small
   dishonesty to a parent –

but to make a resolution will not help,
Greece needs liberating but not by me,
I am likely to find my Sapphics not verses
   but ladies in Queensway,

so I am piling on fuel for the dark,
jamming the pilgrims on tubular chairs
while the NHS doctor checks my canals,
   my ports and my purlieus,

praying that the machine may work a while
longer, since I haven't programmed it
yet, suiting it to a divisive music
   that is the mind's swell

and which in my unchosen way
I marked out so many years ago
in the hot promises as a gift I must follow,
   'howling to my art'

as the master put it while he was still young –
these are the epiphanies of a poor light,
the ghosts of mid-channel, the banging doors
   of the state sirocco.

Sex and the Over Forties

It's too good for them,
they look so unattractive undressed –
let them read paperbacks!

A few things to keep in readiness –
a flensing knife, a ceiling mirror,
a cassette of *The Broken Heart*.

More luncheons than lust,
more meetings on Northern Line stations,
more discussions of children's careers.

A postcard from years back –
I'm twenty-one, in Italy and in love!
Wagner wrote *Tristan* at forty-four.

Trying it with noises and in strange positions,
trying it with the young themselves,
trying to keep it up with the Joneses!

All words and no play,
all animals fleeing a forest fire,
all Apollo's grafters running.

Back to the dream in the garden,
back to the pictures in the drawer,
back to back, tonight and every night.

Affair of the Heart

I have been having an affair
with a beautiful strawberry blonde.

At first she was willing to do anything,
she would suck and pump and keep on going.

She never tired me out and she flung
fireworks down the stairs to me.

What a girl I said over the telephone
as I worked her up to a red riot.

You are everywhere, you are the goddess
of tassels shining at my finger ends.

You set the alarm clock to remind us
to do it before leaving for the office.

You are classic like Roman gluttony,
priapic like St Tropez' lights.

She put up with a lot: I forgot about her
and went on the booze – I didn't eat or ring.

I borrowed from her in indigence.
I was frightened and fell back on her.

An experienced friend told me in his flat
among the press cuttings: they've got to play the field!

Of course, I said, but I knew where that was –
down my left arm, my left side, my windy stomach.

She was sometimes late and when alone
hammered me on the bed springs like a bell.

She was greedy as a herring gull and screamed
when my dreams were of Arcadian fellating.

I woke in her sweat; I had to do something,
so called in Dr Rhinegold and his machine.

Meanwhile, the paradigm was obvious:
it's me that's in you said a polar couple –

me, the love of hopeless meetings, the odd biter;
no, me, the wife by the rotary drier

with the ready hand. Dr Rhinegold moved
mountains for me and said the electric hearse

might not run. But you're sick, man, sick,
like the world itself waiting in Out Patients.

I know how the affair will end –
but not yet, Lord, not yet. It isn't hope,

it's being with her where the scenery's good,
going to concerts with her, eating Stravinsky.

It's something more. I haven't finished explaining
why I won't write my autobiography.

These poems are my reason. She knows
she can't leave me when the act's improving.

She could imagine our old age: a black-
fronted house in a Victorian Terrace

or a cat-piss Square. Working on Modernism
while the stark grey thistles push to the door.

She can't let me go with my meannesses intact,
I'll write her such letters she'll think it's

Flann O'Brien trapped in a windmill. I'll
say her the tropes of tenebrae (or Tannochbrae).

I'll squeal in fear at her feet – Oh, stay with me
I'll plead – look, the twentieth century

is darkening like a window; love is toneless
on the telephone with someone else to see –

only memory is like your tunnelling tongue,
only your fingers tinkering tell me I'm alive.

'In the New World Happiness is Allowed'

No, in the New World, happiness is enforced.
It leans your neck over the void and the only
recourse is off to Europe and the crowded hearts,
a helplessness of pasta and early closing days,
lemons glowing through the blood of Acre.

It is the glaze of galvinism – why are there
so many madmen in the street? O, my countrymen,
success is an uncle leaving you his fruit farm.
The end of the world with deep-freezes, what if
your memories are only made of silence?

In one year he emptied the sea of a ton of fish.
He wasn't one to look at the gardens of Greenslopes
and wish they were the verdure of the Casentino.
Living with the world's reserves of ores,
no wonder our ruined Virgils become democrats.

Masturbation has been known in Europe too
and among the gentiles. Why did nobody say
that each successful man needs the evidence
of a hundred failures? There is weekend leave
from Paradise, among the caravanning angels.

Here's a vision may be painted on a wall:
a man and a boy are eating with an aborigine
in a boat; the sun turns up the tails of fish
lying beside the oars; the boy wipes surreptitiously
the bottle passed him by the old man.

Rain strums the library roof. The talk tonight
is 'Voluntary Euthanasia'. Trying to be classical
can break your heart. Depression long persisted in
becomes despair. Forgive me, friends and relatives,
for this unhappiness, I was away from home.

The Easiest Room in Hell

At the top of the stairs is a room
one may speak of only in parables.

It is the childhood attic,
the place to go when love has worn away,
the origin of the smell of self.

We came here on a clandestine visit
and in the full fire of indifference.

We sorted out books and let the children
sleep here away from creatures.

From its windows, ruled by willows,
the flatlands of childhood stretched
to the watermeadows.

It was the site of a massacre,
of the running down of the body
to less even than the soul,
the tribe's revenge on everything.

It was the heart of England
where the ballerinas were on points
and locums laughed through every evening.

Once it held all the games,
Inconsequences, Misalliance, Frustration,
even *Mendacity, Adultery* and *Manic Depression.*

But that was just its alibi,
all along it was home,
a home away from home.

Having such a sanctuary
we who parted here
will be reunited here.

You asked in an uncharacteristic note,
'Dwell I but in the suburbs
of your good pleasure?'

I replied, 'To us has been allowed
the easiest room in hell.'

Once it belonged to you,
now it is only mine.

Talking to You Afterwards

Does my voice sound strange? I am sitting
On a flat-roofed beach house watching lorikeets
Flip among the scribble-gums and banksias.

When I sat here last I was writing my *Exequy*,
Yet your death seems hardly further off. The wards
Of the world have none of the authority of an end.

If I wish to speak to you I shouldn't use verse:
Instead, our quarrel-words, those blisters between
Silences in the kitchen – your plainly brave

Assertion that life is improperly poisoned where
It should be hale: love, choice, the lasting
Of pleasure in days composed of chosen company,

Or, candidly, shitty luck in the people we cling to.
Bad luck lasts. I have it now as I suppose I had it
All along. I can make words baroque but not here.

Last evening I saw from the top of Mount Tinbeerwah
(How you would have hated that name if you'd heard it)
A plain of lakes and clearances and blue-green rinses,

Which spoke to me of Rubens in the National Gallery
Or even Patinir. The eyes that see into Australia
Are, after all, European eyes, even those Nationalist

Firing slits, or the big mooey pools of subsidised
Painters. It's odd that my desire to talk to you
Should be so heart-rending in this gratuitous exile.

You believe in my talent – at least, that I had as much
As anyone of a commodity you thought puerile
Beside the pain of prose. We exchanged so few letters

Being together so much. We both knew Chekhov on marriage.
The unforgivable words are somewhere in a frozen space
Of limbo. I will swallow all of them in penance.

That's a grovel. Better to entertain your lover with sketches
And gossip in a letter and be ever-ripe for death.
You loved Carrington as you could never love yourself.

I think I am coming within earshot. Each night
I dream comic improvements on death – 'Still alive
In Catatonia', but that's no laughing matter!

Perhaps I had Australia in me and you thought
Its dreadful health was your appointed accuser –
The adversary assumes strange shapes and accents.

And I know, squinting at a meat-eating bird
Attempting an approach to a tit-bit close to me,
That our predatoriness is shut down only by death.

And that there are no second chances in a universe
Which must get on with the business of living,
With only children for friends and memories of love.

But you are luckier than me, not having to shine
When you are called to the party of the world. The betrayals
Are garrulous and here comes death as talkative as ever.

And No Help Came

Where would you look for blessing who are caught
In published acres of millennia
By ravishments of salt and raucous saints
Or janissaries drilling a Big Bang?
The parish of the poor you'd seek, far from
The high grandstands of words and notes and paints.

And when you drove your flagged and honking jeep
Among the huts of starving, brutalised
Dependents, you might chance to hear them playing
Sentimental songs of flowers and moons
Chiefly to keep them safe from art, whose gods
Build palaces adorned with scenes of flaying.

What I Have Written I Have Written

It is the little stone of unhappiness
which I keep with me. I had it as a child
and put it in a drawer. There came
a heap of paper to put beside it,
letters, poems, a brittle dust
of affection, sallowed by memory.
Aphorisms came. Not evil, but
the competition of two goods
brings you to the darkened room.
I gave the stone to a woman
and it glowed. I set my mind
to hydraulic work, lifting words
from their swamp. In the light from the stone
her face was bloated. When she died
the stone returned to me, a present
from reality. The two goods
were still contending. From wading pools
the children grew to darken
gardens with their shadows. Duty
is better than love, it suffers no betrayal.

Beginning again, I notice
I have less breath but the joining
is more golden. There is a long way to go,
among gardens and alarms,
after-dinner sleeps peopled by toads
and all the cries of childhood.
Someone comes to say my name
has been removed from the Honourable
Company of Scribes. Books in the rooms
turn their backs on me.

Old age will be the stone and me together.
I have become used to its weight
in my pocket and my brain.
To move it from lining to lining
like Beckett's tramp,
to modulate it to the major
or throw it at the public –
all is of no avail. But I'll add

to the songs of the stone. These words
I take from my religious instruction,
complete responsibility –
· let them be entered in the record,
What I have written I have written.

BRUCE DAWE

Elegy for Drowned Children

What does he do with them all, the old king:
Having such a shining haul of boys in his sure net,
How does he keep them happy, lead them to forget
The world above, the aching air, birds, spring?

Tender and solicitous must be his care
For these whom he takes down into his kingdom one by one
 – Why else would they be taken out of the sweet sun,
Drowning towards him, water plaiting their hair?

Unless he loved them deeply how could he withstand
The voices of parents calling, calling like birds by the water's edge,
By swimming-pool, sand-bar, river-bank, rocky ledge,
The little heaps of clothes, the futures carefully planned?

Yet even an old acquisitive king must feel
Remorse poisoning his joy, since he allows
Particular boys each evening to arouse
From leaden-lidded sleep, softly to steal

Away to the whispering shore, there to plunge in,
And fluid as porpoises swim upward, upward through the dividing
Waters until, soon, each back home is striding
Over thresholds of welcome dream with wet and moonlit skin.

The Family Man

'Kids make a home,' he said, the family man,
speaking from long experience. That was on Thursday
evening. On Saturday he lay dead
in his own wood shed, having blown away
all qualifications with a trigger's touch.

Kept his own counsel. It came as a surprise
to the fellows at work, indeed like nothing so much
as a direct snub that he should simply rise
from the table of humdrum cares and dreams and walk
(kindly, no man's enemy, ready to philosophise)
over the edge of dark and quietly lie
huddled in the bloodied chips and the morning's kindling,
as though, in the circumstances, this was the proper end.

I liked him. He had the earmarks of a friend,
and it wanted just time, the one thing fearfully dwindling
on Thursday when we talked as people will talk
who are safe from too much knowledge.
                              The rifle's eye
is blank for all time to come.
Rumours flower above his absence while I,
who hardly knew him, have learned to miss him some.

Renewal Notice

From a passing train at twilight
suddenly I began to notice once more
how a stand of trees in the middle-distance takes on
darkness, means night will be cold-damp in there,
chill sweat on the knuckled roots
and the sunless bark, means also
small awakenings to death in the dim aisles where grass
is the only mourner.

Suddenly the world about me
moved from its long trance, like a family-group after
the camera's click, the tension dissolving, breaking up
into a kaleidoscope of laughter and movement and
people slumping joyfully back into their customary
postures, one saying Another second and I'd have
burst! and another There was this awful feeling my nose
was about to drip . . .
                                    Only here its emblems were:
in a paddock a chestnut horse swollen in death, upset
like a child's toy, a barefoot boy on a brand-new
silver bicycle with plastic streamers,
and, later, as the train rocked slowly over a rusted
bridge, the thought of fish in the darkening water,
diving like planes.

On the Death of Ronald Ryan

I dreamt you stood upon the trap of the world,
the rope of your forty-one years
around your neck,
your fugitive days, your prison days, the days of your trial ended.
You waited there for word of your last appeal,
the one no lawyer in the land could make
and only God uphold.
The morning sunburst beat on the dusty glass
with fists of gold.
I dreamt you stood
white-faced beneath your hood
above the lime-pit and the namelessness.
Annealed, un-tranquillised,
scorning a final statement
 – however you lived, I dreamt that day you died
with far more dignity than the shabby ritual
which killed you gave you credit for. You died
most horrifyingly like a man.

Drifters

One day soon he'll tell her it's time to start packing,
and the kids will yell 'Truly?' and get wildly excited for no reason,
and the brown kelpie pup will start dashing about, tripping everyone
      up,
and she'll go out to the vegetable-patch and pick all the green
      tomatoes from the vines,
and notice how the oldest girl is close to tears because she was
      happy here,
and how the youngest girl is beaming because she wasn't.
And the first thing she'll put on the trailer will be the bottling-set she
      never unpacked from Grovedale,
and when the loaded ute bumps down the drive past the blackberry-
      canes with their last shrivelled fruit,
she won't even ask why they're leaving this time, or where they're
      heading for
 – she'll only remember how, when they came here,
she held out her hands bright with berries,
the first of the season, and said:
'Make a wish, Tom, make a wish.'

Homecoming

All day, day after day, they're bringing them home,
they're picking them up, those they can find, and bringing them
      home,
they're bringing them in, piled on the hulls of Grants, in trucks, in
      convoys,
they're zipping them up in green plastic bags,
they're tagging them now in Saigon, in the mortuary coolness
they're giving them names, they're rolling them out of
the deep-freeze lockers – on the tarmac at Tan Son Nhut
the noble jets are whining like hounds,
they are bringing them home
 – curly-heads, kinky-hairs, crew-cuts, balding non-coms

175

– they're high, now, high and higher, over the land, the steaming
   chow mein,
their shadows are tracing the blue curve of the Pacific
with sorrowful quick fingers, heading south, heading east,
home, home, home – and the coasts swing upward, the old ridiculous
   curvatures
of earth, the knuckled hills, the mangrove-swamps, the desert empti-
   ness . . .
in their sterile housing they tilt towards these like skiers
 – taxiing in, on the long runways, the howl of their homecoming
   rises
surrounding them like their last moments (the mash, the splendour)
then fading at length as they move
on to small towns where dogs in the frozen sunset
raise muzzles in mute salute,
on to cities in whose wide web of suburbs
telegrams tremble like leaves from a wintering tree
and the spider grief swings in his bitter geometry
 – they're bringing them home, now, too late, too early.

Homo Suburbiensis

for Craig McGregor

One constant in a world of variables
 – a man alone in the evening in his patch of vegetables,
and all the things he takes down with him there

Where the easement runs along the back fence and the air
smells of tomato-vines, and the hoarse rasping tendrils
of pumpkin flourish clumsy whips and their foliage sprawls

Over the compost-box, poising rampant upon
the palings . . .
               He stands there, lost in a green
confusion, smelling the smoke of somebody's rubbish

Burning, hearing vaguely the clatter of a dish
in a sink that could be his, hearing a dog, a kid,
a far whisper of traffic, and offering up instead

Not much but as much as any man can offer
 - time, pain, love, hate, age, war, death, laughter, fever.

The Copy-writer's Dream

Hoardings screened the landscape from his sight
    He drove for power-thrust miles, his head thrown back,
Down avenues of breasts and teeth whose white
    Everlastingness oppressed him. A neat flak
Of jingles burst above him, a coupé
    Howled up alongside - at its wheel a German
Who flailed him with a baton until they
    Crashed in a ditch. He was listening to a sermon
And waiting for the punch-line, someone came
    (Her hair brushed over him: it smelt of flowers).
He was being carried, strapped into his name,
    And then into his car. He drove for hours,
Always ending in the ditch, with the slow wheels burning,
The sermon, the scent of flowers, the smell of burning.

Going

for my mother-in-law, Gladys

Mum, you would have loved the way you went!
One moment, at a barbecue in the garden
 - the next, falling out of your chair,
hamburger in one hand,
and a grandson yelling.

Zipp! The heart's roller blind
rattling up, and you, in an old dress,
quite still, flown already from your dearly-loved
Lyndon, leaving only a bruise like a blue kiss
on the side of your face, the seed-beds incredibly tidy,
grass daunted by drought.

You'd have loved it, Mum, you big spender! The relatives,
eyes narrowed with grief, swelling the rooms
with their clumsiness, the reverberations of tears, the endless
cuppas and groups revolving blinded as moths.

The joy of your going! The laughing reminiscences
snagged on the pruned roses
in the bright blowing day!

Morning Becomes Electric

Another day
roars up at you out of the east
in an expressway of birds gargling at their first
antiseptic song, where clouds are
bumper-to-bumper all the way back to the horizon.

Once seen, you know
something formidable, news-worthy,
is about to happen, a gull hovers
like a traffic-report helicopter over the bank-up,
one-armed strangers wave cigarette hellos from their cars,
an anxious sedan's bellow floats above the herd
  – the odour of stalled vehicles
wickedly pleasant like an old burned friend,
still whispering to you from the incinerator.

Broad day is again
over you with its hooves and re-treads,
its armies, its smoke, its door-to-door salesmen,
irrational, obsessed, opening sample cases in the kitchen,

giving you an argument of sorts
before you have even assembled your priorities,
properly unrolled your magic toast
or stepped into the wide eyes of your egg.

FAY ZWICKY

from: *Three Songs of Love & Hate*

   1 The Stone Dolphin

I have prayed for the end of his breath
(and mine)
to what end?

Anger's words have been hugged
and released.
The language of tyranny had to be
learnt if anything were to be said.

What has been said has been said
is still said after the panting
mouth has been clamped by despair.
But led by the devils
do angels leave too?

True grief is tongueless when the dumb
define love's death.
In a fiercely fathered and unmothered world
words are wrung from the rack.

Bury love's face
Bury love's bones
Bury love's tongue
in a place where the cataract groans,
where water is wedded to stones.

My dolphin, you'll leap in the sun,
caught sweet, without hate,
without grief in perpetual summer.
I sang you through gentler seas
than you knew, nor will know never.
Time full and perfect made heaven to

laugh in its mercy, made flower the apple,
showered me with innocent petals,
shook birds and fish in the lightning
tides where wind and water merge, melt,
melt and forever melt.

Drowned in the boon of his breath
I gave thanks for his dolphin pride,
for the creatures of water and air
keeping our pace.
Even the airs of the oncoming night
couldn't chill our far fathoming.

Warned, yet unwarned, beguiled by far
kinder griefs, swimming alone and
drowning, I embraced in one
shining sun track a dolphin of stone.

2 Jack Frost

To sit upon her belly warm
Jack Frost has come.
His cold sweet weight
Does not alarm the night
Or shake belief.

Too cold to ache
She parts her leaves
And welcomes thrust of snow
And stretches fingers past all pain
To stroke the teasing foe.

The cold creeps on
The buds unfold and burn
Her into night. Traversed
She lies and powerless to
Thaw the subtle guest.

JENNIFER STRAUSS

Love Notes

1

Thinking of you
the light of your name
dazzles thought.

2

Around a circle of light
shadows waver, darken;
this was the future we wrote
when you turned my palm to the lamp
to read its lines.

3

Blind with love's beginnings
I slammed a fingertip
in your car door;
months later I trim away
the last of that vivid bruise;
my nail looks very pure,
blank as a sheet of paper
on which I see you write
'You know that all things pass . . .'

4

All my intelligible life
is stored in the layout of houses;
feet can trace
old passages in the dark,
hands remain familiar
with switches for lights
and the sequence of cupboards;
until in childhood there's a door
opens only on orchard light
and the sound beyond of the sea;
as now, beyond your door
nothing but stairs
that mount to your bed and you;
I learn the pattern of your body
we keep no house.

5

This handkerchief from the pocket
of an unwashed summer skirt –
smelling of sand and sex
smells of you;
behind closed lids
the sun's wild catherine wheel
spins again,
the sea's surge resounds
in dizzied ears.

6

Hearing them praising your fire and wit
I think of you riding
passion's waves
with your cool fingers
and eloquent skin.

7

Thinking of you
the light of your name
dazzles thought . . .

CHRIS WALLACE-CRABBE

The Windows

First, at a window of the vacant house
A starveling manikin appeared
To glare through dusty mullions
With frank hostility:
He vanished in a flash as we came near.

Later we sprawled and picnicked on the lawn
But swung abruptly toward that house –
Decrepit, shadowy, blank –
As at another pane my son cried out,
Rubbing sleep from his eyes.

What sight, I asked, had hustled him from sleep
Behind those liverish walls?
And in what realm of metaphor
Should innocence
Rise up in answer to a leering dwarf?

No one could answer: least of all my son
Under the web-festoons
Of history's yawning house
Where seven oleanders in a row
Scraped their green spears along a wall.

Some fifteen years we dawdled through that meal,
Then two French windows creaked
As out stepped a young man,
Tailored, a subaltern
With brass in his profile and iron in his heart.

The Collective Invention

Wanting a myth for blowing up the gods,
In his flowing silver cape and plastic wings
Captain Melbourne zooms over Lonsdale Street.

His faithful girl assistants screech below
In their custom runabout:
Their T-shirts bear the sweet inscription JUSTICE
And they wear it well.

Admiringly, the crims and their dwarf henchmen
Hustle away,
Skulk underneath overpasses,
Terrified of the sterling Captain
And those just bosoms busy on their trail.

Glancing up from our sandwiches, if we're lucky
We might spot him gliding overhead
In his line of business,
Doing the common good all day long,
A handful of thunderbolts in his shoulder holster.

O Captain Melbourne, man of the wind and rain,
You are our hero,
Save us from northern weakness,
Continue still to zap and biff and pow.

The Mental Traveller's Landfall

O miraculous blown country
smelling of grass and hucksters' money,

rejoined stem of my sappy world
rising in this bird-riddled sunlight,

streets as wide as oceans full of nothing
but good humour and middle-octane corruption,

enormous anthills plumfull of Greeks and Sicilians
dropped here and there by parenthetical chance,

turfy meadows punctuated by batsmen
and neoplatonic fauna that Eros devised once

and tucked away south of the Wallace Line,
Yoo-hoo, I'm back. Let your furry paws go clap-clap,

roll out the ivory carpets, the spectral champers,
your childhood slides and the tin of cocky's joy.

The dead are alive, they are diamond-coloured dancers
on a triumphal cart as the weird bankers

accumulate dung in their vaults (growing votes and such).
The dancers are risen, they are great rustic virtues

and metaphysical decencies, straw in mouth,
they are bright as tinfoil, they burn like martyrs' blood,

they meet the full moon wedged in a yellow-box fork.
They are one's better, baptismal self,

hater of history and motivational sludge,
wouldbe titanic cousin of the sapphire waters.

A sort of amniotic stillness dissolves me
full of mineral salts, trace elements

and the secret circuits of association:
my veins are iridescent

while black dwarves find gold in my bowels,
phantasmal country like a blowing map . . .

Abhorring a Vacuum

Pearlmother dawn. It is fairly true,
'The mind divests itself
of any belief in the mental'

but my slept fragments
fall back together into a shape
doing things with cutlery.

Outside the pane, frondage and dewdrop-cluster,
tiny birds in their twelve-tone clamour
recommend continuity;

no one I can see observes me,
who fade like blown steam.
Dozy-dim, I battle back as

the fiction of personality
nimbs me for a moment like
slant light through a tram door.

It passes. I am lived
by who knows what, the gene's blind way
of making another gene.

Whatever has been writing this down gets out
from behind the wheel and
walks away.

Nub

Gro-ink. Kopita, kopita, ko-pi-ta . . . *konk*.
Were it not for the fact that I'd recognized the brickwork
of the previous station, coming out of my daze

I'd not have known. Out. I ran a whole block
at dream's peculiar slowness to catch my tram;
grey blocks of a city abstractly slid.

I came to the upside-down house,
its walls were folksified with Virginia creeper
and it looked as cheerful as a month of Sundays. I went in

being bent on finding the future, the logic of which
led me hotfoot up the stairwell to mother's bedroom
where, plumb on her chest of drawers, lay a single jewel-case

of tortoiseshell. Snap: open: there lay the future,
a perfectly polished chromium steel ball-bearing
round about five-eighths of an inch across.

I stared, closer and closer into its surface
so that the room, my face, were warped and bulgy
as through a fisheye lens, but rather fun.

In such a concentrating situation
what can you do but stare? – that's what I did
feeling immense waves of sadness in my legs

and chest all the while. I contracted the world's pain.
It was then, smaller at first than a bee's foot,
that something drew in closer over my shoulder,

an artefact as much as a consciousness,
jointed, threaded and cogged, full of spindles and heads,
a bronze-and-silver toy of elaborate construction

with a sharp weather-eye open. It knew the game.
It was the future. It gave away nothing at all
but a friendly tap on the shoulder. I shut the box.

from: *The Bits and Pieces*

   Opener

is an astonishingly slim
metallic biped,
that is if you call
Captain Ahab a biped;

knees together while
his two teeth bite down hard
if you twiddle his ears round and round
and he skates round the edge
of a silvery rink
on his head,
in his frustration
biting right through that tin crust.

from: *Sonnets to the Left*

IV

The writer depersonalises his dreamwork,
A single being in search of voices,
But change is learned from the outside world
Preoccupied with drink and kissing.
Unhappiness is the funniest thing,
It is a play about the ego
Needing to choose a lifelong project
Through tea and comfortable advice.

How can anyone be called guilty
From the perspective of the trapped
And struggling fly? Perhaps the itsy-
Bitsy is proof against despair,
Knowing between the fork and the knife
All our beyond is in this life.

And the World was Calm

Sandbags of sugar cannot conceal the gloomy fact
That we are inserted headlong into life
As a new pen is dipped in lavender ink.
We take up a space amid the comings and goings
Haphazardly, wanly. Velvet wrappings of eternal night
Contain our small blink, pitiless in their Logos.
Powderblue through gentle distance, lyrical mountains
Look at our passing span with incomprehension:
We never read their huge minds, and we die.

Why was the serpent given access to language and stuff?
Awareness becomes a different kettle of fish when eked
Out in a long line: the clipped image gives over
Until your modulation from rambunctiousness to grief
Is felt as a matter of slow brown flow, all river
And no cute islands. Remember, grace yields to Valium
Down on this late-in-the-century flood plain
Where even the fodder and grain crops are postmodern;
That is to say, containing no vitamins.

I'd like to build a cabin or humpy for awareness,
Something rustic like the Bothie of Tober-na-vuolich
Where I could hum and tootle against the wind,
That long grey stranger skirling through everything.
Grammar is always complete, but the world is not,
Shrugging and folding, surely hatching out of magma.
'You see what you are dreaming, but not with your eyes',
Said a chap who met little sailors down in the park
But grew austere as the case went on wearing him down.

Light is more mysterious than anything else –
That is, except for having to shit and for loving,
Categories you could not have invented, supposing
You were God for a while.
                              Am I alive or dead?
A question basalt or sandstone could never ask.
Awareness becomes a different kettle of herrings
When it's applied to the psyche of a whole country,
Something quite rosy, hydra-headed and fat:
Public opinion did a jig on the carpet of madness.

In the beginning green verbs went bobbing in space
Which was pearly or golden in its painterly turn
And we do not think about gales in the Garden of Eden
Nor about any distinction between plants and weeds
So that Adam is constantly doing something with roses.
Rubric, baldric, erotic, I brood on these terms,
He could have reflected, leaving his pruning aside
While he rolled the well-made words on his tongue like stone:
For the main thing then was learning how to think crudely.

Subtle as ivory handles, we think we are now
Umpteen years on from that scene in the Olduvai Gorge,
Outside the gates of which St Michael struts with his sword.
Pining, we find little paragraphs in which to lament
That we are inserted headlong into life;
Poetry survives with its coppery glint of gnosis
Along one edge.
                It is a drug that endures
Riding atop the bubbles of evanescence.
The river we step in will burn us off at the knees.

DAVID MALOUF

The Judas Touch

for J.M.

Meeting by chance and speaking
of you, we climb
in the huge print of your footsteps
to folded clothes, then silence
 – the view to a death.

And always the same landscape
looms in my head:
I recognise my face
in his face; smug survivors,
we're two of a kind.

The kind I mean whose friends
get lost, end up howling
in a public cage, or lie
streaming with salt
on a coroner's slab.

Is this the conclusion
you came to, dropping out
of air into deep water? Three
decades to touch bottom.
Full throttle, full stop.

Your good friends busy meanwhile
establishing elsewhere
all we have in common:
the judas touch, and a talent
for holding our breath.

Bicycle

for Derek Peat

Since Thursday last the bare living-room
of my flat's been occupied
by a stranger from the streets, a light-limbed traveller.

Pine-needle-spokes, bright rims, the savage downward
curve like polished horns
of its handlebars denote

some forest deity, or deity of highway
and sky has incognito set up residence, the godhead
invoked in a machine.

To the other inmates of the room, a bookcase,
two chairs, its horizontals speak
of distance, travelling light. Only the mirror

remains unruffled, holding
its storm of light unbroken, calmly accepting
all traffic through its gaze. Appease! Appease! Even

this tall metallic insect,
this angel of two geometries
and speed. So much for mirrors. As for myself

I hardly dare look in. What should I offer
a bicycle? Absurd
to lay before its savage iridescence –

grease-drop's miraculous resin,
the misty Pleiades –
my saucer of sweat.

Now time yawns and its messengers appear.
Like huge stick-insects, wingless, spoked with stars,
they wheel through the dusk towards us,

the shock-wave of collision still lifting
their locks, who bear our future
sealed at their lips like urgent telegrams.

For Two Children

Lelo and Alex Tesei

Across the lake the small houses appear
to be real, or to imagine themselves somehow
painted on the view and leaning toward
their shaky selves in water, taking the sun
for granted, stretching their timbers, half asleep
in a dream of such apparent permanence
that we hire a boat and would row across to visit,
or walk there if we could, watching fishes
snap their tails beside us and the mirror
scales reflect us tiny on their backs.

Instead we trail our hands under a jetty
and stay close in to shore. The water is clear,
metallic, deep, with an edge so keen our hands
are struck off at the wrist, set in Peru, say,
or Alaska, in a reliquary of solid
rock crystal. No longer ours, they seek
adventures. In the houses opposite, across
the blue-black glassy lake they stroke a cat
or crumble cup-cakes, saying we should have come there
too. And indeed we should, in a hired dinghy

and a swirl of smoke over icy pebbles, trailing
our oars and flicking crumbs of rainbowed sunlight
at fishtails in our wake. But the houses seem
no nearer. At arm's distance our hands give up
a career of pins-and-needles and drift back
to a warm, a known continent. Only the fish
rise to the surface and their round mouths gape.
We lean to where the boat tugs at its shadow
down there, blue-black and deep. Where have you been
all day? they ask at the boatshed on the beach.

RANDOLPH STOW

The Calenture

1

The natives camped on the hatches, who sang through the
   leeching mornings,
red ramis raw in the sunlight, dreaming of, hymning shade,

fearing a little, feeding, sending the smell of yams
to curl through the stagnant noon to the cuddy where I lay
   listless,

I must reckon dead now, or rescued; and all the sailors among
   them.
Abandoned I heave in fever, the calenture's heretic pupil.

2

Mary, star of the ocean! confound all witchcraft so lovely,
all fields so fair and deceitful. Believe me, I do not forget,

gentle indeed though the grass is, unlike the grass of these
   regions
(tender, ah tender-shooted, like winter-grass in my boyhood)

do not, and will not, so help me, forget that I am a seaman.
In spite of the endless calm, let me never forsake my standards.

3

Reminding myself therefore, continually of the ocean,
imaging under my eyelids its known and agreed appearance.

examining, questioning all, from the standpoint of common
    sense,
of common report and practice, of the usage of the Service,

I am not deceived, I find, by the waving grass; whose scent,
crushed out by tranquil sleepers, crowds every porthole.

Landfall

And indeed I shall anchor, one day – some summer morning
of sunflowers and bougainvillaea and arid wind –
and smoking a black cigar, one hand on the mast,
turn, and unlade my eyes of all their cargo;
and the parrot will speed from my shoulder, and white yachts
    glide
welcoming out from the shore on the turquoise tide.

And when they ask me where I have been, I shall say
I do not remember.

And when they ask me what I have seen, I shall say
I remember nothing.

And if they should ever tempt me to speak again,
I shall smile, and refrain.

The Singing Bones

> *'Out where the dead men lie.'*
> Barcroft Boake

Out there, beyond the boundary fence, beyond
the scrub-dark flat horizon that the crows
returned from, evenings, days of rusty wind
raised from the bones a stiff lament, whose sound
netted my childhood round, and even here still blows.

My country's heart is ash in the market-place,
is aftermath of martyrdom. Out there
its sand-enshrined lay saints lie piece by piece,
Leichhardt by Gibson, sealing the wind's voice,
and Lawson's tramps, by choice made mummia and air.

No pilgrims leave, no holy-days are kept
for these who died of landscape. Who can find,
even, the camp-sites where the saints last slept?
Out there their place is, where the charts are gapped,
unreachable, unmapped, and mainly in the mind.

They were all poets, so the poets said,
who kept their end in mind in all they wrote
and hymned their bones, and joined them. Gordon died
happy, one surf-loud dawn, shot through the head,
and Boake astonished, dead, his stockwhip round his throat.

Time, time and time again, when the inland wind
beats over myall from the dunes, I hear
the singing bones, their glum Victorian strain.
A ritual manliness, embracing pain
to know; to taste terrain their heirs need not draw near.

ANTIGONE KEFALA

Sunday Visit

We listened to the music,
carefully tracing the blue patterns
of the Persian rug.
Time waited, dusted, polished,
faded like the china cups.
Through the glass doors
the spring wind moved the trees;
unsettled wind,
unsure and full of boldness.

Another cup of coffee?
They had shrunk slightly
and their eyes looked dimmer.
The Greek in the next flat had died
during the winter, the poor man.
They still went for their walks,
had planted a new daphne by the wall,
watched the resilience of the new shoots
children's arms, firm, round,
shaded so slightly by blonde silky hair.
In the evenings
they returned to the old country.

Industrial City

We drove towards the city
past carcasses of cars
rotting in treacle by the
roadside, giant chimneys
topped by puffs of cream,
the black dust raining
on a landscape
that no longer cared.

At night, the railway clock
struck stubbornly the hours,
the room groggy with heat,
dogs barked furtively at the
new moon, out in a humid sky.

The first train left at dawn
the whistle marking slightly
the low sky, bleached blue
above a sea of moonstone.

The Party

The guests moved restless
caged under the sky
the strong wind swept away
the music, but the beat
came back to slap your face
with the sea air.

The hero came quite late
sniffing the air
his face like a skinned animal
eaten by maggots with ice heads

a musty smell about him
as he danced
his hollow eyes turned inward,
bleak tunnels with no end.

Freedom Fighter

A freedom fighter, she said
lighting the gas stove.
In the mountains we fought . . .
great days . . .
the words stubborn
weary in the shabby kitchen
with the yellowed fridge
and the tinted photograph
of the dead husband.
The house full of morose
rooms suffocated with rugs.

We came out on the low verandah
her heavy stockings pitch black
the rough spun dress the
indigo blue of some wild flower
the Sunday neighbourhood still asleep.
Come again, she said indifferently,
watching the windy street
and the Town hall squatting
on its elephant legs,
come again.

TOM SHAPCOTT

Shadow of War, 1941

We had never seen black cockatoos, though in the park
at home sometimes we'd begged our mother along
to the safe wire to stare at the white cousins
for a taunt of trained vowel and diphthong;
but here, up in the country where our father had sent us
(evacuees from a real and newspaper terror),
one morning we were shown on the dead tree near the
   kitchen
black cockatoos gathering, over and over

crowded in warfare of black wings, black feathers,
quarrelling for a few stiff branches in their thick dozens.
'Look at them!' we cried to the farmer our taciturn host,
as they covered the charred tree with acrid blossoms,
jagged and torn by red shadows, red crests.
He stood in the dry yard where we shouted and pranced.
'I see them,' he said: then 'It's the corn they're after.
A gun would shift them.' But he only walked away, and
   cursed;

while we crowded and shrieked to see the birds keep the tree,
not like the sleek crows, sly and silently,
but angrily, arrogantly, with black and red noise,
forcing their own terms triumphantly.
We were too young to price the waste of a crop,
or the shrug of that grim man, whose son was new dead
in a battle out of reach. On the dead verandah
we played at soldiers, khaki and black and red,
and our cries were jeering birds on fire overhead.

The Blue Paisley Shirt

My friend the blue paisley shirt is always assured
like eyes that crinkle up with goodhumour
he walks in the room
and is made welcome. Like laughing eyes
he seems a multiplicity of welcomes.
I bought my blue paisley shirt to make me friendly
to offer the grin of my shirt, its brisk handshake.
It is a dark blue, and the paisley white curls even its toes.
When I first put it on I felt good, so
this afternoon I walked into the crowded room
and my wife's deodorant under my armpits strewed petals
as I moved. Surely your saw me?
  Saw me standing
a middle-aging fool in white jeans and last season's sideburns
my face made naked above its shirt of skulls?

Turning Fifty

Surprisingly easy to cook a meal now.
I can iron shirts too, and bank managers
are people learning the ropes. Habits
express themselves in food
and the automatic tongue-tip
when concentrating: you will go
to your grave like a schoolboy.
Five p.m. and the rite of the wine cask.
(Australian patent, thank you Wynns)
(another habit: knowledgeability).

I have decided to learn all the operas of Wagner
(even Der Feinsholt) and the cantatas of Janáček.
Schoenberg lost his way at fifty, Webern
might have revised his. That defines me.
Some discoveries disprove what we hoped for.

To dream of death is not to ask why
but to ask how. I wear glasses
and I keep misplacing them. Is it true
my penis is shrinking? 'If you want to do anything,
do it yourself' my mother said.
Her sister in dying became almost my grandfather
right to the Ravenswood nose and the blue eyes
that haunted me when grandpa told Ned Kelly yarns
or the bankruptcy of ideals in the Great Depression.
Genes hold the trump card though I have
invented myself continuously. When I was fifteen
I had a sharp tongue and did everything myself
because nobody in my family understood.
My daughter makes her own way with the gestures
of her great-grandmother. Turning fifty
is a way to arbitrate between all these claimants
and to catalogue the library of Alexandria
in the drive-in video supermarket.

Post Operative

I came to the end at an inappropriate midnight.
It was so like a beginning, say one of those plane flights
that do not put down until Hong Kong. But it was
truly the end and I whispered 'I can take it no more'
though of course I considered that theatrical.
It is a long while, the end.
My father took months.
At midnight my body prepared to lay itself out
for ridge and blade, for the tug of sensation
and sensation drugged, pulled inwards.
Alone in my bed, in the end, I considered my gut
as an annex of god. I reached out to the phone.
In the distance the phone voice was angry. What to do?
'Ring the doctor' but I had lost decisions.
Five hours, then another five. The important things

were the animals that began grazing in my stomach,
licking its poison with slow tugs. Their breath
took me over, I was cud, mass, a process. Yes,
I could believe their calmness, even their incuriosity.
They had some further end in mind.

But it is true that later I was wheeled
in a metal frame onto the slab
with tubes up my nose and my penis. I looked at the surgeon
and his masked attendants: they had joined the beasts
there at the carcase, could it be worth so much?
For them
I was something different, a navigation chart.
I woke, and the animal breath was merely my own.
My torso was plugged in like a car engine, all sockets
and wires.
When you have been to the end you do not come back.
I live now in the afterlife. Had they told me
it would be the same I would have chewed like the animals
but yes, yes once you have seen this is death,
this is life, you do not return.
You make do with the sparks of your body as if it were
another. In borrowed time you remember
the incuriosity of hunger. You remember the distance
of pain: though it tugs in your very entrails
it nags with the voice, merely, of one lost on the phone.

The City of Home

The City of Home is reached only in dreams.
It has a town centre, a river with curved bridges

and the famous clocktower. There are always pigeons
which signify abundance not overpopulation.

There are no walls, no toll gates, no ribbon developments
full of hoardings, carpet Emporia or used car allotments.

The City of Home has retained only stone monuments and spires
and the shady maze of the Municipal Gardens

or perhaps secret childhood wildernesses of bramble
 - the smell of lantana still clings to an old pullover.

You approach from the air, it is a plan, a totality.
It is worthy of all your best secrets and the secrets of others.

Like all great cities, the City of Home reaches back
into all the generations, all the inheritances

though you have your own special associations
and insist on the second seat outside for your coffee.

There is no other coffee, no taste in all the world
to compare with that coffee! Yes, you insist, the second chair

the one under the awning where you can glimpse the fountain
and the bronze angel. The City of Home is like no other city

not even the City of Remembering or the Cities Of The Plain.
The City of Home has only one drawback, but that is terrible:

The City of Home is empty of people.
All its songs are the songs of exile.

JUDITH RODRIGUEZ

The Mahogany Ship

in memory of John Manifold

How I would have the poem rest:
that European circumstance, the ship
storm-blind
and unaccompanied
beating along by shelved cliffs, gulfs, west
under the gales' whip,
the length of her
urged at the last ashore
prow abutted on hummocks
to sift, to burrow like a burr.

And the passionate connection to begin:
thrown once for all too far up to be manned,
sea-jarrings
and the speaking charts
of sea-roads stilled, their known ports shunned to earn
a pilgrimage in sand –
the timbers weigh,
sailors run crouching, bayed
by fears, and snatch at brush
for watch-fires in her lee –

night-long at the flickering edge
of their race and language. Fires sicken. The dark
land dawns,
dunes packed by rain
mass, shoulder aside Europe. At the ridge
a face flares, turning last
from sand-bloated breakers
after water, timber, game.

Un-history cancels them. The Yangery
like the long wind hurling and raking

take them, unravel and stow
their genes between the dark thighs of the tribe.
Coast songs
and the wry cross
possess their children, the songless ship-ropes go
for nets that childbearing wives
three centuries on
re-knot for fishing – Jim Cain's
black Kitty and yellow Nellie – in their flesh.
Captain Mills notes the strain

surfacing, a legend's landfall,
even while the wind-grey panels of the hull
knives slip on
and farmers pillage
wear out of sight like the Great Expedition, founder
in wastes, and bearings fail.
The poem, consigned
and claimed, deepening in sand,
shifting, reaches among layers
to a beginning, to ends . . .

The long stain in the mind.

This wreck lay among the sand dunes near Warrnambool, in
the tribal land of the Yangery. No remains have been seen
since the 1890s. The Portuguese Grand Expedition of 1536
has been suggested as the origin of the wreck.

In-flight Note

Kitten, writes the mousy boy in his neat
fawn casuals sitting beside me on the flight,
neatly, *I can't give up everything just like that.*
Everything, how much was it? and just like what?
Did she cool it or walk out? loosen her hand from his tight
white-knuckled hand, or not meet him, just as he thought

You mean far too much to me. I can't forget
the four months we've known each other. No, he won't eat,
finally he pays – pale, careful, distraught –
for a beer, turns over the pad on the page he wrote
and sleeps a bit. Or dreams of his Sydney cat.
The pad cost one dollar twenty. He wakes to write
It's naive to think we could be just good friends.
Pages and pages. And so the whole world ends.

Nu-plastik Fanfare Red

I declare myself:
I am painting my room red.
Because they haven't any
flat red suitable for interiors,
because their acres of colour-card
are snowy with daylight only,
because it will look like Danger! Explosives,
or would you prefer a basement cabaret?
a decent home where Italians moved in,
Como perhaps (yes, I've gilded the mirror)
or simply infernal –

I rejoice to be doing it
with quick-drying plastic,
for small area decoration.
I tear at the wall, brush speeding:
let's expand this limited stuff!
It dries impetuously in patches,
I at edges too late scrub; this is a fight.
I sought the conditions,
and the unbroken wall is yet to come.
Clear stretches screech into clots,
streak into smokiness.
Botched job this, my instant
hell! and no re-sale value, Dad;
cliché too. Well, too bad.

It's satisfying to note
this mix is right for pottery.
Good glad shock of seeing
that red-figure vases *are*.
Not 4th-edition-earthy, but stab-colour,
new vine, red-Attis-flower, the full howl.
My inward amphora!

Even thus shyly to surface:
up we go red, flag-balloon,
broomstick-rocket!
Brandishing blood and fire, pumping
lungs external as leaves!
This is a red land, sour
with blood it has not shed,
money not lost, risks evaded,
blood it has forgotten, dried
in furnace airs that vainly
figure (since mines are doing well)
the fire. Torpor
of a disallowed abortion.

Why not a red room?

About this Woman:

green-eyed and could not give them to her children,
caresses her friends in thought, doubts they do likewise,
malingers and charms in fits and starts, dies daily.

About this woman:
wears no ring. Hangs on her husband, hang him,
to be the husband he could be, if he was;
if it takes fifty years. Faithfully mangles him
in words and thoughts, precarious vindications.

About this woman:
has heard of nymphs like wine; savagely inside
copes with turbid storm-water, and walls of sludge
it piled and can't shift now. The calm nymphs braid
light-runnels, a summer stilled. She dredges
in mixed minds at a quarry-mount of muddle:
where to dump, where gouge, whether
to abandon the site to flood,
worked faces flayed
with rubble in the flurry;

this woman.
Tuned to a tangible mode,
score half-composed, corrupt,
exultant, inharmonious, full of trouble . . .

Nasturtium Scanned

Ropey, lippy, loopy, scribbly
over a brick's edge, she's a riot,
straggly as random and tricky as a diet,
tiddly, wobbly, oddly nibbly
and flashy as a landmine on her vine-meandrine
Alexandrine tangle-scanned line.

PHILIP HAMMIAL

Automobiles of the Asylum I pull the huge book down from the bookcase. Rich full-color photographs of the cars & their drivers, page after page. But first the text: it seems the inmates have races in these vehicles; they start on the roof & roll down a spiraling ramp to the ground floor. No one knows when or how these races originated.

Each vintage car is a true work of art: magnificent chrome-plated radiators through which (so one of the captions says) only the rarest blood can circulate; huge highly-polished brass head & tail lamps, their wicks trimmed by special attendants; brass horns that curl to animal & vegetable bulbs with the scaled reality of the mermaid; spoked wheels with the shimmering complexity of fire-rimmed, god-filled mandalas . . .

And the bodies of these small vehicles – no larger than go-carts – each one is shaped like the torso of its creator-driver, a fur or silk-lined outer skin into which the limbless inmate may be comfortably placed for his or her one-way roll at dazzling speeds down, always down the ever-narrowing ramp to the shock-rooms.

Petit Guignol

The gas is good
It makes them dead.
We like them dead, & the dance before.

When they shuffle in we never look up.
We know nothing & never smile at these parties.
They shuffle in wearing gloves & thick glasses & take their
   seats.
They balance on their stools like goggled & gloved motor-
   cyclists on the starting line.
Goggles to keep the insects from their weak eyes, gloves
   to hide the liver spots on their hands.
It's a race to the finish, & as it progresses these motorcyclists
   cum skin divers begin to swim.
First the winner & then the others press their faces against
   the wall of the aquarium.
It's our aquarium, & the conversation bubbles.
The bubbles rise to a surface & burst, & it's good when that
   happens.
We like what happens when they burst, & and the dance that
   follows.

Treason's Choice

Either I'm swimming toward a floating discotheque its dancers
have all stopped dancing they're cheering me facetiously on
or I'm cowering in a dinghy towed by a racing sailboat its seven-
member crew is pointing me out to the spectators as an object
of ridicule.

Jane

> of her Jacks, Latin
> if they please

> of speech
> held while they fondle her map
> of the hog mine with its engine
> of snout in heavenly pink seemingly
> insatiable

> of body
> they'll ask her to leave, her shame
> if she does while they quarrel
> over veins, while they nibble
> & nip

> at her Jills, pig
> whom they please.

Sadie

She works with the Moors. Showing some skin she lures a tattooed sailor to an alley where the Moors are waiting with their knives. Two words, LOVE & HATE are found on the knuckles & removed. The sailor gets his just deserts.

When Sadie & the Moors take some LOVE & HATE they must do the 800 Celebrations. They must perform each other in the first & private person until they reach the last & public person. This last & public person is always behind a locked door. When Sadie & the Moors reach this door they must knock on it with LOVE & HATE. It opens, invariably.

The sailor is given his second chance. He must speak some lines in the third & every person that, unknown to him, can be spoken only by Sadie in her second. He trembles invariably, & spills the wine. As the first had his, so he is given them again.

He must be shoved aside or stepped over. The sanctuary must
be entered. 1600 hands must be washed. Every hand must hold
every other lest one of them disturb one of the thousand veils.
Sadie's dance

of LOVE & HATE could last forever, but again & again the last veil,
a sailor's blouse, is removed by LOVE & HATE for the last time until
she stands naked before them who, as always, would take her
in that person, in turns.
It's

now
& never that she must kneel on the stage & do the *telephono*,
to perfection. As always

she pours the wine without spilling it.   As always the words are
perfectly there as she calls them across the lines.

LES MURRAY

from: *The Bulahdelah–Taree Holiday Song Cycle*

1

The people are eating dinner in that country north of Legge's Lake;
behind flywire and venetians, in the dimmed cool, town people eat
    Lunch.
Plying knives and forks with a peek-in sound, with a tuck-in sound
they are thinking about relatives and inventory, they are talking
    about customers and visitors.
In the country of memorial iron, on the creek-facing hills there,
they are thinking about bean plants, and rings of tank water, of
    growing a pumpkin by Christmas;
rolling a cigarette, they say thoughtfully Yes, and their companion
    nods, considering.
Fresh sheets have been spread and tucked tight, childhood rooms
    have been seen to,
for this is the season when children return with their children
to the place of Bingham's Ghost, of the Old Timber Wharf, of the
    Big Flood That Time,
the country of the rationalised farms, of the day-and-night farms,
    and of the Pitt Street farms,
of the Shire Engineer and many other rumours, of the tractor
    crankcase furred with chaff,
the places of sitting down near ferns, the snake-fear places, the
    cattle-crossing-long-ago places.

2

It is the season of the Long Narrow City; it has crossed the Myall,
    it has entered the North Coast,
that big stunning snake; it is looped through the hills, burning all
    night there.

Hitching and flying on the downgrades, processionally balancing
    on the climbs,
it echoes in O'Sullivan's Gap, in the tight coats of the flooded-
    gum trees;
the top of palms exclaim at it unmoved, there near Wootton.
Glowing all night behind the hills, with a north-shifting glare,
    burning behind the hills;
through Coolongolook, through Wang Wauk, across the Wallamba,
the booming tarred pipe of the holiday slows and spurts again;
    Nabiac chokes in glassy wind,
the forests on Kiwarric dwindle in cheap light; Tuncurry and
    Forster swell like cooking oil.
The waiting is buffed, in timber villages off the highway, the waiting
    is buffeted:
the fumes of fun hanging above ferns; crime flashes in strange
    windscreens, in the time of the Holiday.
Parasites weave quickly through the long gut that paddocks shine
    into;
powerful makes surging and pouncing: the police, collecting
    Revenue.
The heavy gut winds over the Manning, filling northward, digesting
    the towns, feeding the towns;
they all become the narrow city, they join it;
girls walking close to murder discard, with excitement, their
    names.
Crossing Australia of the sports, the narrow city, bringing home
    the children.

    6

Barbecue smoke is rising at Legge's Camp; it is steaming into the
    midday air,
all around the lake shore, at the Broadwater, it is going up among
    the paperbark trees,
a heat-shimmer of sauces, rising from tripods and flat steel, at that
    place of the Cone-shells,
at that place of the Seagrass, and the tiny segmented things
    swarming in it, and of the Pelican.
Dogs are running around disjointedly; water escapes from their
    mouths,
confused emotions from their eyes; humans snarl at them Gwanout
    and Hereboy, not varying their tone much;

the impoverished dog people, suddenly sitting down to nuzzle
    themselves; toddlers side with them:
toddlers, running away purposefully at random, among cars,
    into big drownie-water (come back, Cheryl-Ann!).
They rise up as charioteers, leaning back on the tow-bar; all their
    attributes bulge at once;
swapping swash shoulder-wings for the white-sheeted shoes that
    bear them,
they are skidding over the flat glitter, stiff with grace, for once
    not travelling to arrive.
From the high dunes over there, the rough blue distance, at
    length they come back behind the boats,
and behind the boats' noise, cartwheeling, or sitting down, into
    the lake's warm chair;
they wade ashore and eat with the families, putting off that up-
    rightness, that assertion,
eating with the families who love equipment, and the freedom
    from equipment,
with the fathers who love driving, and lighting a fire between
    stones.

Lament for the Country Soldiers

The king of honour, louder than of England
Cried on the young men to a gallant day
And ate the hearts of those who would not go

For the gathering ranks were the Chosen Company
That each man in his liefetime seeks, and finds,
Some for an hour, some beyond recall.

When to prove their life, they set their lives at risk
And in the ruins of horizons died
One out of four, in the spreading rose of their honour

They didn't see the badge upon their hat
Was the ancient sword that points in all directions.
The symbol hacked the homesteads even so.

The static farms withstood it to the end,
The galloping telegrams ceasing, the exchanges
Ringing no more in the night of the stunned violin,

And in the morning of insult, the equal remember
Ribaldry, madness, the wire jerking with friends,
Ironic salutes for the claimants of the fox-hunt

As, camped under tin like rabbiters in death's gully
They stemmed the endless weather of grey men and steel
And, first of all armies, stormed into great fields.

But it was a weight beyond speech, the proven nation
On beasts and boys. Newborn experiment withered.
Dull horror rotting miles wide in the memory of green.

Touching money, the white feather crumpled to ash,
Cold lies grew quickly in the rank decades
As, far away, the ascendant conquered courage,

And we debauched the faith we were to keep
With the childless singing on the morning track,
The Sportsmen's Thousand leaping on the mountains,

Now growing remote, beneath their crumbling farms,
In the district light, their fading companies
With the king of honour, deeper than of England

Though the stones of increase glitter with their names.

The Broad Bean Sermon

Beanstalks, in any breeze, are a slack church parade
without belief, saying *trespass against us* in unison,
recruits in mint Air Force dacron, with unbuttoned leaves.

Upright with water like men, square in stem-section
they grow to great lengths, drink rain, keel over all ways,
kink down and grow up afresh, with proffered new greenstuff.

Above the cat-and-mouse floor of a thin bean forest
snails hang rapt in their food, ants hurry through Escher's three
    worlds,
spiders tense and sag like little black flags in their cordage.

Going out to pick beans with the sun high as fence-tops, you find
plenty, and fetch them. An hour or a cloud later
you find shirtfulls more. At every hour of daylight

appear more that you missed: ripe, knobbly ones, fleshy-sided,
thin-straight, thin-crescent, frown-shaped, bird-shouldered, boat-
    keeled ones,
beans knuckled and single-bulged, minute green dolphins at suck,

beans upright like lecturing, outstretched like blessing fingers
in the incident light, and more still, oblique to your notice
that the noon glare or cloud-light or afternoon slants will uncover

till you ask yourself Could I have overlooked so many, or
do they form in an hour? unfolding into reality
like templates for subtly broad grins, like unique caught expressions,

like edible meanings, each sealed around with a string
and affixed to its moment, an unceasing colloquial assembly,
the portly, the stiff, and those lolling in pointed green slippers . . .

Wondering who'll take the spare bagfulls, you grin with happiness
 – it is your health – you vow to pick them all
even the last few, weeks off yet, misshapen as toes.

The Mitchells

I am seeing this: two men are sitting on a pole
they have dug a hole for and will, after dinner, raise
I think for wires. Water boils in a prune tin.
Bees hum their shift in unthinning mists of white

bursaria blossom, under the noon of wattles.
The men eat big meat sandwiches out of a styrofoam
box with a handle. One is overheard saying:
drought that year. Yes. Like trying to farm the road.

The first man, if asked, would say *I'm one of the Mitchells*.
The other would gaze for a while, dried leaves in his palm,
and looking up, with pain and subtle amusement,

say *I'm one of the Mitchells*. Of the pair, one has been rich
but never stopped wearing his oil-stained felt hat. Nearly everything
they say is ritual. Sometimes the scene is an avenue.

from: *The Sydney Highrise Variations*

3 *The Flight from Manhattan*

It is possible the heights of this view are a museum
though the highrise continues desultorily along some ridges,
> canned Housing, Strata Title,
> see-through Office Space,
> upright bedsteads of Harbour View,
> residential soviets,
the cranes have all but vanished from the central upsurge.

> Hot-air money-driers,
> towering double entry,
> Freud's cobwebbed poem
> with revolving restaurant,
they took eighty years to fly here from Manhattan
these variant towers. By then, they were arriving everywhere.

> In the land of veneers,
> of cladding, of Cape Codding
> (I shall have Cape Codded)
> they put on heavy side.

The iron ball was loose in the old five-storey city
clearing bombsites for them. They rose like nouveaux accents
and stilled, for a time, the city's conversation.

Their arrival paralleled
the rise of the Consumers
gazing through themselves
at iconoclasms, wines,
Danish Modern ethics.

Little we could love expanded to fill the spaces
of high glazed prosperity. An extensive city
that had long contained the dimensions of heaven and hell
couldn't manage total awe at the buildings of the Joneses.

Their reign coincided
with an updraft of ideology,
that mood in which the starving
spirit is fed upon the heart.

Employment and neckties and ruling themes ascended
into the towers. But they never filled them.
Squinting at them through the salt
and much-washed glass of her history, the city kept her flavour
fire-ladder high, rarely above three storeys.

In ambitious battle at length, she began to hedge
the grilles of aspiration. To limit them to standing
on economic grounds. With their twists of sculpture.

On similar grounds we are stopped here, still surveying
the ridgy plain of houses. Enormous. England's buried Gulag.
The stacked entrepôt, great city of the Australians.

Equanimity

Nests of golden porridge shattered in the silky-oak trees,
cobs and crusts of it, their glory box;
the jacarandas' open violet immensities
mirrored flat on the lawns,
weighted by sprinklers; birds, singly and in flocks
hopping over the suburb, eating, as birds do, in detail
and paying their peppercorns;

talk of 'the good life' tangles love with will
however; if we mention it, there is more to say:
the droughty light, for example, at telephone-wire
height above the carports, not the middle-ground
distilling news-photograph light of a smoggy Wednesday,
but that light of the north-west wind, hung on the sky
like the haze above cattleyards;
hungry mountain birds, too, drifting in for food, with the sound
of moist gullies about them, and the sound of the pinch-bar;
we must hear the profoundly unwished
garble of a neighbours' quarrel, and see repeatedly
the face we saw near the sportswear shop today
in which mouth-watering and tears couldn't be distinguished.

Fire-prone place-names apart
there is only love; there are no Arcadias.
Whatever its variants of meat-cuisine, worship, divorce,
human order has at heart
an equanimity. Quite different from inertia, it's a place
where the churchman's not defensive, the indignant aren't on the
    qui vive,
the loser has lost interest, the accountant is truant to remorse,
where the farmer has done enough struggling-to-survive
for one day, and the artist rests from theory –
where all are, in short, off the high comparative horse
of their identity.
Almost beneath notice, as attainable as gravity, it is
a continuous recovering moment. Pity the high madness
that misses it continually, ranging without rest between
assertion and unconsciousness,
the sort that makes hell seem a height of evolution.
Through the peace beneath effort
(even within effort: quiet air between the bars of our attention)
comes unpurchased lifelong plenishment;
Christ spoke to people most often on this level
especially when they chattered about kingship and the Romans;
all holiness speaks from it.

From the otherworld of action and media, this
interleaved continuing plane is hard to focus:
we are looking into the light –
it makes some smile, some grimace.
More natural to look at the birds about the street, their life

that is greedy, pinched, courageous and prudential
as any on these bricked tree-mingled miles of settlement,
to watch the unceasing on-off
grace that attends their nearly every movement,
the crimson parrot has it, alighting, tips, and recovers it,
the same grace moveless in the shapes of trees
and complex in our selves and fellow walkers; we see it's indivisible
and scarcely willed. That it lights us from the incommensurable
we sometimes glimpse, from being trapped in the point
(bird minds and ours are so pointedly visual):
a field all foreground, and equally all background,
like a painting of equality. Of infinite detailed extent
like God's attention. Where nothing is diminished by perspective.

Louvres

In the banana zone, in the poinciana tropics
reality is stacked on handsbreadth shelving,
open and shut, it is ruled across with lines
as in a gleaming gritty exercise book.

The world is seen through a cranked or levered
weatherboarding of explosive glass
angled floor-to-ceiling. Horizons which metre
the dazzling outdoors into green-edged couplets.

In the louvred latitudes
children fly to sleep in triplanes, and
cool nights are eerie with retracting flaps.

Their houses stand aloft among bougainvillea,
covered bridges that lead down a shining hall
from love to mystery to breakfast,
from babyhood to moving-out day

and visitors shimmer up in columnar gauges
to touch lives lived behind gauze
in a lantern of inventory,
slick vector geometries glossing the months of rain.

There, nudity is dizzily cubist, and directions
have to include: stage left, add an inch of breeze
or: enter a glistening tendril.

Every building of jinked and slatted ledges
is at times a squadron of inside-out
helicopters, humming with rotor fans.

For drinkers under cyclonic pressure, such
a house can be a bridge of scythes –
groundlings scuffing by stop only for denouements.

But everyone comes out on platforms of command
to survey cloudy flame-trees, the plain of streets, the future:
only then descending to the level of affairs

and if these things are done in the green season
what to do in the crystalline dry? Well
below in the struts of laundry is the four-wheel drive

vehice in which to make an expedition
to the bush, or as we now say the Land,
the three quarters of our continent
set aside for mystic poetry.

The Drugs of War

On vinegar and sour fish sauce Rome's legions stemmed avalanches
of whirling golden warriors whose lands furnished veterans' ranches;
when the warriors broke through at last, they'd invented sour mash
but they took to sugared wines and failed to hold the lands of hash.

By beat of drum in the wars of rum flogged peasant boys faced front
and their warrior chiefs conversed coolly, attired for the hunt
and tobacco came in, in a pipe of peace, but joined the pipes of war
as an after-smoke of battle, or over the maps before.

All alcohols, all spirits lost strength in the trenches, that belt-fed
    country
then morphine summoned warrior dreams in ruined and would-be
    gentry;

stewed tea and vodka and benzedrine helped quell that mechanised
    fury –
the side that won by half a head then provided judge and jury.

In the acid war the word was Score; rising helicopters cried Smack-
    Smack!
Boys laid a napalm trip on earth and tried to take it back
but the pot boiled over in the rear; fighters tripped on their lines of
    force
and victory went to the supple hard side, eaters of fish sauce.

The perennial war drugs are made in ourselves: sex and adrenalin,
blood, and the endomorphias that transmute defeat and pain
and others hardly less chemical: eagles, justice, loyalty, edge,
the Judas face of every idea, and the fish that ferments in the brain.

The Tin Wash Dish

Lank poverty, dank poverty,
its pants wear through at fork and knee.
It warms its hands over burning shames,
refers to its fate as Them and He
and delights in things by their hard námes:
rag and toejam, feed and paw –
don't guts that down, there ain't no more!
Dank poverty, rank poverty,
it hums with a grim fidelity
like wood-rot with a hint of orifice,
wet newspaper jammed in the gaps of artifice,
and disgusts us into fierce loyalty.
It's never the fault of those you love:
poverty comes down from above.
Let it dance chairs and smash the door,
it arises from all that went before
and every outsider's the enemy –
Jesus Christ turned this over with his stick
and knights and philosophers turned it back.

Rank povery, lank poverty,
chafe in its crotch and sores in its hair,
still a window's clean if it's made of air
and not webbed silver like a sleeve.
Watch out if this does well at school
and has to leave and longs to leave:
someone, sometime, will have to pay.
Lank poverty, dank poverty,
the cornbag quilt breeds such loyalty.
Shave with toilet soap, run to flesh,
astound the nation, run the army,
still you wait for the day you'll be sent back
where books or toys on the floor are rubbish
and no one's allowed to come and play
because home calls itself a shack
and hot water crinkles in the tin wash dish.

Dog Fox Field

*The test for feeblemindedness was, they had to make
up a sentence using the words* dog, fox *and* field.
                                    Judgement at Nuremberg

There were no leaders, but they were first
into the dark on Dog Fox Field:

Anna who rocked her head, and Paul
who grew big and yet giggled small,

Irma who looked Chinese, and Hans
who knew his world as a fox knows a field.

Hunted with needles, exposed, unfed,
this time in their thousands they bore sad cuts

for having gazed, and shuffled, and failed
to field the lore of prey and hound

they then had to thump and cry in the vans
that ran while stopped in Dog Fox Field.

Our sentries, whose holocaust does not end,
they show us when we cross into Dog Fox Field.

MUDROOROO

from: *The Song Cycle of Jacky*

Song Thirty-Four

Long ago, his skin itches as men enter his pores
And run their fingers lightly along his walls,
Or scratch faintly diagrammatic lines.
From then on they touch Jacky in other ways:
The Wandjina eat themselves through his skin to become his bones.
White, yellow-haloed figures with gapped eyes
Searching for the tribal dead and the touching fingers
Of the living marking out the living.
In other places his skin is dotted, tapped and corroded by shapes;
Even the wraithlike Mimi emerge from between his cells
To line a rock with stick-like figures of grace
Which men might copy or trace with wondering nails.
The dancing Kwinkin quiver across his skin,
A hand is stencilled and a thylacine sketched.
Jacky's flesh shivers with thousands of tracks and figures and
    signs –
To be followed by strange horrific shapes,
Stranger men with stranger weapons,
To be etched and kept for all to see
That life is ever-moving, changing across his skin.

Hide and Seek

Hidden in hidden rooms,
Afraid to face
A glimmer of truth,
Wives and kids
Hardly speaking a word,
Except to demand.
Speak, reply, mumble.
Once men were mythologies;
Once spears were clutched;
Once our words ran together,
In complex sentences of intent;
Now we have become monosyllables,
Lonely in straight streets,
As long as the sentences
We once formed
From our initiation marks,
Cut deeply into our living flesh,
By masters of our languages.

Peaches and Cream

You like peaches and cream,
And white bodies made urgent
With a flare of injustice;
You talk of oppression and hate,
And are often written up in newspapers,
While those who know you
Talk of your liking of Bundy-and-Coke,
And porno movies made
For the touches of peaches and cream gone commercial.

You hide parts of your life in superior flats,
Then wander proud into a black hotel
As if you owned the place, maybe you do,
But you stutter in your words,
And the drover's hat sits askew on your head.

You talked and talked like a white fellow,
Till the gins grew tired,
And said you raved out of your head.
Then you swore retirement,
And how it hurt, no unity
In your fight for us fought on
Till your health suffered
In too many Bundies-and-Coke,
And peaches and cream,
Which you ate with little compassion.

Last night I saw you on the telly,
Projecting Jesus and his message,
Perhaps one day I'll understand,
Though many didn't and called you hypocrite;
But they didn't know
That even Christian peaches and cream
May be sweet with a taste of injustice,
And try to sweeten it more with you.

J. S. HARRY

Walking, when the Lake of the Air is Blue with Spring

A dark chocolate fungus
soft as the nose of a deer
nestles
into the soft,
moss-hollow,
between two
forest pine-trees

A pair:
yellow-winged honeyeaters turn
their black and white striped
bellies earthward
as they curve   into flame flowers;
one gives a gentle
come-on-now
peck at the other,
then, as if held
by invisible string
they fly fast
out of the overhead tree,
over two hundred yards
of unchosen flame trees,
into another

Out on the lake
one solitary pelican:
when the pelican
flaps his wings
his reflection
flaps back at him

Humanflung bread pellets
flip in an arc
up into air
down into water

The seagull diving
into the lake for bread
breaks into his own
white reflection

Little black waterbirds
are diving out on the lake
vanishing into ripple
their necks rise thin as snakes

A crowcoloured dog
gallops over the hill
while the voice of his colour
caws above him

A Shot of War

while those disintegrated by exocet
are unable to be present,
mrs thatcher – well wrapped
against the 'killing' chill
by a several foot
thickness of photographers
& 'fortified'
by the champagne-bubble-knowledge
that the war
was 'justified' – politically –
by being a success – in general –
with the british public –
& – in particular –
had improved
her popularity,
in january 1983

visits the falkland islands,
lays wreaths   on the ground
           above
'the british war-loss' –
& 'plays'
at being the one
to 'fire'
a military gun

a salon hair-do 's blown to pieces
by the force of the falkland gales
which, earlier, pushed up those seas
through which, on which, & under which
particular, british, & argentinian,
soldiers, sailors, & de-planed airmen
were struggling, freezing, & dying,
& she 'jumps' like an ordinary
first-time-soldier
pushed back   by the noise
& power of the gun

'kittenish'
behaviour drops from her
at this sound   so 'like'
a shot of war

underground the
recovered, drowned, burned, shot,
blown up, or frozen
are unable to oblige
by 'doing it again'
for the publicity picture

The Poem Films Itself

Down the slimy rope   into the impossible!
The insides heave   somehow they got the camera down inside
                              the alimentary tract
The poem as a historical drama or epic
by shakespeare or a drunken lamington by somebody french whose
    names
our memories'd glided over (elision   marked by ampersand:
    digestion omitted)
will be filmed in prose our new technique (perfect
    for moribund structuralism)   The costumes
will appear to be modern, say crudely

*early*modern   ashbery or o'hara (we will not know either of
    them well enough   to differentiate)
with a few loops of pointlessly-picked-over intestine   (It would
    be 'hard'
to establish   a particular crow was here)
Though our techniques are the shirts we are betting
our horses' lives on, their bloodlines (techniques', shirts', horses')
    like those of the   abused, & fictive, 'crow',
'derive'   from the ancients & cannot be said to be authentically
'ours'   yet still the pace carries us, into the
future with a marvellous momentum We are like

the *élan* about to drive a gothic cathedral
upward   into havens of print/sky-high!/   happy?   heavenly?
    (exit arsehole as might be
expected)   the mixed
naturalism, & the absurd, trade-marking   the content local,
    a few flashes of unparrotlike
environmental realism, yet to be added, for the risk . . .

Notwithstanding
                    dead animals rising on our tongues (soap, soup,
the leather we've been chewing, round the holes
                    in our spirits' feet where the thaw, as a
melting joke leaves gangrene green as agony)
what sincerely gets to us is   : a kind of food-poisoning
: that we are   still here   as if saving cents for a 3rd row seat
                    where

we don't want to sit   & are   already . . . too close up . . .
   from a
3rd row seat, the soundtrack-roar
                's quite deafening . . .
                  (& peering)   : the screen immense in front of us
(Mute Nausea   saving up   to pay
to be itself & dead?) while from the backrow stalls we do
                not have the bread for, they say   you can almost
see, & hear, from there . . .
it could be little boy blue or hamlet   who was the one . . .
              by the needs of the drama managed . . .
to get   the shiv dug in   himself: right
              place &
job well-done . . . the real, irrelevant bagpipes wailing
              frail but true, outside, (us liking them – but better:)
next role will play us into death

GEOFFREY LEHMANN

from: *Roses*

For Nancy Steen (author of *The Charm of Old Roses*)
and Charles and Barbara Blackman

I

At night, circling weightless, we dreamed of roses,
But woke to shrapnel whining over the tundra,
Faces drained in the time of immense bombardments,
Staggering through gas and mud, eating from tins.

Clutching the crumbling edge of nothing, our minds
Reached for the tiny bursting and popping of space.
Then the guns fell silent, men climbed from their holes,
We laboured back along the roads of pain

To our first house and garden of the world,
Veterans of all denominations, lame
And agile, the convoys thundering back at sunset
To a place of weeds, cattle munching wild peaches.

The expensive hybrid roses which we bred,
Unnatural blue and scarlet had gone back
To briar, were lost, and in their place the shy
Neglected cousins, the simple climbing roses

Had rampaged high as houses, trunks as thick
As trees, sailing with a vast freight of blossoms,
Scattering fragrance to moths and rain-wet grass.
Dust-stained we stood in the roses' soundless welcome.

In a house of fading brick on dusty floor boards
We dreamed of our natural and archaic pleasures,
Lawnmowers coughing grass, rain talking on roofs,
Leather and butter, wine and cream in the mouth.

By our heads an old ghost stood in calico trousers,
A mattock damp with earth glittered in his hands.
'Come out. The roses are calling under the moon.
Walk out in your sleep in the garden which is yours.'

VI

There is no absolute rose, there are the names
And differences, the roses of a night.
The Musk, the Green Rose, the extraordinary Mosses.
Where do these strangers come from with their gifts?

Tangled in snow, the shapes, the names, the families,
No mind, no system can contain the rose.
A rose in a glass of water waits by a bed.
A child with a pencil draws a singing bird.

IX

The harvest moon above the thistle forests,
The cattle snuffling follow at a distance,
Dust rising from their hocks, browsing in briars.
Wild ducks and apricots, and weathered sulkies

On purple plains of Patterson's Curse,
Mint under foot, fresh roses in a glass
On a veranda lit by a flickering lantern,
And fingers darning clothes torn on a journey.

from: *Ross's Poems*

16

'What's that bird, Mr Long?'
'That's a chipper.'
'What's that small bird over there?'
'That's a fly-bird.'

There's a forest I'll never see again
where birds with exotic names
whistle to each other,
flashing blue and scarlet
as they dart and fan their wings.

'What will you have for breakfast, Mr Long?'
asked my father.
'I could eat the leg of the Holy Ghost,'
replied Mr Long (meaning toast).
'I would *not* have expected that of *you*!'
said my father with ice –

But Mr Long was rarely put out.

On a wooden chair by my bed
there's hot chocolate I'll drain quickly
because these autumn nights
are taking the warmth out of things
as they loosen the poplars' yellow leaves.

Then I'm going on that journey
Mr Long always promised
with a covered wagon and a cockatoo,
cooking fish on river stones,
to Palm Valley and its wild blacks
through the spinifex.
'What's that bird, Mr Long?'
'That's a parson-bird with the white collar.'
'And that one over there?'
'That's a grey hopper.'

Walking all day
out on the western plains, Mr Long
could sustain himself
with a line of trees on the horizon.

29

Music is unevennesses
of pressure on the ear-drum.
Sight is the vibration
of rods in the eye.
My dog's called Joe.

Meaning to ask for Ock her son
I asked Mrs Wearne
'Where's Olly?' (Her dead husband)
'You tell me,' she said.
Waking in winter –
a big bush cat was sitting in the starlight
scratching at green parrots in a cardboard box.
And where was Olly?
You tell me.

36

This house hasn't known much music
except Sally sitting in the dust,
tightening the wire strings of a bee-box frame
and plucking them.

At night the trees rush with different sounds
or a bull is restless
and dogs interrupt the darkness,
these are a sort of music –
or sleeping in a travelling car my ear
listens to the change
from bitumen to gravel and back again,
the chassis vibrating.

Young, I needed an occupation,
felt myself going mad without it.
Older,
I find music in anything,
sounds of nature, personal idiom,
doing nothing –

57

Lying on the back of my brother's utility
my head propped among chaff bags
I watch falling stars
flicker down the sky,
like the neurons in my brain
going one by one.

Which one of those million lights
melted and fell?
There's no gap to say.

Country and western music is playing
from my son's corrugated iron bedroom.
At about ten each night a small bat
visits his room and flies out again.

67

A motor-cyclist's head
skimming high grass
promises a summer of fires.

And it's a hot summer
at the moment for barbers,
with more white clippings
than black,
on barber-shop floors.

Every young man is Adam
with his hair on fire,
while out-of-work barbers have nervous breakdowns
as the rules of a generation collapse.

They say collapse,
but I call it change.
It's not hard to choose between
low infant mortality and an art nouveau tile.
There's no nostalgia
about women nursing dying children
on finely carved cedar beds
with embroidered linen.

Our time is on fire,
the barbers say,
but time is always on fire
with good fires and bad.

Through the dusk my wife with quick steps carries
from our old house to the new
my favourite pressure lamp.
Moving across the buff paddocks

its light is softly yellow and archaic,
as today
they've put up power-lines through the trees.

I prefer a world
that's modern, vulgar, and well lit.

GEOFF PAGE

Road Show

At the end of his act
the softshoe possum,
the spotlights hard
upon him,
                   danced
one step and made
a final bow.

The Holden, however,
not brought up
to vaudeville,
swept on,
                   printing
the bitumen with
a whiskery gesture.

Smalltown Memorials

No matter how small
Every town has one;
Maybe just the obelisk,
A few names inlaid;
More often full-scale granite,
Marble digger (arms reversed),
Long descending lists of dead:
Sometimes not even a town,

A thickening of houses
Or a few unlikely trees
Glimpsed on a back road
Will have one.

1919, 1920:
All over the country;
Maybe a band, slow march;
Mayors, shire councils;
Relatives for whom
Print was already
Only print; mates,
Come back, moving
Into unexpected days;
A ring of Fords and sulkies;
The toned-down bit
Of Billy Hughes from an
Ex-recruiting sergeant.
Unveiled;
Then seen each day –
Noticed once a year;
And then not always,
Everywhere.
The next bequeathed us
Parks and pools

But something in that first
Demanded stone.

Late Night Radio

On tape and late at night
the great man's friends
remember him alive at lunches

staring from a ferry prow
intoning Latin in a toilet –
his brilliance could detach itself

and hang there in the air.
The poems somewhere else
are edited and final

between a set of covers.
The quiet man with his spools and questions
is gone also, a writer of

mild forgotten poems.
The voices he preserved
drift in and out of time

(more than half their owners dead)
speaking of alcohol, scandal, children.
From all six capitals

beneath the westward moon
their voices radiate and thin
away into mountains and into the sea

and into certain rooms
where on a shelf in a single book
in maybe half a dozen poems

the spaces between his words
still speak
even as the dust falls through them.

The Elegist

Sleek, dark-suited
as if on the payroll
and with an undertaker's
nervousness of hands

he has touched down this morning
having smelt out the news.
No poet's death
can possibly evade him –

the shifty
sentimental eye,
the steady nose for grief.
Sidelong in the silence

of oregon and stone
he places like an usher
the mourners either side –
remembering old photos,

guessing from the clothes.
Later at the graveside
the breeze cannot
unslick his hair;

his eyes assume
the texture of the sky
and in the rhetoric
of dust and ashes

his images
begin to harden.
A necessary friendship blooms.
Saturday next

their two names meet
across a matter
of four or five stanzas –
though one is always

better known
the printer's ink
unites them nicely
over coffee in the morning sun.

Jerry's Plains, 1848

Living alone in a sad-looking house
his brother's house in Jerry's Plains
the year of Europe's revolutions

a man turns through his life by lamplight,
poems pasted in a ledger
rescued from the Sydney papers

and swept around with annotation.
He snips them too from the *Mercury*
and does its local correspondence

(*the aspect of the clouds is promising*),
a keeper of the pound also
(one roan mare of 14 hands)

master of Queen Victoria's post
agent for Holloway's Pills and Ointments.
Three miles out on the Singleton road

is the woman he waits for (*the Eulengo lass*)
post-and-railed by cool relations
and, closer in, the daily gossips

who take their news across the counter
and wonder at his forehead's height
that restlessness of change and hands

but they are lying straight in bed now
or maybe watching suspect windows
as a nib is dipped and starts to write:

I am 'a bard of no regard'
in my own Australia
but my countrymen

and the world
will yet know me better.
I doubt not indeed

but that I shall yet be held in honour
both by them and by it;
that is when I have lived down

certain calumnies
that are now afloat against me.
One of these is

that I am a drunkard.
This is mainly a lie.
Another of these calumnies is

that I am somewhat lax
in my sexual moralities.
This is also

mainly a lie.
I have lived chastely
upon the whole

throughout my entire life.
Another evil belief
to my prejudice in certain quarters

is that I am somewhat
atheistically given
in my conversational speculations.

Now this is wholly a lie
and has been originated by incapables
who did not understand me.

And this, tonight, might almost be enough.
They'll all be there tomorrow
and out of town

the critics with their London quips
the squatters and their jumped-up lawyers
the aristocracy of bunyips.

He leaves the ledger open now
and follows his lantern away down the hall
drags off his boots and stares at the ceiling

which, when he pinches out the wick,
is suddenly a total blackness
uncomprehending as the sky.

ANDREW TAYLOR

Developing a Wife

In the one cool room in the house
he held her face two inches under the water
rocking it ever so gently
ever so gently. Her smile
of two hours earlier came back to him
dimly at first through the water, then with more
boldness and more clarity.
The world is too much with us
on a hot day (he thought); better
this kind of drowning into a new degree,
a fraction of a second infinitely
protracted into purity. Her smile
free now of chemical and the perverse
alchemy of heat dust and destroying wind
free from the irritation, the tears
and the anger that had finally driven him
down to this moment,
was perfect, was
irreversible, a new reality.
Is it, he thought, that there is truth
here which she imperfectly embodies?
Or is it I that I'm developing here –
my dream, my vision of her,
my sleight of hand?
Perhaps, he thought, our marriage is like this? –
flimsy, unreal, but in its own way real:
a moment, a perfection glimpsed, then gone, gone utterly,
yet caught all the same, our axis, stationary,
the other side of drowning?
                              He bore
her smile out in the heat to her, as a gift.

Clearing Away

Today I chopped back irises
spear-sharp
layers of leaves
long as our memories –
Vietnam, savage green
in the March decline;
paler, lank low leaves
almost brittle – Korea;
then a tangle of grey –
dusty, forgotten rubbish –
the last war, Second World War –
crumbling to the blade.
Beneath –
the red-backed spider
angry at being disturbed.

Fitzroy

It's only at Christmas and New Year
you can see the lights of Brunswick
twinkle like crystal chandeliers
here and that's because
the factories are shut and pollution's
down, she said, snapping
open a bottle of gin. The baby
pugnacious all day, pugnates sullenly
in its basket, punching its way
down bluestone alleys glittering
with the pretty hues of broken
bottles and teeth. I want to say
various things about inner-urban
living, I want to comment
on why this house is worth so much more
than we are, she said, since the baby

was beyond speech, cornered behind
a knitwear mill by a bunch of hoons
with steely claws and little respect
for baby. Tonight
it looks like fairyland, next week
they'll think up another freeway or
antiquated highrise and the whole bloody
battle begins again. By now
baby has a broken nose and a knife
and crawls from the cobbled cul-de-sac
behind the burnt café and finds the road
clear to the thirties, the Depression
no one today remembers. Who'd want to?
I don't even know how we afford
this semi-renovated slum that cost us
eight years ago 25,000. Baby,
installed in the streets now,
follows the horses, carries a gun
and wonders if Archbishop Mannix
will ever die. When he does
he hopes the shamrock in his lapel's
as green as his neighbour's. The terrace
needed so much *restoration*
it was a joke. He'd opted
for treeferns in the front and a modern
concrete back yard with a patch
for silverbeet and tomatoes. Tomatoes
returned to Carlton with the Italian
invasion of the fifties, but these
were the *original* tomatoes, all seed
string and a hide that would blunt
a flick-knife. When the baby gnaws
fitfully and noisily in its sleep
on a plastic gun or something, she runs
frightened by a latent outbreak of care
to its nursery in the deceased estate.

from: *Travelling to Gleis–Binario*

X Goethe and Brentano

Of course they had servants, dressed for dinner
and though they themselves hardly washed
their linen was spotless. They didn't squat
on a bed in a room three metres square
in underwear, or in torn jeans,
drinking red wine, scrawling their poems
on their knees, or grab a stand-up meal
from the fridge. It must have been hard really
to be Romantic then, which I guess
is why they were best, serious
with the help of money, servants, limitless leisure
a religious background and the knowledge
they were the first. Today anyone
can act the part, but could we manage
any sex life, two litres of wine a day, and some
great poems, all with a valet looking on?

ROGER McDONALD

The Hollow Thesaurus

Names for everything I touch
were hatched in bibles, in poems cupped by madmen
on rocky hills, by marks on sheets of stone,
by humped and sticky lines in printed books.
Lexicographers burned their stringy eyeballs black
for the sake of my knowing. Instinctive generations
hammered their victories, threaded a chain,
and lowered their strung-up wisdom in a twist
of molecules. But with me in mind
their time was wasted.

When the bloodred, pewter, sickle, sick or meloned moon
swells from nowhere,
the chatter of vast informative print
spills varied as milk. Nothing prepares me
even for common arrivals like this.

Look. The moon comes up. Behind certain trees are bats
that wrench skyward like black sticks.
Light falls thinly on grass, from moon and open door.
This has not happened before.

Incident in Transylvania

Black in a tentlike cloak, at rest
near the roots of an ancient oak on a hillside
the count awaits a two-legged bottle.

Soon, awkward astride a mule, plunking with lurches
his winded guitar, a corpuscular friar
with lymphocytes fizzing like spa water
rides through a curtain of sweat
till his chin clicks up
on the outstretched arm of the Count who is waiting.

A surprise, like cactus clapped to his neck:

'I've been watching your ride,' lips the Count,
with ruby politeness. The friar has bubbles
of breakfast loose in his throat,
and riffles a pack of escapes:
'I'mer, willyar, issalltoo . . . too . . .' and slumps
to the pit of his belly, waiting.

But the Count draws back from capture, strangely,
and it isn't the friar's fat, or the odour of fear
that deters him, nor even a whiff of chubby religion.
There are personal bones that give trouble –
nights of competing with shadows,
the knuckle and knee-bruising hunts,
the general ascent in the land
of inferior blood.
'It's a pain in the fangs,' he snaps,
heeling the mule in the butt,
bouncing the friar in whistles downhill.

Back at the castle the groom has observed that the Count
seems no longer himself, no longer deliciously flensed
by the howl of his creatures (those slack
acres of flesh in cylindrical pits)
no longer – the servants gather and mutter –
no longer the Count of the cloak and the eye, the limp,
and the dreaded formula.

He calls for a glass of milk, he calls
for news of the world and a hot brown bun,
while a little old wife appears in the room's far corner,
clucking and knitting, nursing a cat,
blinking her blue old eyes and snicking her lips for a chat.

NIGEL ROBERTS

Max Factor Pink

in yr absence/i
flip through
the spread shots
& the memories
other
Xeroxed images –
you
shaving yr legs
or
you
tinting yr nipples
max factor
pink

The Mona Lisa Tea Towel

Not
in the Louvre behind
bullet proof glass
but liberated by
The Tiger Mountain
Tea Towel & Printing Collective
in homage
to Duchamp
& the dadaist spirit

of the peoples republic
of China –
The Mona Lisa
on linen / printed
as linen / washed
as weathered flag
pegged to the Hills Hoist
upside down.

The Gulls' Flight

The gulls' flight
is low
flat
& hard

they go
to sea
to the edge / where
the day's fire
is lit

they go
as shiftworkers
to the dawn.

A Nigger & Some Poofters

The support act
at 'The Club'
is a drag show –
Their silicone & outrageous

razzle dazzle of Tallulah
Judy, Marlene, Bette
& Mae
plays to the indifference
of the poker machines
& to
the dull & predictable wit
of the schools
thick and safe
at the bar.

The main act
is a circuit black
of such clubs
& talk shows –
He works & excites
the passing interest
of an obituary –
&, at the bar provokes
a renewed assault
of whose shout, until
the m.c. suggests
'Fair go for the nigger, or
we'll bring the poofters back'

& so it is,
they hold it down
at the bar
& give the nigger
a fair go;
until a handful begins
to bark a preference
for bringing
the poofters back.

RAE DESMOND JONES

Shakti

down under the bridge you
could still feel the water rub
onto the stone

& because it was late the
grass crushed a juicy perfume
under our shoes

at luna park the lights
were out & the trains droned
the koran across the high rise
minarets & laundromats

you took your coat off
beside the pylons & rested back
& in the deeper grass an old man
coughed

& you were open & thick as
an apricot overripe with blood

& in the city huge pillars
of light burned the ancient
corpse of god

& the empty ferris wheel
creaked & worked its hooks
into the eyeball of the clouds

The Front Window

it is raining softly
as an old greek woman
dressed in black walks
along the path with
a big brown paper
parcel
      the spray tapers on
      the roof opposite like dürer's
      hands & i know if i take a rubber
      i can obliterate the world
the old woman looks
at me & her face is folded & cracked
& her eyes are small
      i take the rubber
      & she looks down as she
      begins to disappear
because she is heavy i rub harder
& she becomes gradually faint
& weak
      she drops the parcel &
      it splits on the wet ground
      & sets loose a swarm of angry
      bees
their tails are fat &
they beat against the glass & live
although i rub them out one by one
they are a plague

James Dean

1

where if you glance behind
you can see the monochromed bars of taxis
swivelling at the bend

the car still burning there its flame
crawling up the sky hesitant as a crippled fly
on glass

& beside the white emptiness of billboards
stylised coppers watch blank faced
from motorbikes

in the rear-vision mirror you catch
him looking through your eyes narcissist
as ever the flowers of his mockery recurring

eternal late movies on television

2

with valentino he escaped
a destiny of soap commercials but has served
to keep the repressive myth alive

beauty & honesty are easy distorted but
as with rimbaud they could have done without
his energy. an unforgivable imperfection –

although the creases have never deepened
on the sides of his face

3

a few lengths ahead
an old customline her fins swept back ducktail
& sleek brakes at the stoplights

the slow single flicker
on off on off & the regular heartbeat
of gas & the delicate pulse of her timing

move slowly past him the manual gear change
up when the lights go green

the speedometer needle climbing & the sleeve
caught in the door & leave him
& america

pissweak reflection & creator of a generation
now gone to parenthood & the suburbs
& the chicken still screaming on the verandah

the tragic screen widening to cinemascope
the sun coming up & the huge mandala of the wheel
easy in your palm

JENNIFER RANKIN

Old Circles

Red berries wiping rain at the window
staining in a black and white winter day

wet leaves flattened on a marble stair
veined like an old man's eye

birds huddled in the forked aviary roof
blinking at stiff-legged death

garden trees tamed and round
waiting while the sky completes its turn

a woman crouched inside by the hearth
unwinding her wet face hissing to burning wood.

Forever the Snake

Awkward on a hillock of grass
feet falling forward over the edge
cramped close to the children
away from the snake.

And in that patch of long reed it is waiting.

You pick up a spade.
Eyes pace out the ground.
Your left hand is clenched on itself
nails bite into your skin.

A heavy grey rock lies in the reeds.
With one move you upend it.
The children edge closer on the hilly rise
they stand on my feet.

I see you consider and bend
you probe with the spade.

And then it is here.

Snake. Flashing its back
arrowing through grass
black missile with small guiding head
firing off reflexes, straight into attack.

And the spade. Lifeless and foreign
under your hand raised in the air.

This black speeding nerve is cutting through space.

Somewhere forever your hand is raised
in far-off space fields the snake is racing.

Now the thick spade crashes down from above
snapping the nerve that even in death sends its messages.

We inch about on our hillock of earth.
The back of the snake is still thrashing.
You stand with its head under your spade
you are locked to its spine.

Far-out in space the snake is still speeding
rushing through grass to attack.

Closer in space the spade has been raised.

Here on the grass the black nerve is broken.

Yet always the snake is now striking
in the quiet, in the space beyond time.

Sea-bundle

I carried you to an island.

A thousand years of sailing
and the reef still stretching away.

Wrapped in old sails you ate
out of my hand

you drank from the sea

you gazed ahead in the morning
returning each night.

I handled you gently in your bandages
I brought you safely to shore.

Now I squat on the sand.
It is mid-summer and I am unwrapping you.

I hold you within my hand
and you twist in the sun.

The sea spins its mirror over our heads.

Here in the sand the worn calico unravels.
I have come to the end.

You stretch and flap up into my face.
I am old and I cry into your hands.

'A man is following me . . .'

A man is following me

I hurry away from the tram-stop
straight into the street of laurel trees

I hear him close behind stepping faster
we crisscross the street together

I check the distance to the end
my school shoes ringing out too loud

I feel his shadow in all the shadows
I feel his faltering

A man is following me
and I am getting to know him

all my life I have moved with his shadow
pacing the street in this slow mad dance.

Tale

Rotund, stubby fingered
I feel him fumbling
stumbling his body against mine.
But where is his head?
Over there, discoursing with Aristotle
on the mantelpiece.

Love Affair 36

On the seventh day

in the late afternoon
with shadow already entering the valley

I watched your biceps.

They were flashing and beeping.
They were signalling confidence.

And I knew that my eyes were darkening
I knew that my eyes were slits when I glanced

as you walked on the balls of your feet through that house

your hips quite taut below your brain
and your lips too sweet by far.

And I stayed behind in the bedroom.

I was tossing and turning
I was considering the stars
I was laconically flicking a page
I was reading the dictionary
I was brushing my hair
I was wrapping myself in a shroud.

I lay on the bed with my terrible eye
and you strutted outside the door.

I ate a crisp apple
bursting the skin with my teeth.

You whistled so lightly in the bathroom
I very nearly stabbed you there
blood all over the green-tiled floor

toothpaste in your beard
a smile on your lips
apple between my teeth.

Instead I slowly turned the page
and the paper smelt of ink and a summer breeze.

Old Currawong

After the sudden rain
the heavy after-drops still thudding

a large black currawong slipping
gripping rasping in the corrugations of the iron roof

and the lorikeets flying in only as colour
and the talking of the koels and the crows circling above

I see the black neck stretching
the opening beak the awkward sliding feet

always unbalancing trying to regain to stand up straight

while the great heavy weight of the body
slips on and over the roof

The last of the rain falls hard and separate and of its own

But the beak of the bird is still there high on the roof.

Yes the beak is still there pinned to the iron ridge.

I see it open I see the long dark shaft of the beak open

From deep below the earth it pulls out its cry.

LEE CATALDI

It's Easy

to take a woman in your arms
when she's falling apart
if you need her
it's easy
to pull her together

but you need the experience
to see
how easy

it's the falling apart
not the remedy
that causes the panic

women
are not the creatures of comedy
they were supposed to be

they fear
the laughter   they doubt
they are taken seriously

and arms
assure them they are

it's something you need to know
because
it's easy

We Could Have Met

in some cool room in college after
hours of arguing about metaphysics and men to slip
into a bewildered recognition hand in hand
while outside in the hot night ambulances wailed
striking us with panic

or one afternoon
sun burnishing dust above the wooden floor
voices from tennis courts echoing in an open window
to stumble upon an irresistible but unwelcome truth
about the nature of our skin

or perhaps in a café eating pound cake and tea
in a booth full of boots, coats, scarves and misting breath
I would have come from Duke Humphrey's library
from old texts and familiar complaints
another Australian would have introduced us
we might have both been pregnant
going to exercise classes together
delightedly watching ourselves grow bigger

or at a meeting
deploring the failure of university women
to recognise their unequal chances
in the rat race you would have noticed my accent
not put off by my ostentations, my hat full of drugs
my house full of tattooed men

or having dragged bags and children through the endless corridors
of airports to catch the last delayed flights
to anywhere in Africa
come to rest against a counter in an obscure corner
singled out by bureaucratic failure

children screaming with fatigue
unable to get to Lagos or Oran
we might have cashed this string of coincidences
in for two hours of blissful tranquillity

but finally to wind up here
in this outpost of empire dust crows the ancient
inheritance of original cultures
at the crossroads of language
stripped of the paraphernalia of class and style
what is plain to see is

plain to see

13 November 1983

these Americans   I see
floating in a tide of money

in the photo in the art magazine sent by Katherine library I
recognise myself

a well-groomed middle-aged dyke called a
'personality' who indifferent to content paints

women   birthday cakes   goats

I too could have exercised minor tyrannies of style
always buoyed up and blinded by the fronds
of inconsequence trailing like weeds and admirers

from the rocks of possession

whereas here   I subject myself
to cultural dismemberment
trying to understand a people
who possess nothing

and ask everything

Advice

he plays
with no cards   you have
the pack

      the toyota   the axe
      history as they say
      is in your hand

but don't put yourself in his power
he can't forget how your father
with a white face and a gun
shot his father just for fun

BOBBI SYKES

Cycle

The revolution is conceived
as a babe in the womb;
It is, as a foetus,
An idea – a twinkle only
in men's eyes and a silent knowing
in women;
Yet it lives.

The revolution is alive
while it lives
within us;
Beating, making our hearts warm,
Our minds strong, for we know
that justice is inevitable –
like birth.

Unaware of what they see,
They watch us;
We grow stronger and threaten
to burst our skin;
They do not realise
that the revolution
is near birth

That it threatens to spill
from this succoured womb
To the long-ready world
Which has not prepared
Even in this long time of waiting.

We do not always talk
of our pregnancy
for we are pregnant
with the thrust of freedom;
And our freedom looks to others
As a threat.

Yet we must be free, we know it,
And they know it,
For our freedom is not a gift
To be bestowed,
But torn from those
Who seek to keep us down.

We must stand up, raise our arms
To the sun, breathe deep the free air,
And our children
Cavort as new-born, trouble-free.

The revolution lives. It lives
within us. Birth is imminent.
It cannot be bought off,
pushed back, held off.
The revolution will spring forward
As surely
As the child will leave the womb
 – When it is ready;
We must make haste preparing
while biding our time.

One Day

Moving along Main St. /
  Whitesville /
Digging all them white faces /
  (Staring, or 'not staring')
Until I felt surrounded /
  Lost / bobbing on a sea I didn't know /

I began to concentrate so hard /
   (Head down)
On the lines and cracks
   Of the footpath . . .

And I felt you / unknown Brother /
   Across the street /
Over the heads /cars /
   Throwing me your glance /
Your salute / clenched fist /
   Smile . . .

Fellow Black /
   You were majestic /
Your sparks lit up the street /
   Whitesville /
And I was no longer moving along /
   But / Brother /
            Moving up!

JOHN TRANTER

The Moment of Waking

She remarks how the style of a whole age
disappears into your gaze, at the moment
of waking. How sad you are
with your red shirt, your features
reminiscent of marble, your fabulous
boy-girl face like a sheet of mist
floating above a lake.

Someone hands me a ticket
In Berlin a hunchback
is printing something hideous;
my passport is bruised with dark blue
and lilac inks. Morning again,
another room batters me awake
you will be haunting the mirror like silver.

Now the nights punish me with dreams
of a harbour in Italy – you are there
hung in the sky on broken wings
as you always have been, dancing,
preparing to wound me with your
distant and terrible eyes.

from: *The Alphabet Murders*

23

We could point to the poem and say 'that map',
the heart's geography, and words enact
the muscley parable of exploration: on your right
Maugham's club foot which tromps the clay of life into
a lovely chorus line of English prose; on your left
the dead Romantics, gone into that same earth
that took their tears and all their unforgivable
syntactical mistakes. The land is cruel
with existentialists, though lyric poets
wander through like crippled birds . . . but this map
is false and crazy – here the Doppler shifts
convert to analogue then back to pulse-code modulation
information full of news and noise, so the heart's
continent abandons form and drifts out into the night sky
full of parachutes, and we feel the mind's mountains
bonking against our head like knobs,
for the little 'heart' grows 'dark' at night
and lacking infra-red photometry and radar
we rave down along the flare path looking like
an anxious moth, don't we? In the flight plan?
But there you go again, plotted out of your simple wit
and this is the second-level problem: observers
without the keys to fit their own responses
so that a poem is merely rhyme and meaning, or a gift
of gaudy trash, and nothing else. So we slog on
to navigate the fading resonance of our capacities
and find the luminescent map of armies
burning on the plain.

Enzensberger at 'Exiles'

At the back of the bookshop a Karate expert
keeps a pot of coffee brewing, in the window
a man exhibits his bandages and the lights
flash red, amber, blue; all night long
the sex magazine quiz gets filled in.
What am I doing here? That cloud layer
threatens nothing, and speaks casually
of a distant beach; everybody's laughing . . .
they trained beautiful men and women
to meet me at the airport, they
follow me around and buy me lunch,
they point out the misfits and the deviants
and keep me amused at parties where young men
fight and make up like emotional Brownshirts.
In Martin's Bar the topless waitresses
are all sober, their perfectly matched tits
jump at the drunks while upstairs
a poet listens to the race results,
next door at The Balkan a cloud of burnt fat
gushes up the ventilator; these
are the good times, Australian style,
this has become a new vernacular
and waits for my Adler to turn it into German.
Europe is a ruined Paradise buried under
books; here, nothing important was promised.
I'm drinking coffee and writing
in English on a piece of crumpled paper;
soon I'll learn the native dialect and ask
Where are the ovens? Is it true that you never
learned to kill each other? Are you happy?

The Un-American Women

One, they're spooking, two, they're opening letters,
three, there's a body at the bottom of the pool
labelled 'Comrade X', and you've been asked to
speak up truthfully or not at all. It's like Einstein
lolling on the lawn – somebody *gave* him the telescope,
he wouldn't 'buy' one – and our investigator has him
trapped in the viewfinder. Albert! Tell us everything!
We won't blame you for the Atom Bomb! After all,
you're dead! Four, cancel the code and burn the cipher.
It's no laughing matter when the shit hits the fan –
why are you grinning like that? Are you now
or have you ever been a woman? That's a tricky one,
I know you'd like a stiff rum and coke and ten minutes
alone on the patio to think it over, but
the G-men in the back room are getting anxious;
the Mickey Finn's invented, the hand that
feeds you's quicker than the eye, and in a wink
the powder's in the drink! Our Leader's dozing
in a tank and in his memory we labour mightily.
Are you a German Jew? We sympathise; do you?
The Memory Bank is sad tonight, it's asking
for your friends, they have a future there.
Let's share a Pentothal and take a ride;
the garden's full of Government Employees
but I'll hold your hand. You make a movie,
I'll write the dialogue: One, we're laughing,
two, we're breaking rules – I'm finished, you're
dead, and as the cipher smoulders on the lawn
a cold glow rises from the bottom of the tank:
our Leader starts to speak, and so will you.

The Great Artist Reconsiders the Homeric Simile

He looks back over the last metaphor
and his eyes shift their focus, his gaze weakly
taking in the litter on the desk and then
the blurred garden, its order and composition:
bare trees, a path strewn with leaves,
a distant figure dawdling at the gate –
light dazzles the window-pane with brilliant
diamonds of dew – he sighs, and drops his pen.
As when a detective in the spring has found
a junk-struck hippy crouching in her pad
at the dead end of Desolation Alley, and
has faked the evidence and booked her, soon
her man returning giftless from his rounds
sees the flat empty and his girl-friend gone;
at that he freaks out, and checks his stride
and with short uneasy steps circles the block,
with smothered groans repeating her name; but she
lies on the cell floor, overdosed,
a heap of bright rags – never again
will those disco mirrors catch her image
floating by, nor the bathroom echo her
withdrawal screams – as that poor addict
hides in horror till the heat cools off,
nor knows his loss, so Matthew Arnold brooded
on his failing similes. His cup of tea
grew cold as he stared out at the Autumn
leaves; a change of air was what he needed,
a holiday at Dover, or Torquay . . .
and as he mused, the lounger at the gate –
the Future – turned his back, and walked away.

* See Matthew Arnold's 'Sohrab and Rustum', lines 556–75

Backyard

The God of Smoke listens idly in the heat
   to the barbecue sausages
speaking the language of rain deceitfully
   as their fat dances.

Azure, hazed, the huge drifting sky shelters
   its threatening weather.
A screen door slams, and the kids come tumbling
   out of their arguments,

and the barrage of shouting begins, concerning
   young Sandra and Scott
and the broken badminton racquet and net
   and the burning meat.

Is that a fifties home movie, or the real
   thing? Heavens, how
a child and a beach ball in natural colour
   can break your heart.

And the brown dog worries the khaki grass
   to stop it from growing
in place of his worship, the burying bone.
   The bone that stinks.

Turn now to the God of this tattered arena
   watching over the rites
of passage – marriage, separation; adolescence
   and troubled maturity:

having served under that bright sky you may look up
   but don't ask too much:
some cold beer, a few old friends in the afternoon,
   a Southerly Buster at dusk.

Debbie & Co.

The Council Pool's chockablock
with Greek kids shouting in Italian.
Isn't it Sunday afternoon?
Half the school's there, screaming,
skylarking, and bombing the deep end.
Nicky picks up her Nikon
and takes it all in, the racket
and the glare. Debbie strikes a pose.

In a patch of shade a grubby brat
dabbles ice-cream into the cement.
Tracey and Chris are missing,
mucking about behind the dressing sheds,
Nicky guesses. Who cares?
Debbie takes a dive. Emerging like a
porpoise at the edge of the pool
she finds a ledge, a covered gutter,
awash with bubbles and chlorine's
chemical gossip. Debbie yells there,
and the rude words echo.
The piss-tinted water slaps the tiles.

Debbie dries off, lights a smoke,
and gazes at her friends fading out
around the corner of a dull relationship
and disappearing.
                        Under the democratic sun
her future drifts in and out of focus –
Tracey, Nicky, Chris, the whole arena
sinking into silence. Yet this is almost
Paradise: the Coke, the takeaway pizza,
a packet of Camels, Nicky's dark glasses
reflecting the way the light glitters on
anything wet. Debbie's tan needs
touching up. She lies back and dozes
on a terry-towelling print of Donald Duck.

She remembers how Brett was such a
dreamboat, until he turned into
somebody's boring husband. Tracey
reappears, looking radiant. Nicky
browses through an Adult Magazine.
Debbie goes to sleep.

Glow-boys

Four a.m. At the reactor an alarm begins
howling. The core's full of shit: get out
the gloves, the phosphorescent rakes.

A burnt-out star hangs low on the horizon.
The Harrisburg glow-boys knuckle down
to work, poking around in the ashes.

They gaze out through glitter: behind the visor
putty imitates a human face, the lips
gritty, frayed, as they reach for speech

across the static field. Now a bell rings
and they wade thigh-deep into the muck,
their eyes the colour of lightning.

Five years of that and they're
too hot to touch; they wake screaming
before dawn, the pillow soaked.

What have they seen: their children's future
flare and crackle, a vast Christmas tree
flashing up from the skyline?

Rake it up, Ratshit! In a month
vacation in the Rockies, drinking rye and
blowing rattlesnakes away with a shotgun.

Now, like any cleaners, they go to work
deft and grumbling, their wives awake
in nylon nighties staring at the ceiling

and the glow of the luminous clock.
The pot of coffee popping on the stove.
The kids asleep, dreaming fitfully.

Having Completed My Fortieth Year

Although art is, in the end, anonymous,
turning into history once it's left the body,
surely some gadget in the poet's head
    forces us to suffer

as we stumble through the psychology of it:
the accent betraying a class conflict
seen upside-down through a prism, the bad luck
    to be born in a lucky country –

yet in the end it is our fault, i.e. my fault
not to be born Frank O'Hara and cursing
a whole culture for it – it's no excuse
    not to be run over at thirty,

to live on, turning out couplets
with the fecundity of a sausage machine
but without the cachet of the Imperial drawl,
    not even a cute lisp;

above all to miss out on drugs and Sodom
in the mindless mid-afternoon heat among
the nylon swimsuits and the beery surfers,
    a trial, not a vacation –

the girl around the corner gagging on whisky
in the school-yard after dark, the boss
clocking off and weaving out the back door:
    'I'll be at the pub . . .'

well, at forty, the pieces lie about
waiting to be picked up and puzzled over
and fitted into a pattern, after a fashion,
  one I'm not fond of –

there are two sorts of people: those who say
with an owlish look 'There are two sorts of people',
and those who don't; then there are the writers
  who live on another planet,

their droppings bronzed like babies' booties
and we're glad to see things so transmogrified
though we suspect that life's not always rhymed
  quite as neatly as that,

and then there are those for whom every voyage
is an opportunity to lash the rowers,
the sun rising over something absolutely
  dreadful every day:

a people totally given to the cannibal virtues,
a set of laws designed to confuse and punish,
an art that shrinks experience into a box then
  hermetically seals the lid;

but squabbling over Modernism won't help,
England needs liberating but not by me,
she has concocted her own medications after all
  for marsh fever and the sinks,

so I'm stocking the fridge with Sydney Bitter,
checking the phone numbers of a few close friends
while the conservatives see to it that I conserve
  my sad and pallid art

and I'm hoping that the disk drive holds out
at least till the fag-end of the party
so my drunken guests may go on bopping till they
  drop into their mottoes

as I did some twenty years ago,
embarking on this yacht, this drudger's barge,
being 'absolutely modern' as my mentor taught
  from the embers of his youth,

and hardly guessing then what would turn up:
these postcard views from a twinkling and distant
colony, of the twin cities: dying heart of Empire,
    sunset on the Empire State.

Lufthansa

Flying up a valley in the Alps where the rock
rushes past like a broken diorama
I'm struck by an acute feeling of precision –
the way the wing-tips flex, just a little
as the German crew adjust the tilt of the sky and
bank us all into a minor course correction
while the turbo-props gulp at the mist
with their old-fashioned thirsty thunder – or
you notice how the hostess, perfecting a smile
as she offers you a dozen drinks, enacts what is
almost a craft: Technical Drawing, for example,
a subject where desire and function, in the hands
of a Dürer, can force a thousand fine ink lines
to bite into the doubts of an epoch, spelling
Humanism. Those ice reefs repeat the motto
whispered by the snow-drifts on the north side
of the woods and model villages: the sun
has a favourite leaning, and the Nordic flaw
is a glow alcohol can fan into a flame.
And what is this truth that holds the grey
shaking metal whole while we believe in it?
The radar keeps its sweeping intermittent promises
speaking metaphysics on the phosphor screen;
our faith is sad and practical, and leads back
to our bodies, to the smile behind the drink
trolley and her white knuckles as the plane drops
a hundred feet. The sun slanting through a porthole
blitzes the ice-blocks in my glass of lemonade
and splinters light across the cabin ceiling.

285

No, two drinks – one for me, one for Katharina
sleeping somewhere – suddenly the Captain
lifts us up and over the final wall
explaining roads, a town, a distant lake
as a dictionary of shelter – sleeping elsewhere
under a night sky growing bright with stars.

TIM THORNE

Whatever Happened to Conway Twitty?

My bakelite mantel set pulled him in
Through the whine and crackle of KZ and I
Drummed on a dented pencil tin
To *Danny Boy* or *Mona Lisa*,
Tensing my hands and jaw as his art
Made seven syllables of 'heart'.

Five p.m. was too early to get
Anything like a good reception
And I broke the volume knob off that set
Trying to bring America closer,
Or if not America, then at least
Stan the Man, oracle and priest.

Masturbation and vandalism
Came with darkness, but first the radio
Would spurt its sweet, commercial chrism,
The god would descend through static, lift up, up,
Up to the top of the *Cashbox* chart
All seven syllables of my heart.

High Country

1. Homecoming

Button-grass flats, pale through the drizzle: my eyes
Unhinged, unhingeing; patch-brown pools:
My body's own still liquids.

After the climb, hard through the spine's country,
Where leatherwood and myrtle drip
Holes into the bent flesh,

After the droplets running off the tight skin
Around the vein-riddled gullies
Stretched on a hairpin bend,

This is the homecoming, arriving at this level –
The brain laid open in the wet,
Nerve ends like sags, open.

2. The Hut

The plastic strips flap in the doorway still
Sad alchemical colours to ward off evil.
The poet comes home like a blue-arsed fly
Too late for the real summer, too soon
For the winds that take the corner of the year
On two loud tyres – the screech of March.

I light the fire and wait for my life's details
To dry out – buckled paperbacks,
The sleeve of an early Dylan record
(Young jew-angel's face, cowboy mystery,
Holding his guitar's neck like a flowering tree)
A man could die waiting between these hills.

Outside in gumboots, moving rocks around,
Channelling off the water, watching it take
Used-up petals like brain cells with it, down
To the flats where my brackish eyes are set like traps,
I am immune here, acting without itch,
Connections all leached, open, waiting.

One day, too late for insects, bleak with peace,
After a month of my turning stones by the moon,
The hills will hear the brash harmonica
And send a patly scored reply in gusts.
And in that instant as the axis tilts
Someone will cross the sags, his clothes blown dry.

ROBERT ADAMSON

Action Would Kill It / A Gamble

When I couldn't he always discussed things.
His talk drew us together;
the government's new war, the best french brandies
and breaking the laws. And it seemed
a strange thing for us to be doing;
the surf right up the beach, wetting our
feet each wave.

On that isolated part of the Coast, counting over
the youngest politicians.
Huge shoulders of granite grew higher
as we walked on, cutting us from perspectives.
He swung his arms and kicked
lumps of quartz hard with bare feet, until I asked
him to stop it . . .

He didn't care about himself at all, and the sea
just licked his blood away.
The seemingly endless beach held us firm;
we walked and walked all day
until it was dark. The wind dropped off and the surf
flattened out, as silence grew round
us in the darkness.

We moved on, close together almost touching;
he wouldn't have noticed, our
walk covered time rather than distance.
When the beach ended,
we would have to split up. And as he spoke
clearly and without emotion
about the need for action, about killing people,
I wanted him.

Passing Through Experiences

I lived on drugs and understood the pushers
As the crackup came on
There was nobody to blame and I confessed for hours
Until the police were in tears

The prison had a few prophets but they
Understood themselves
During the night the lucky ones burnt their tobacco
Each morning I feigned silence

The experience of prison remained behind bars
I dwelt on the idea of freedom
And folding *The Prince* away when afternoon appeared
Went after pain

The ideas crowded around like pushers
And fed on my doings
I discovered thought as powerful as cocaine in winter
As a screw off duty I tapped my foot

All experience pointed to Saint Theresa
The Prince reassured me
I escaped from the books but names kept coming up
Pain alone said nothing great

I ask her *why you know it all though say nothing*
Believe me pain replies *You don't falter*
You move

Sibyl

Then with my white sails and bad luck
with the wind I am beautiful
each dawn there is more resentment towards me the
    fishermen
cannot look as sun
catches my hair turning the spokes
on their decks

So again I depart from the side of the planet
the boy who sleeps with me
Why speak

from: *Sonnets to be Written from Prison*

1

O to be 'in the news' again – now as fashion runs
everything would go for 'prison sonnets': I'd be on my own.
I could, once more, go out with pale skin
from my veritable dank cell – the sufferer, poking fun
at myself in form, with a slightly twisted tone.
My stance ironic – one-out, on the run.
Though how can I? I'm not locked up: imagine a type-
    writer
in solitary. I dream my police unable to surrender –
I'm bored with switching roles and playing
with my gender; the ironies seem incidental, growing thin.
Here's the world – maybe what's left of it –
held together by an almost experimental sonnet.
Surely there must be some way out of poetry other than
Mallarmé's: still-life with bars and shitcan.

2

Once more, almost a joke – this most serious endeavour
is too intense: imagine a solitary typewriter? Somehow
fashion runs its course; and I'm not in pain.
So there's hardly any need to play on abstract repetitions
to satisfy a predecessor, poet or lawbreaker: I won't be
    clever –
all the clever crims are not inside the prisons.
Here's the world – maybe what's left of my pretences –
I dream of being carried off to court again:
a sufferer, where all my deities would speak in stern
almost sardonic voices. 'Your Honour, please –
bring me to my senses.' There, I love confessions!
Imagine writing prison sonnets four years after my
    release.
If only all my memories could be made taciturn
by inventing phrases like: imagine the solitary police.

3

Yes Your Honour, I know this is ridiculous – although –
I'm 'in the news'. I couldn't bring myself to do
one of those *victimless crimes*: I must suffer in more ways
than one. My crime's pretence is not to overthrow
social order, or to protest – it's my plan
to bring poetry and lawbreaking where they interplay:
imagine newspapers in solitary. I'd walk right through
the court taking down copy 'catch me if you can' –
Defendant in contempt. There has to be a fight,
I can't imagine anything when I'm not up against a law.
Now here's the world – our country's first stone institution,
where inmates still abase themselves at night.
If I was in solitary I could dream – a fashionable bore,
writing books on drugs, birds or revolution.

6

We will take it seriously as we open our morning paper.
Someone's broken loose, another child's been
wounded by a pen-knife. A small fire down the bottom
of a suburban garden smells of flesh. Dark circles under
the mother's eyes appear on television; she's seen
her baby at the morgue. Our country moves closer to the
    world:
a negro's book is on the shelves. The criminal's become
mythologised; though yesterday he curled
over and didn't make the news. So the myth continues,
    growing
fat and dangerous on a thousand impractical intuitions.
The bodies of old sharks hang on the butcher's hooks.
In broad day somewhere a prisoner is escaping.
The geriatrics are suddenly floating in their institutions.
The myth is torn apart and stashed away in books.

My House

My mother lives in a house
where nobody has ever died

she surrounds herself
and her family with light

each time I go home
I feel she is washing
and ironing the clothes of death

these clothes for work
and for going out
to the Club on Sunday
and for Jenny to take her baby
to the doctor in

death comes on the television
and mum laughs

saying there's death again
I must get those jeans taken up

My Tenth Birthday

We went to Pumpkin Point
for my tenth birthday

the best picnic beach on the river

the mud is thinner
and doesn't smell as off

and there is a swing
made from a huge truck tyre

I wore my first jeans
and got a cane rod and a bird book

Dad washed the rabbit blood
out of the back of his truck
and we spread blankets
and pillows over the splinters

A storm came up after lunch
and I cut my foot open
on a sardine can as I ran into a cave

it was the same cave
I found again four years later
on a night my father set out the nets

and slept beside me
for the only time in his life

The Private

Take this man with an axe

alone

in a rented house

setting out his cups

Rimbaud Having a Bath

To have been held down in a park
the animal breath on your face
hands tightening on the throat
grappling at you in the dark
a life lashing out to embrace
the flesh and green bones under it
and then the infected slime
injected by the half-erect cock
Remains a flesh wound until
morning and poetry begins its work
in the carnage under the skull
The great poet goes home again
to his mother and becomes
the boy he is and then feels the pain
subside his senses numb
by the fire boiling the water
and the yellow soap in the copper
he takes a rag and pumice-stone
and then slides his naked body in
Because he has taken this bath
he has betrayed his art
having washed the vermin from both
the body and the heart

The Home, The Spare Room

I am the poet of the spare room
the man who lives here

with television's
incessant coloured noise

between the ads keeping the children
at bay

At night I walk the seagrass
down the hall

my head rolls before me
like some kind of a round dice

which room tonight?

I think of my wife-to-be
who has thrown herself down

into a foetal shape onto her bed

I am a hard man, a vicious seer
who simply wants

to go on living – love is beyond me

if its exists – my heart,
so called, is as efficient as a bull's

and as desperate
for the earth's treasures –

I turn into the spare room
and begin to write a poem of infinite

tenderness

Gutting the Salmon

The blade touches the fish heart, over
the kitchen floor, over the newspaper
it's body meat; the cat circles
the outside edges of blood-drenched type,
the boys look on, taking it in –
This isn't like weekend fishing, cleaning
other fish: down into nets of veins,
severed arteries; the ritual goes on
out of control – fillets of red meat, fillets
of white, flesh almost black
dark blue with blood; the cat now howling
its Burmese meat-mantra, the boys
turning to tv football. No feelings
of remorse though how to stop, how to clean-up;
back into the content of the gut, husks
of prawn, fragments of worm; the liver spilling
through fingers.

Dreaming Up Mother

Understanding is all, my mother would tell me,
and then walk away from the water;

Understanding is nothing I think, as I mumble
embellished phrases of what's left of her story.

Though I keep battering myself against sky,
throwing my body into the open day.

Landscapes are to look at, they taught me,
but now the last of the relatives are dead.

Where do these walks by the shore take us
she would say, wanting to clean up,

after the picnic, after the nonsense.
I have been a bother all the years from my birth.

Look out – the river pulls through the day
and Understanding like a flaming cloud, goes by.

An Elm Tree in Paddington

Branches of grape-vine thick as ankles
grow through the terrace iron,
the fruit is a bitter wood; I think

of Brennan standing on similar joinery,
in the same suburb, soured by love
and Symbolism. A black beetle waves

a feeler, its lasso, involves itself
with the security mesh before the panes
of rain-printed glass. I drink

American whiskey from a champagne flute
and think of Lawson at The Rose & Crown,
he knew the price of a beer

cost more than the blackest sonnet.
The drinkers choose not to hear
parody in a voice, see the rag of a suit,

know the terrible hour it took
to shave up and comb for this sad front.
Out in the yard an old elm shoots

out from the acid dirt at an angle,
its boughs spokes of sylvan thought, here
where form eats content to a gloss.

CAROLINE CADDY

Three-Inch Reflector

They've taken it apart
      dusted the mirror's little desert
            with camel's hair
and centred the diagonal
          disembodied eye.
Together again
      it looks like the real thing
          which it is –
working model of the mahout guided
        Licks and Kitt Peaks.
It's the shape of sophistication
and the let me see of a young child
        watching someone peer through
a piece of rolled-up cardboard.
White and black   who moves who
        calipers their legs
as they walk it around the yard
        in search of
enough dark for gathering
       tiny fit-start suns –
       instant time-lapse
and me volunteering
      or conscripting information.
I have to lie down to get rid of
this pain in my neck
      and repeat   who said it first?
that sometimes the only way
        not to re-invent the wheel
        is to re-invent the wheel
         or the moon.

Bat squeak adjustments and they've got it
            rich yellow load
and what strikes us
                 with the impact of inspiration is
that it's just like its pictures –
                  perfect *Geographic* N.A.S.A.s –
reproduction to old master and back.
           Not order but the catch that matters
                     in the throat
                     of the breath
like the time I heard
         – heresy to admit hearsay as knowledge –
     a concise account of North American history
                from a Spiderman comic
and nit points shimmied
as the old radar moved under its housing
               appreciating in every direction
out here in the wide open dark
               listen to the discovery of
the boundlessly reflected
            Rand-McNally Moon.

PETER SKRZYNECKI

Hunting Rabbits

The men would often go hunting rabbits
in the countryside around the hostel –
with guns and traps and children following
in the sunlight of afternoon paddocks:
marvelling in their native tongues
at the scent of eucalypts all around.

We never asked where the guns came from
or what was done with them later:
as each rifle's echo cracked through the hills
and a rabbit would leap as if jerked
on a wire through the air –
or, watching hands release a trap
then listening to a neck being broken.

Later, I could never bring myself
to watch the animals being skinned
and cleaned –
             excitedly
talking about the ones that escaped
and how white tails bobbed among brown tussocks.
For days afterwards
our rooms smelt of blood and fur
as the meat was cooked in pots
over a kerosene primus.

But eat I did, and asked for more,
as I learnt about the meaning of rations
and the length of queues in dining halls –
as well as the names of trees
from the surrounding hills that always seemed
to be flowering with wattles:

growing less and less frightened by gunshots
and what the smell of gunpowder meant –
quickly learning to walk and keep up with men
that strode through strange hills
as if their migration had still not come to an end.

ROBERT GRAY

Journey: the North Coast

Next thing, I wake up in a swaying bunk,
as though aboard a clipper on the sea,
and it's the train, that booms and cracks,
it tears the wind apart.
Now the man's gone
who had the bunk below me. I swing out,
cover his bed and rattle up the sash –
there's sunlight to come teeming
on the drab carpet. And the water sways
solidly in its silver basin, so cold
it joins together through my hand.
I see from where I'm bent
one of those bright crockery days
that belong to so much I remember.
The train's shadow, like a bird's,
flees on the blue and silver paddocks,
over fence posts carved from stone,
and banks of fern,
a red bank, full of roots,
over dark creeks, with logs and leaves suspended,
and blackened tree trunks.
Down these slopes move, as a nude descends a staircase,
the slender white gum trees,
and then the countryside bursts open on the sea –
across its calico beach, unfurling;
strewn with flakes of light
that make the whole compartment whirl.
Shuttering shadows. I rise into the mirror
rested. I'll leave my hair
ruffled a bit that way – and fold the pyjamas,
stow the book and wash bag. Everything done,

press down the latches into the case
that for twelve months I've watched standing out,
of a morning, above the wardrobe
in a furnished room.

Flames and Dangling Wire

On a highway over the marshland.
Off to one side, the smoke of different fires in a row,
like fingers spread and dragged to smudge:
it is an always-burning dump.

Behind us, the city
driven like stakes into the earth.
A waterbird lifts above this swamp
as a turtle moves on the Galapagos shore.

We turn off down a gravel road,
approaching the dump. All the air wobbles
in some cheap mirror.
There is a fog over the hot sun.

Now the distant buildings are stencilled in the smoke.
And we come to a landscape of tin cans,
of cars like skulls,
that is rolling in its sand dune shapes.

Amongst these vast grey plastic sheets of heat,
shadowy figures
who seem engaged in identifying the dead –
they are the attendants, in overalls and goggles,

forking over rubbish on the dampened fires.
A sour smoke
is hauled out everywhere,
thin, like rope. And there are others moving – scavengers.

As in hell the devils
might pick about amongst our souls, for vestiges
of appetite
with which to stimulate themselves,

so these figures
seem to wander disconsolately, with an eternity
in which to turn up
some peculiar sensation.

We get out and move about also.
The smell is huge,
blasting the mouth dry:
the tons of rotten newspaper, and great cuds of cloth . . .

And standing where I see the mirage of the city
I realise I am in the future.
This is how it shall be after men have gone.
It will be made of things that worked.

A workman hoists an unidentifiable mulch
on his fork, throws it in the flame:
something flaps
like a rag held up in 'The Raft of the Medusa'.

We approach him through the smoke,
and for a moment he seems that spectre with the long barge
    pole.
 – It is a man, wiping his eyes.
Someone who worked here would have to weep,

and so we speak. The rims beneath his eyes are wet
as an oyster, and red.
Knowing all that he does about us,
how can he avoid a hatred of men?

Going on, I notice an old radio, that spills
its dangling wire –
and I realise that somewhere the voices it broadcast
are still travelling,

skidding away, riddled, around the arc of the universe;
and with them, the horse-laughs, and the Chopin
which was the sound of the curtains lifting,
one time, to a coast of light.

The Dusk

A kangaroo is standing up, and dwindling like a plant
with a single bud.
Fur combed into a line
in the middle of its chest,
a bow-wave
under slanted light, out on the harbour.

And its fine unlined face is held out in the cool air;
a face in which you feel
the small thrust-forward teeth lying in the lower jaw,
grass-stained and sharp.

Standing beyond a wire fence, in weeds,
against the bush that is like a wandering smoke.

Mushroom-coloured,
and its white chest, the underside of a growing mushroom,
in the last daylight.

The tail is trailing heavily as a lizard lying concealed.

It turns its head like a mannequin
toward the fibro shack,
and holds the forepaws
as though offering to have them bound.

An old man stands on a dirt path in his vegetable garden,
where a cabbage moth puppet-leaps and jiggles wildly
in the cooling sunbeams,
the bucket still swinging in his hand.

And the kangaroo settles down, pronged,
then lifts itself
carefully, like a package passed over with both hands –

The now curved-up tail is rocking gently counterweight behind
as it flits hunched
amongst the stumps and scrub, into the dusk.

JOANNE BURNS

revisionism

king lear in a mr. whippy van
ulysses in a greyhound bus
heathcliff in a honda
miss havisham waiting for the lights to change

henry lawson in a holden commodore
silas marner in a mercedes
gertrude stein as a taxi driver
jane austen in a panel van

tennyson in a toyota
emily dickinson in a cadillac
voss in a campervan
hamlet in a valiant

huck finn in a volvo
lady macbeth as a removalist
the man from snowy river in a rolls
sartre as a petrol tanker driver

dickens in a mini moke
lawrence in a jaguar
hardy as a hearse driver
whitman in a four wheel drive

sylvia plath as an ambulance driver
eliot as a chauffeur
evelyn waugh as a rickshaw driver
proust with a flat tyre

marble surfaces

ever since i was knee high to a grasshopper they said i had cute cheeks. theyd lean down into the stroller and pinch them. hes almost good enough to eat. ive always maintained a good cut. i sell a prime product. no horse. these bones are a bit stiff today. they say i was quite creative as a kid. had a neat stroke with the paint brush. painted lots of farm scenes. had some little wooden animals. used to play with them in the dirt for hours. anyway to cut a long story short dad said id have to have a trade. uncle sid had a butchers shop so there i was. the butcher boy. he gave me a rough trot at first. sweeping the sawdust, wrapping parcels delivering parcels stuffing sausages. he wasnt so bad. bark was worse than his bite i guess. finally i got to cut the meat. i'll never forget how proud i was when my shining new knife cut clean through the lamb. mum had had it engraved. as if id been doing it all my life. 6 beautiful lamp chops. what a thrill. everyone liked me. i never looked back after that. they called me smiley. i saved my money. worked long hours. have never regretted it. guess its in my blood. pound of pigs trotters and an ox tongue for mrs. stern shes been a good customer stuck by me through thick and thin. they say i havent changed much though ive filled out a bit. in my prime now. she still comments on my smile. service with a smile tommy she says. shes a funny one. treats herself to something special once in a while. asked for pigs head a few times. dont know what she does with them. says it reminds her of a toy she had as a child. or some story. often she stays for a chat. runs her hands across the counter. what a beautiful marble surface. ive got some good customers. loyal. stayed with me when berts opened down the road. even though he offered cheaper prices. real cut throat bastard he was. tried to push me out of business. and the time of the 4 car pile up. easter a few years ago. one of them smashed up my window. the display was ruined. meat all over the footpath. you can imagine. dogs came from everywhere. then the ambulance and police. just chaos. but my regulars still came to pick up their holiday orders. round the back entrance. im not surprised i won the service award. ive always been aware of the benefits of pleasant surroundings. i like the customers to like shopping here. we use real fern in the meat display. none of that cheap plastic stuff. im very particular about the meat display. people say i would have made an excellent window dresser. i always try to create soft effects in the centre. i put the veal the yearling the pork there. pink has such a soothing effect doesnt it. then i put the redder meats around these. rumps and roasts look good in the window. i never put out the brains and livers. they seem to spoil the colour scheme. occasionally i put out a bit of tripe. looks fine next to the fern. doesnt take that long to make things look nice. some of the fellows here kicked up a bit of a stink when i decided we'd all put on black bow ties. when i was a little fellow i wore one out to family gatherings and i didn't like it but i know it looked good. pale blue. people would always say what a cute little fellow. pink and blue are so nice together. im thinking of opening up another shop. might specialise in gourmet type meats. wont have much trouble getting a loan from the bank. theyre really pleased with the gross profits for the year. the mural had a good psychological effect on the profit rate i think. painted it myself. real country scene isnt it. got a few ideas during the annual holidays. we were driving through the country and one of the kids was quite taken with the lambs grazing in some paddock. very green it was. when i went back to work i thought we need something to brighten up the shop. didnt take long to do. just one sunday afternoon. dont get out to the country much. except on holidays. too much of a rush on weekends and the roads are always so busy. too many maniac drivers these days. youre lucky to get home in one piece.

reading

there were so many books. she had to separate them to avoid being overwhelmed by the excessive implications of their words. she kept hundreds in a series of boxes inside a wire cage in a warehouse. and hundreds more on the shelves of her various rooms. when she changed houses she would pack some of the books into the boxes and exchange them for others that had been hibernating. these resurrected books were precious to her for a while. they had assumed the patinas of dusty chthonic wisdoms. and thus she would let them sit on the shelves admiring them from a distance. gathering time and air. she did not want to be intimate with their insides. the atmospherics suggested by the titles were enough. sometimes she would increase the psychic proximities between herself and the books and place a pile of them on the floor next to her bed. and quite possibly she absorbed their intentions while she slept.

if she intended travelling beyond a few hours she would occasionally remove a book from the shelves and place it in her bag. she carried 'the poetics of space' round india for three months and it returned to her shelves undamaged at the completion of the journey. every day of those three months she touched it and read some of the titles of its chapters to make sure it was there. and real. chapters called house and universe, nests, shells, intimate immensity, miniatures and, the significance of the hut. she had kept it in a pocket of her bag together with a coloured whistle and an acorn. she now kept this book in the darkness of her reference shelf. and she knew that one day she would have to admit to herself that this was the only book she had need of, that this was the book she would enter the pages of, that this was the book she was going to read

how

how these pieces of paper: lined unlined small large crinkled smooth smudged spotless, become pieces of first draft scribble, of typescript, of 'writing', become texts for performance, works in progress, submissions to magazines and journals, become copyright, enter folders in filing cabinets, become manuscripts, literature, the numbered pages of published books isbn-d.

how these books are launched admired read reviewed squeezed alongside within between a crowd of others on the shelves in private and public places. how these books will be remaindered, garage saled, dumped in glad bags along with old newspapers, junk mail and ageing christmas cards, turn up as brief mentions in fifty years time in someone else's biography, or within the meticulous index in the work of a fastidious literary historian securing a career.

how these books will return to pulp, through diligent efforts to beat the world's timber crisis, how these books will turn into serviettes paper towels and parking tickets, into pieces of paper, become torn food wrappings lifting in the wind

KRIS HEMENSLEY

Sulking in the Seventies

there is no language for the present time.
we are vested with heartlessness. the
language of times past. neither recognition
at the theatre nor the jackpot for the line
that clicks. whatever are the right words?
my stuttered 'quelle heure est'il?' isnt
heard by the gallery of cool movers combing
each other's auburn hanks thru their fingers
flicking that illicit ash all over the foyer's
high pile. observe me merge with fantasy's
skyline. they scan thru smoke & burn me there.

they are the linguists. a row of bronze heads
by the famous sculptor. there's
nothing so humdrum as lousy work by
the famous. they belong in the
open air but no one will have a
bar of that. some sit & twitch
before a Bridget Riley. you can
but sympathise even with hypocrites.

this isnt the language of last
night's soiree. consider that matter
closed. saved by the show's
second half. consider instead
the roses monsieur et madame. they are
the best. they come from my home town.
i don't expect you to know that! 'why me?'
is *my* favourite tune. accused by Maria
Schneider's painful pleasure is hardly
poetry. the game nowadays is
filling out the timeless spaces with

lines of the cleverest talk. *not*
the one about Everest or 'Ross's'
desert song or even 'have you got
the time''s infernal variations. it's
called 'sulking in the seventies.'

from: *A Mile from Poetry*

1

for John Thorpe

a poem by John Thorpe

is something i must show to every
one although
that's a problem before i even start
to whom? for there is no
one (John!
you wouldn't believe me). it seems to be
prose
    not a swish but a craggy-legged
movement
        grounding all that flits
        between the top left-hand corner &
        the rightwards meander. his
        poem ends with the inscription
        on a local's grave or
        something somebody says pre
        occupied with a hard life.

his poem

        receives its independence in the middle of the page
        brave as a little boat in the choppy marina.

2

my poem's in the oven where it
gathers the slurred words of Joe
Garvey's latest anecdote. despite
his older brothers' disapproval he relates
how Lennie or Lonnie one or the other
bugger asked the wee tale's hero how
he regarded that Lenin.   Lenin?
barked the hoary correspondent.   he's nothin
but a Cunt.   it's here the gun-toting guardians
of poetry start shoving not to mention the
story-teller's kin.   we both get it on
the chin.   as if we've got to ration
familiarity & save passion
for the real subjects of poems
the gallivant of Mars or the frequent
crimes of passion involving cars.   we'll
not cavil.   we're easy in the public bar
tippling beer & tasting cheeses toasting
the mile between poetry and us.

47

look! she said you can see
his study light. i went out
side to see. the rose-
bushes held all the rain

of the night. i withstood
the pour calculating the time
he would be enabling me
the time with her. but

even before a stolen kiss
he called her. & more :
he was on his way. i
met him in my room. i

avoided his honest eye &
urged upon him evidence
of my fecundity. he
was a man of scruples. he

said i had given him the
heart to get back to it.
the lady returned in proper
haste proffering a wealth

of breasts & kisses. i
stole away to the water
logged garden & once
more stood barefoot

on the gravel to
attend her old man's
light & kept a chaste
vigil all thru the night.

48

the place was famed for
murder. it will be
armed said My Lady.
i didnt care that

a passing couple heard
me protest though i was dead
scared of being stabbed in
the subway. but why this

America was so small-towny
didnt dawn upon me until
My Lady called it Norway.
entering our first de luxe café

was so much easier then. there was
no end to my cheek or the dollars i
furled in my pocket. i had to protect
My Lady's chair from other

girls. & then i spied an old
friend clowning with a tray.
i lost my head! o! we were closest friends
i yelled when we just eighteen!

BILLY MARSHALL-STONEKING

Passage

The oldest man in the world wears shoes.
The oldest man in the world has a cowboy hat on his head.
The oldest man in the world speaks to me in English.
He rides in motor cars.
His body: fluid, capable – a perfect shock absorber.
One tooth knocked out in front, a red bandanna tied
around his neck, he names Names
as we bounce over the dirt track in the back
of a four-wheel drive.

'That tree is a digging stick
left by the giant woman who was looking
for honey ants;
That rock, a dingo's nose;
There, on the mountain, is the footprint
left by Tjangara on his way to Ulamburra;
Here, the rockhole of Warnampi – very dangerous –
and the cave where the nyi-nyi women escaped
the anger of marapulpa – the spider.
Wati Kutjarra – the two brothers – travelled this way.
There, you can see, one was tired
from too much lovemaking – the mark of his penis
dragging on the ground;
Here, the bodies of the honey ant men
where they crawled from the sand –
no, they are not dead – they keep coming
from the ground, moving toward the water at Warumpi –
it has been like this for many years:
the Dreaming does not end; it is not like the whiteman's way.
What happened once happens again and again.

This is the Law.
This is the power of the Song.
Through the singing we keep everything alive;
through the songs   the spirits keep us alive.'

The oldest man in the world speaks
to the newest man in the world; my place
less exact than his.
We bump along together in the back of the truck
wearing shoes, belts, underwear.
We speak to each other in English
over the rumble of engine, over the roar of the wheels.
His body: a perfect shock absorber.

Picture Postcard

the picture on the front
cannot tell you what it is like:

T. gets drunk on Saturday afternoon
and runs down H. (who is three) and
the whole settlement comes
for payback,
with nulla-nulla and spear.

the naked woman swinging her crowbar
outside the shop this morning
sings as she swings it round her head:
'where is my husband? where's that bastard?'

in the picture, you can see,
the places I have circled:
the missionary's house
when M. ran amok because
the devils were attacking en masse,
and the cops came down and
took him to heaven.

and the road, leading into town,
marked with an X,
where S. finished up
with a bullet through his brain.

the landing strip
where the prime minister's wife exclaimed:
'the flags, the flags,
where are all the children with the flags?'

running out of space

wish you were here.

On the Death of Muriel Rukeyser

Old Sister Death bit you off
maybe dreaming of my backdoor;
I'd sent you a letter explaining it all:
(living in ancient Aboriginal land
at the foot of big dinosaur hill); I said,
drop in and see me . . . and you said
maybe I will.

But as Annie says,
all's got teeth:
cups and card tables,
drawers and feet.
In New York, death might be
fifty storeys high;
a railing that gives way
too easily; the last beat
of a dry martini.

I don't know how it came to you –
not that poetic, certainly.
More likely dead in a dirty brasserie
or impatiently with a pen

after the heat leaked out.
The news I received was impersonal,
the cost of *Time* magazine:

Sixty-six, poet of social protest,
Heart attack;
proselyte of the dissident muse
(not Sappho, Sacco) –
the message more important
than the way it's read.
But

if I could reach you now
past solemnity, past Death,
past fame, we might laugh
at that last grim joke;
pointing to the dinosaur hills
you never visited,
your thick, woman voice gesturing:

'Those mountains waited two billion years
for me to be born, and
before I could see them
I was dead.'

RHYLL McMASTER

Clockface

Night licks the backyard with its reptile tongue.
The baby gives her windy death's-head grin;
no comfort.
Who's awake? Is there anyone?
The illuminated clockface
tells the truth;
it shakes the future out with metal teeth.
A breeze picks out a damp patch
on my lap.
The baby squirms and turns her eyes on me.
They're wet and lustrous like an animal's.
The road lights dip and stutter
through the trees.
No engine noise. The dark's malevolent.
I see the warmth and closeness
of our bed like a brown heaven
down the corridor;
I love sleep.
They watch me watching them,
darkness and death,
and hold hands inside the gate.

Back Steps Lookout

A cross-framed square of kitchen light
outlines the tomato bed.
A silhouette of my head boats the shallows
of one particular
frilled and spiky pumpkin leaf.

The dark behind the brief dark
that I can see
is very deep.
Footpads with no feet stop, then pass;
the leaves get up and walk.
The mangoes stalk with crabs' eyes through their tree.
In a wet temper night skates about the grass
like a maniac in a black
rectangular overcoat.

MARTIN JOHNSTON

The Sea-Cucumber

for Ray Crooke

We'd all had a bit too much that night when you brought out
     your painting,
the new one, you remember, over Scotch in the panelled
     kitchen,
and my father talked about waiting. Well, he was doing that,
     we knew,
or it could have been the dust you'd painted, the way you'd
     floated
a sfumato background almost in front of the canvas
so your half-dozen squatting dark figures couldn't see it
that moved him in that moment softly, in damp stone, outside
     time.
He was as garrulous as ever, of course, but somehow,
in a time of his own, it seemed that he was pressing
every word-drop, like the wine of a harvest not quite adequate,
to trickle in brilliant iridules across the stained table:
what sorts of eucalypt to plant – so that they'd grow quickly –
art dealers, metaphysics, three old men he'd seen
at Lerici, playing pipes and a drum under an orange sky.
Memory finds a nexus, there in your image,
people just waiting, not even conscious of it,
or of ochre and sienna pinning them in an interstice of hours.
None of this, you see, will really go into writing,
it takes time to leech things into one's sac of words.
The bloated sea-cucumber, when touched, spews up its
     entrails
as though that were a defence; my father's old friend
the gentle little poet Wen Yi-tuo, who collected chess sets
and carved ivory seals in his filthy one-room hut,
is gutted one night and flung into the Yangtze.
The dark river runs through your dusty pigments.
Ferns, moss, tiger-coloured sun beat at the window with banners
but the dust ripples between trees, and among the waiting

322

glints of earth and metal are wiped from the fading hand.
These people of yours, Ray, they are that evening
when we first saw them, or the other one when my father
planted nineteen saplings in our backyard, or when you looked
    at them
later and said, They're coming on, and his fingers
drummed a long nervous question on the table, though he
    agreed.
And we were all waiting, though not in your style of art:
more of a pointillism in time, disconnected moments,
a flash of light over an empty glass, a half-finished volume of
    Borges,
the cabbage palm stooping at dusk into the chimneys,
certain paintings, Corelli, or a morning like the fuzz of a peach,
all bright and disparate. But I think, remembering that painting
of yours, that if one could step away, ten yards, or twenty, or
    years,
at an angle perhaps, a frame would harden into cedar
and through a haze of dust we would see all the brilliant dots
merge into a few figures, squatting, waiting.

In Memoriam

for John Forbes

A painting would have been the best way to get things over
but my father's old Winsor & Newtons still sit in their tin
    box
unused for three years except for when I painted
a shoddy flamboyant number on our front door.
They have hardened and cracked like introverted poets.

Coloured inks will soak through the best bond paper
in a soft fuzz of amoebas, a sunset blur
of fruit-coloured clouds, a weak ambiguous vision.
I could never use chalk or charcoal.
The poem must stalk on its own thin mantis legs.

We become, in any case, too attached to colour.
Graphite and lignite, slate and marble
that make cliff-faces, monuments, holes in the ground
have a greater permanence in their crumbling way
but aren't what we like to look at

or not in themselves. Ever since we learned about emblems
and correspondences, we have mirrored ourselves in the sea
and the rock; and the subtle shadowed faces
of our friends and rivals, as the light changes, reflect
the obliquities of our shadows, our syntax, our blood.

O'Hara, Berryman, Seferis, Pound
have a lot in common. Not only are they all dead poets
but they make up a metrically perfect line
running on iambic sleepers to whatever personal
ameliorations I think, for me, they're good for.

And that's the way the game goes. Reading the Saturday papers
and the cultured magazines, I find my nightmares visited
by a terrible vision of contemporaries writing elegies
notebooked and rainslicked at the graveside
or serial as Magritte's windows or Dunne's time

in a recession of identical rooms.
Whether there is particular grief in the deaths of poets
is a question that much engages us,
that we answer always in the affirmative,
a priori, because it's very useful to us to do so.

Pale watercolour lovers in the pastel sun
we can rape and chomp our friends' corpses at midnight,
hunch and sidle in the morgue, our eyes
a tracery of red veins in the Gothick crypt, and the tourist
maps show Transylvania's regular trains, its ordered roads.

Because it does come down to rape, this invasion
of one's substance by that of another
without connivance. And not the strongest or fiercest
can fight it, but must lie back and open
up to the slime and spawn.

Death and rebirth myths are made by poets, and no wonder:
one Dransfield can feed dozens of us for a month,
a Webb for years. And they're fair game, we can plead
    continuance,
no poet ever died a poet: as the salt muck filled Shelley
the empyrean gave way to the nibbling fish and the cold.

I should have hauled out the oils and tried to do a townscape
after all, a grey square with stoas and colonnades
toothed with eroding busts, their long shadows staining
each other and the foreshortened watchers'
death-watch beetle-scuttle across clattering bleached stone.

For the fan of letters opens and shuts and the wind blows
errant zig-zags of light and night through the phrases,
chops, remoulds, effaces. Theologians
have always found dismembered cannibals tough.
The whole thing becomes too tight, which is not at all

what's needed, whatever sensualists may say.
Too like Zen archery, too painful somewhere around
what used to be called the heart. The parataxis
of time and light could have flowed around and through
these dead and living poets and myself.

That would have been a pretty nonsense. Instead the flicker-
flicker of a zoetrope. In this peepshow world
all styles come down to punctuation. O Mayakovsky,
Buckmaster, all of you, they're circumventing Euclid.
They knew that parallel lines in curved space meet

eventually, somewhere: in the black hole between spaces,
the full stop with no sentence on either side,
between the moving magic-lantern slides.
Not that you wouldn't have gone there yourselves willingly:
where the blood pours out the dead come to the feast.

from: *In Transit: A Sonnet Square*

6 The Café of Situations
for Grace Edwards

In this café they have solved the problem of names.
Orders go to the bar: 'Coffee for Calendar,
two cognacs for Backgammon Board and Football Poster.'
You are where you are. They know names must be revealed
most cautiously and that numbers only serve numbers.
In the café of situations they have found the golden mean:
sit there often enough and you'll win a table and name,
Clock, say, or Air Vent, which feeds not on you but you,
drop in occasionally and you're still gifted
while you're here with just that identity-in-place
you've been so long in quest of. Wherever I go
I wear the café walls around me, and the shuffling step
of the invisible waiters brings subtly misconstrued orders
to Broke or Loving or Drunk or wherever I happen to be.

12 Drinking Sappho Brand Ouzo
after Vassilis Vassilikos

Crackup, last day of Carnival, first of Lent,
an ouzo-sodden moony pall hangs over the city
where we swim, soft wet flies, mad and silent
and American sailors on leave, their faces covered
with moist red apertures, buy Greek pornography.
'I only come to observe the audience.'
Cheap ouzo, Sappho brand, the dawn
*b*rododaktulos, in the Lesbian dialect. The normal
awaking hangover this time is milky white not blue,
has the half-twist of sexual origami. Try being stoic
in the Stoa five minutes' walk off – crackup – the sherds
carry dialect variants of your name, and a gypsy
follows everywhere singing: 'I shook down
the flowers from the blossoming almond-tree.'

Gorey at the Biennale

The vaporetto founders in green slush,
wickerwork masks are hanging in trees
aslant, with half-glimpsed smiles. A vague unease
seems to be centred on a certain bush.
Those little birds seem not quite right for birds,
these beetles have an odd seductive air.
Who ever heard of willow trees with hair?
Words keep suggesting other unwanted words.
It's not that it's not pretty in the park,
not that you feel there's anything afoot,
but when you hear the little steamer's toot
you hurry to get out before it's dark.
Of course the gate is locked; of course you knew
the star attraction of the show was you.

JOHN A. SCOTT

'Changing Room'

The breath's slow
drum-brush marks the end of Gillian's time.
Her hair's haphazard marathon, swaying
with the slowest jazz of afternoon. Detectives
wandering at her breast; the nipple's darker trilby.
A black thief hair, returning to its crime.

*

Now, amongst the sheets, there is
a trace of blacker hair, curled and blunt
as shorthand. I watch her move, the blankets
fanned across the mattress like a deal of cards.
Her foot beside an ashtray shell, its butted
cigarettes settled into parquetry. She dresses
as a child might in a changing room, all
half-under things. And what she'll do tonight
comes out of silence like a talking in her sleep.
She's leaving; and the similes are gone.
A borrowed room, and everything quite suddenly
and only like itself: this coat, this coat.
This floor, this floor.

Plato's Dog

Thirty years ago, Marseilles lay burning in the sun, one day. That's Dickens. Tonight when I go home, everything's going to be exactly where I left it, this time. That's me. I'm good with words. For example, this bar reminds me of someone eating with their mouth open.

Tonight's a bad night. Tonight I'm on milky drinks because I've seen people drink them and the barmaid told me how some older blokes order 'koala and milk' – and not joking either – because they've just heard it wrong. When you swirl them round the glass they settle into these curves. Like the rings of Saturn. I'm good with words. Though someone once told me I 'possessed a humour incompatible with sexuality'. That is, I entertain, but at the end of the night they go home with someone else.

Tonight's not a good night. At the table behind me there's an argument about Human Nature. Someone brings up Plato's dog. And someone else says 'who?' and the first bloke explains, except I know it's not *Plato's* dog, and be blowed if I can think whose dog it should be. I stare at the ashtrays, all an equal distance above sea-level. Like lane-markers in the pool of the bar.

The barmaid's pegging out bottles; lost in her unrequited dance. I swirl the last of my milky drink and engage this couple across from me in conversation.

– Excuse me, I say. Remember when you were a kid and listening to the radio, and there'd be songs you'd sing all the way through, and years later you'd hear the song again and realise you'd been singing the wrong words.

They look up and wait a bit.

– You know *She Loves You*, she says. There's a line in that that says 'Pride can hurt you too' and for years I thought it was 'Invite her to your room'.

– And sometimes you never *knew* the words, I add. But you could imitate the sounds. And you'd be singing along with all these nonsense words. That's how I figure life. You're either misunderstanding or not understanding at all.

We fall silent. The way you do after laughing a lot.

– I never knew if it was 'inside a zoo' or 'in Xanadu' in *Baby You're a Rich Man*, the man offers. But the moment's passed.

Maria would've been fixing me something to eat right now, so I'd have something to sit down to when I got in. A bowl of soup, say. And the idea of the soup almost makes me cry – the way I almost cried when I caught a glimpse of her standing on the front porch in that dreadful pink wrapper as I drove off. And the slippers she wore that looked like she was treading on two poodles.

You see, I can cope with the people, and the arguments. But the objects defeat me every time.

Outside it's drizzling again. But tonight's been OK. No-one asked me to leave. They just watched me – maybe listened to me. I was probably the centre of a dozen conversations back then, while I sat there, and while I walked out, one day.

Helen Paints a Room (1984)

In the prose version
she would be painting
the end room.
Calling breathless at ten,
stopping for a jasmine tea
 – perhaps – but then
retiring with her brushes
out of sight.

Here it is more difficult.

In the prose version,
a peach luminosity.
The questions of light
to be brought inside
as against the noises
to be kept away:
    the radio
    persistent carpentry
    a trampoline
    a motor cycle
    a dog
and occasionally
    another dog.
Or how that blossom
by the window

might be persuaded
to create
a willow-pattern story
right here,
within the room.

But all this started
somewhere else.
I am concerned, they say,
that there has emerged
a looseness in your style;
so that, for example,
the achievement of this poem
might be sensibly
compared to that of Helen
who at this very moment
is painting the room
at the end of the house.

In the prose version,
lost inside the large
white 'opportunity' shirt,
she would emerge at twelve
to wash the brushes
and ride away
to her Aikido class
or was it to acquire
a little French?

Anyway, eventually
the room belongs
to someone else.
The colour proves
unsuitable.
The blossom
tends to interfere
with someone's view.
And she has left the room.
And I have left the room.

But here it is
more difficult.
And the poem no place
for honesty.

He Mailed the Letters Himself

*A few years after his return to Italy, suddenly old and silent, he went into the garden
one day and sat down at his typewriter. He wrote letters. He had not written anybody
in years. Were the old fires flaring up again? The despondency and fatigue 'deep
as the grave' rolling away? He mailed the letters himself. Within a week they began
to return. They were addressed to James Joyce, Ford Madox Ford, Wyndham Lewis,
William B. Yeats . . .*

Guy Davenport 'Ezra Pound, 1885–1972'
The Geography of the Imagination

Dear Jim:

*31 I finally got your letter, encloseing your letter, enclocusing your letter which was
so omportant fo me thank quack ob verymuch. In time this fainful business will will
soonful, will soon be onered. Thankanany goodness if ess lossie ely wy oner we sinc
signature, I hope I hope I make it*
  signed,
   Bill

William Carlos Williams, letter to James Laughlin

Typing the Letters

Out back, Lotte's feeding pillow cases
through the wringer like she were
about to type them. Paper through the bail's
   no different. An ordinary task.
'How're those letters going?' he enquires
   from the blanket. From the porch.
He hears. He sees her flock of hair toss back.

A crackling breaks out from the birch leaves. Hurried.
   Like a child's unwrapping them.
Lotte hauls more linen from the tub,
   the whiteness water-marked with caps.
They fit. The handle turning. Notice how
   the moisture smokes off under sun.
Explodes like sweat punched from a boxer's head.

Plat. And it's away. The hammer on
    the rubber tube. A 'd', *plat* 'e',
plat 'a', *plat* 'r'. The Kama Sutra's stroke
    of ecstasy. A chorus line.
The stocking's leafish silver. Searching it
    a letter at a time. It kicks.
And now he's looking up the dress. So far,

so good. The hand drawn from the basin, from
    the hot sudsed water, stings across
his face. He reddens at the thought, that every-
    thing keeps changing places. Turning
out 'Omportant.' There! The pain of these
    unspeakable necessities . . .
As water seeds through Lotte's auburn hair.

Counting. Ten plats gives him 'thankanany'.
    Eight plats, 'goodness'. That's to say
the speaking out's an ordinary task,
    the *said*, an ordinary fear.
He's finished. Tattered out 'I hope I hope
    I make it'. Looking up to see
the raw sun burrowing amongst the twill.

Mailing the Letters

What's nested in the keys? He's on all fours.
    The tufts of lint-fleck soaked in black.
'They've hatched!' he yells along the porch.
'They've

        flown!'
    Should know better. How it's best
to keep the necessary distances.
    But what holds knowledges of flame
from touching all the tinder that is voice?

Wouldn't say himself he might be right,
    but sure as hell knew *they* were wrong!
And now it's out. It's hung out by the scruff.
    A goddam kerchief of a letter.
There's his signature. Initialled in
    the corner. Arabic and punch drunk.
What he's written. In the slap of air and light.

Except she gets to them. In time. Makes sure.
    A gibberish that could mean nearly
anything, which means don't mean a thing.
    Half of it not there. 'Left out!'
he grins. As if. The rest against itself.
    Sees 'thankanany'. Tucks him in.
The fool thinks washing is a letter. Only

this time Lotte's busy. There's a path.
    He hands them on himself. He's slipped
them by. Before she knows it, someone's taken
    them to all the obstinately
silent correspondents. That's enough
    to make us cry. And who's to blame?
She thought they were his handkerchiefs. What
else?

She could've held them, palpable, aloft.
    Head-high. Click! The proof. Like trout . . .
He's got *her* at it now. A letter's just
    a letter. And the first three gone.
He waits the seven days alone. He's written
    to his friends. He's told them all
about the 'fainful business'. Dear, dear, dear.

Receiving the Letters

William, Wyndham, James, . . . the list of friends.
    It's come to this. A washing day,
weeks gone. The flick of sheets a hopeless truce
    waved out to Fall. She shakes her head.
What they never guessed had left, was home
    to roost. She turns. What was he thinking?
All of them moved on? Refused to answer?

One by one, the letters had come back.
    Aged him. Made a fool of him
with death. Lotte hauls the sheet towards
    the wringer. Streaming bolster of
a thing! A bride, pulled from the lake. His fingers
    work, undoing them, alone.
The envelopes. The pointing finger stamped

into the white. Jotting on its cuff.
    Return . . . The leaves blot through the air.
The ground alive with flocks of rotting birch,
    racing, dumb as sheep. The sounds
elude him. Blushed before his own mistakes.
    He crushes all the pages flat.
Holds them on his head. They crackle there.

Who's listening now, to one not worth it? Christ,
    he tells himself, he could remember
conversations leading them into
    the burning risk. Was sure of it.
And drunk. Belonging. Dawn . . . It dawns on him.
    Guess we do it, all of us.
Bewildered by the doing and the done.

They return. And we undo them, don't we.
    Have to, everyone. The sun's
still here. Still at it. Autumn finds us in
    the yard. Heads down. The steady peck.
The poem's struck, more foolish than before.
    The ruddy man has written friends
and lovers. Written this . . . *off he goes!*

VICKI VIIDIKAS

Four Poems on a Theme

Inside of Paradise

We are coming and going. At last you have arrived, your suede shoes like soft faces brushing the floor. Advertising, you say, recognising your face stacked on a library shelf. The thrushes have left the eaves. You are alone inside the tower, respected, working. And elm knocks on the window. I come in wearing blood, a cloak edged from outside. How many times must I walk this threshold? You swivel saying, I have lost Paradise, I thought I was done.

I am bringing you rain and African deserts, animals in need of shelter. We are arriving in a circle, we are coming through cultures and lost continents, sometimes I don't know what to tell you. Act, I think, I never know where to begin. You fall away a glass paperweight, a faded map of lost Peru. I am a stranger in your drawing room, want to take you outside. I say, these are the knives, take one in pledge. You have a history to reject as I recreate idols. Voodoo men own my laughter, they have a claim on me like you. The shaman is out to get you, make you jangle inside of Paradise. Chaotically we're arriving. This time the risk is gold.

I have your feather, I never forget.

A Trunkful of Structures

Daylight hasn't entered this library. Beaded fluorescent lights shine like dominoes on the ceiling. Traffic is steadily flushing its own purpose down the street. No good, you say, meaning I do not fit into your life. No good. The streets are full with animals carrying sharp sticks, handbags, cruel eyes. It's the beginning of another week and we're all moving into familiar patterns. You must keep your car repaired, you who never risks buses.

I am stalking a zebra crossing, lunchtime crammed with shoppers and stale sandwiches. I am in a library, my feet up on a chair. Great Lives, Great Men and Great Words confront me. I don't even flinch. Curtains keep the sun out, readers have fallen asleep in chairs. I am among the shelves looking for a book. I am rummaging among the shelves searching for a word. You're nowhere in sight. And I'm looking for something. Not perfection or great lies. Not complicated gestures. Something to replace your strained eye. You're out of control. And books are leaning posts. These days it's hard to conjure up devils when there's only an hour for lunch.

I've never been in this library with you. Or in a pool room, or on a zebra crossing. I've been in bed with you, kissed you and wanted to draw blood. I imagine that is significant. That I have been in bed with you. That it was you and not a ghost. I imagine I can recognise, claim you, have you in my sensibility. Dream of fire and water and symbols to bind us together. But I can't.

Not you or anybody. I can acquaint myself with the edges of lives, read the intimate journals of some great writer. Tell others about you. Know it won't be you or anyone I'll spend 30 years of my life with. And the books are saying, believe, believe me. I exist. You exist. Readers adrift in dreams exist. Separately. So long into death. Into memories of your eye, 'how it was', the quarrels we never meant to have. My sagging bed, 'our romance', 'our affair'. The bridges you'd built and the water flowed under them. Each of us seeking belief thinking, I am significant. Want no more lies. Loved us away from structures, the closest thing to being free. Made us scent each other's blood. Away from tired defences. So we believe.

It's not true. You have dragged your ghosts with you, unable to fob them off. You've come rattling a trunkful of structures saying, here, try this one, perhaps it will fit. Like hats or shoes. They didn't. So you feel let down. Having my own trunk, and a sagging bed with a cat for a hot waterbottle. You've gone off wearing the old coat saying, no good. The structures like clamps. Leaving me to mine. Each of us squeezed breathless.

It's Natural

It's not enough, looking at you blundering like a turtle against the stream. Prowling my room like caged animals. Mud slinging. Nothing more violent than turning the eye in like a knife. I see. Fingerfuls of affection falling away like flesh. I imagine what her bed is like. You dropping into her like a well, forever lost, bottomless. Another territory.

Madness is in your eye. I want to carry you off and say yes, I've something more than a bed of straw. Yes, you're a coward, want to blow you up with words. Got a match? I can't replace you. I'm saying there's more to life than love. Eh? Yeah. Words. Structures.

The man in the communist bookshop was a capitalistic pig. Personally. And I say I've set up my affections like tin gods to be shot down. Absolutes. Wanting permanence. In and out of the line of vision. Fire. Essences. What more essence is there than your seed? Tomorow night it could be in her. It's natural. I won't accept her. You? Tweed coat betrayer. Nonsense! I'm making a farce of it – this possessiveness, this claim. Removed from cities to mud huts. Honey I'm going to howl. Get your spear. It's my line.

Going Down. With No Permanence

I'm finding it impossible to begin, as you've ended so little. Last night my heart was a cheap flag waving to the nearest mirror in sight. I couldn't believe anything, seeing you drive away into others' arms. I'm no sweet virgin sock-washer either. So it's a matter of priorities I guess, just who wants to gamble. Talk of loving when there is no goal. Of belief when there is no road. My shoes are off and I'm walking barefoot. Down a long avenue of arms and kisses like knots. I'm getting tired and angry and thinking hell, I'm no sock-washer but there must be some other venue. I say my heart's big enough, it is. Every time it's eaten and collapses like a cough.

Today I'm trying to be reasonable. You're having breakfast with her. And there's no wedding ring, baby, fidelity, photo. No day to week token of what we have, a visible future. Crazy thing, it's happening everywhere. You waft into my room bringing delicious words, eyes, every other love you're still attached to, claim.

'I want all love-rites simultaneously.'

'I don't want to negate anything.'

Yes I understand. Incredible egotist! that one cracked heart is your own, gyrating in its uncertainty. Adoration. Adulation. Your heart seeks to reflect itself. Narcissus in the bath. How many loves do you want? Are you never full, leaky bucket?

And now you turn to your sock-washer reasoning socks are better than none. So you're surrounded again. Pursued and claimed. A shroud of outrage going up. Thinking of numbers and lines. It sharpens your humour. While I love this one the others must love me too. I'll keep my heart spinning. You think you're responding, keeping all the doors open. Yes. Yes.

This is the road my bare feet touch. Going down. The avenue with few affirmatives. Going down. With no permanance. This is the alternative to restrictions. So we assume. Without end.

Future

It doesn't really matter if I met him in a bar, picked him up or was picked up; in the morning he pushed me out of bed saying, 'You must go, my wife's due back.' And catching the 7.44 a.m. bus I thought, it doesn't really matter, what did I expect? These are my fingers spread out to touch, the palms turned down, the kisses like nets; these are the lines, when I was a girl the fortune teller said, 'You will travel.'

ALEX SKOVRON

Election Eve, with Cat

A tramstop swarms with schooligans, their brand
is chalked all over the matron's face.

Another busload tapers to the kerb
to take a breath. A briefcase with a watch

runs naked down the street, trips up the step.
The mob disperse, a well-cut

kindly teacher ponders past, he debates
the moralities of moving a snail.

The tramp is dozing richly on a bench
across the way, two schoolboys stand and perve

up at the sky. At fifteen on the brink of sex
a bookworm worries Tacitus

with teeth, tugs at her jeans, braces
herself for home. With the look of a man

ready to age the keeper of cigars and empty chairs
shops for spice on the wind, watches

a tramcar teeming like a Roman bus.
Somebody's wallet vanishes, a black convertible

with painted flames killed by a foolish dent
becalms itself. The traffic clings.

A blushing upstairs clerk scribbles a reply.
Tomorrow we condone another government.

ALAN WEARNE

Go on, tell me the season is over

   but listen,
there is moreover, experience and example:
in his sleepout J. M. Hooke mentions the words
   'computer' and 'motel';
or, is she married? (left hand fool;) and
to find out the origins of the surname
   Delahunty – marvellous!
There's so much to be done in Melb.
 – Crossing Spring from Carpentaria Place,
   climbing Collins
in a morning fog, marking the spires of
Scots and The Independent, to pause at Gibbys,
   Vienna 25c.

Tell me the season is yes, another game, an
other game. Is radio, ole-time with
   Dancing in the Dark,
its author, anonymous now, who'd wish to
say, say: enjoy your Octobers in these,
   our golden-times . . .
(it need not be computer and motel, e.g.
he worked on the computer/they stayed at a motel.)
   But it's still to be done;
   marvellous!

from: *The Nightmarkets*

from: 5 *Terri*

                              Can't be a model, there'd be times I
        wouldn't know whether
my arms or my legs should do that or do this. Haven't very memor-
        able tits.
   'Oh, yeah?' Ian pronounced. 'I'll remember and prove you wrong,'
        grinning, gentle
but serious. Another man wanting to cheer up. That day the music
        played it laid back. Sex? Incidental.
Drugs? There was a drought. But got what we wanted. How often we
        feel, *That one'll do.* If something almost fits
take it, keep it. So we've taken, we've kept. Won't be seeing each
        other much more, but our crazy bits
have jigsawed into something crazier. Memorable, he says. Needed
        to meet someone like Ian. I'd've just chucked a real mental.
   How out of it was he if he was? Yet weren't the rest all so sane, a
        little boring?
Ian arrived early one shift. Yes, a few days after New Year's day.
(St Kilda Road seemed almost empty, certainly wider. All my regulars
        were on vacation. With Ross away,
settling a deal for a crop somewhere, Jacqui and I spent warm even-
        ings at the beach). Yes, it was the morning
after a cool change. I was called to meet him. 'Hi, I'm Terri.' 'Ah ha.
        Right. Right.' (Ignoring
any chance to meet the others.)   Seemed nice. We'd take our time.
        It wouldn't delay
a backlog of fellas. There weren't any. I undressed him, said no he
wasn't a slob, as he wanted 'an opinion'. Told me things. There
        seemed discretion, though not all *hush-hush*
y'never know who'll find out. Bath first. Didn't treat me as an instant
        push-over, so liked him. But wondered if this was to be like
        my doctor, say, someone steady –
friendly and reliable – or a kind oncer slowly getting his rocks off.
        Bits of ourselves were already
given out in the small talk: 'Live with anyone?' 'Used to. Hope to.
        You?'   'My boyfriend's doing business up the bush.
Has these caneware stalls 'n' shops. He's coming home tomorrow.'

Well, wouldn't be spending this hour with some fuming clown
    wishing I'd shuddup. Rather the opposite. Talking as I soaped
    myself, could see he wanted to listen.
Told him: 'Well, had jobs for eight or nine years. First I was a
    strapper years ago –
my last job? Oh, a receptionist, plenty of them 'round town, the
    world, I suppose.'
He told me: 'Sort of work for my brother. He wants to be a
    politician.'
'Send him along, get more than a few MPs here. Notice we're most
    discreet?
'Nah. Bob and I don't talk about things like that.' 'My sister 'n' me
    don't either.
Wouldn't mind where I work. It's just she'd keep on asking. Week-
    ends I need a breather,
y'know, to be normal. See, this job is normal, but it isn't, and, well,
    don't want to cheat
myself *too* much. I try to forget it. Melinda wouldn't let me. Sure, I
    make a bit, don't really treat
myself to anything that special though. Yet. Can't say where it's gone.
    Aren't too clever
with money – not on smack, dumby. Haven't really seen much, but
    what I've seen's enough.
And I'm not like Shelley. She's headfucked on mandies. It's curtains if
    Leon ever discovers.
After a club as good as this, it's all down: parlours next, then the
    street.' 'Club?' he muttered. 'That word covers
a lot of ground about here.' 'You like the Crystal Palace?' Ian
    shrugged, gave a small cough:
  'Oh, maybe there's excitement, but where's the fun in meeting
    someone you're *certain* will have it off?'
Have to change that, I thought. Might need you back. He kept
    calling my regulars, *'Your lovers'*.
Strange how grim that sounded. 'Well, if they want to be like that.
    Everyone plays their parts,
Ian, me, you – ' And he hasn't smiled yet, I thought. Ahh, well, no
    use acting the tease
if he's not relaxed, could snap in half. Get this rabbit at ease:
'Not going to bite you, Darls.' 'Oh, yeah? Pity.' 'So, there is a spark
of something in your head.' 'Please? The biting? I'm harmless. Really
    haven't much of a bark.'

from: 8 *Elise*

1

Life was back lanes, therefore out of bounds
(the fence turned moss rotting into mulch);
and father held us. Rich to say so. Rich
to import, sell, employ: we 'comfortable enough' to enjoy sounds
of Kathleen in the wash-house singing. What?
Irish ditties (sentiment thick as the sod),
white little cottages, mother and the Lord.   Our god
was the tea trade, cocoa and coffee trade. That lot
entered us to 'circles', and better kinds of folk
whose was a world (no, land) of thank you, please.
  We gave and obtained respect, affection, but love? At thirteen
I thought it a bad sad joke;
    'Mmm, just kissed the iceman comely as you like, Elise.'
  Like? I like? I like it not, Kathleen.

  Seeing them in Brighton still, the lanes. If
then, no doubt now, huts by the fence.
(I played near the house, though; father's girl showed sense.)
  Huts? Would I join brother Keith
and his Cannibals Club? (Rather be a coon,
on the moon!) All their *Watch out gang, here's sis!* And
Elise May Merrill, in all her ladies' college hand-over-hand
demureness, froze. A prig? (Oh, but only to the 'helps'.) Soon,
though, when Josie got expelled or left or something
(school and all the bayside a-buzz), it shot to my heart.
Funny, we're ladies now, exempted from, well, naught.
  And later when Keith was coupé-courting,
goodness never knew where or who, I'd lie awake, start
to wonder, When, how, might *I* be something; tempted maybe,
        taught.

  Each Head of the River *Lamberts* was almost on loan
to the crews and their friends. They'd adjourn downstairs
for rounds of squashes, sarsaparilla-spiders, éclairs.
  Once Gwynneth, whose father owned
the Broadway Soda Fountain Company, kissed each member
of the winning crew.   'I couldn't give a hoot,'
she laughed. 'I love you, love you all!' Oh, to cock a snoot
at everything. Oh, maybe I could when older.
And, ahh, to be so-o-o-popular!   'Well, hoo-roo, smarty

pants,' some boy yelled to his friends. With a frantic
chase to the top of the stairs they tumbled over, rugger style.
    Ha. Ha. That night I'd go with Keith and a much maturer party
to the boat race ball. (If I knew I'd meet the dashing, romantic
Jack McTaggart, my face might've eased into a broader smile.)

Often we went to the pictures, Jack persevering. 'Soppy!'
he'd laugh. 'How wet!'   True, being Mister and Missus
would beat any Rialto heart-throb. And our kisses!
Dry electric ones, swoony perfumey ones and sloppy
ones that annoyed him and made me giggle.
    Yet we knew what could happen, we knew
how far was far enough, anything else a brew
that made you never never never want to stop. He wouldn't niggle
me or whinge; as much as he tried, John laughed and tried.   'One
        day,
old girl,' he sighed. 'I know, one day. We understand – '
    A full moon covered the sea and suburbs. Under its light,
singing G and S, we drove home. Sunday
after church and dinner I tried to nap and
    Oh thank, God, I thought, thank God I didn't give in last night!

    from: 9 *The Division of O'Dowd*

    7

We've yet to cohabit. For some we simply arrive and leave parties
at roughly the same time. This here's a low-profile affair. Not that hectic
to rope in a herd (or mainly as she calls herself, Auntie Sue). Louise's
        choice of friends being as eclectic
as my own, we've an overlapping social life, and that rams it up the
        odd smarties
we've still to suffer; those, say, expecting a perpetual couple,
those who treat going against what they consider 'prevailing', as
        some monstrous crime:
    'Everybody does it. It happens all the time.'
    Okay, everybody minus two. We trust our self-respect as suffi-
        ciently supple
not to accommodate the norm. Met Allison for coffee last week:
        'Going with Lou? At least it's what I saw
last party, from a distance.'   And I supposed: ' – like you if we were
        kids, this might be going steady.'
    'I understand. Give her my luck. She'll need it.' Al mentioned how

Eddy will reform the band before the band before the band before
his last tour and album bombed. Everyone felt The Niddries go Meg-
adisco sounded rather absurd, even for them. 'But it isn't slow-
ing the pace,'
she urged.'Call this a consolidation – ' (I got her) ' – and then we
hope to go all over the place,
all over, India, Paris France, Chad, Niddrie, San Francisco.'

8

We've those few hours over. Maybe it's a quirk
of closing a campaign, but here we laze at Bob's: the afternoon
before this final rally,
slow drinking in the garden, with a valley
of shade edging across as the day ages. Louise mentioned some of
the work
she does: childcare counselling. (Single mothers, single fathers for
that matter;
I'd asked once. There'd been three.) It's something as serious as run-
ning for Parliament: ' – then there's the matter of our funding.'
   Maxene wants to have Lou for a return natter,
in a few weeks, after Bob's the member. That's probably enough to
entice her over; the thought of political action. Max, always ready to
shoot you an opinion, says: 'Ian, keep an eye on *her*. Louise really
suits you.'
If we couldn't take such unsolicited advice,
these embarrassments could create fuel
for an awkward exit, if we were really to believe them. But, of course,
we linger.
laughing as my sister-in-law wags an index finger:
   'Now don't miss out this time, Mister Cool.'
   Placards and cheers, the municipal pipe band,
the tang of chopped lawn outside the recreation centre:
campaign and rally time is closing.   As dignitaries enter
through a tee-shirted phalanx of party faithful, the gelati van
vies 'Greensleeves' with the pipes' 'Amazing Grace'.
   '*Direct Action,* socialist news; *Direct Action!*'
   '*Tribune,* fifty cents!'   And each Marxist faction
tries for the conscience, custom, noise-space
of the oh, horror! Nunawading
boosj-whah-zee. Of Nunawading? Can they believe it?
   Ahh, militants, sweet militants, better leave it

to a candidate's slamming local press release, to hacks plodding
the electorate, seeking door-stop conversions. 'Cripes,
Labor, eh? Yeah, why not, why not indeed!'
    Part auction, part exorcism, with a creed
of slogans. Part carnival with tee-shirts, ice cream and the pipes.

9

    Tonight I'd like to feel like a non-aligned nation.
So many of our models were boring, corrupt. I'd relish we'd be quit
        of them.
Top power, top celebrities. Each bit of them
adds to us in preposterous equation
their language and style. Yet Australians are hardly 'into dating'.
That belongs with California: naïve, formal, with a sheen of raunch.
    Well, we've something different, perhaps better, to launch.
    The phrases prepared for my forthcoming phases lie waiting.
(Viz: maybe two thousand and two?)   There's a price
to this proposed non-alignment, Louise. Perhaps it seeds, flowers, in
        a cynic's paradise,
but let's try. I tried the Crystal Palace. I've even 'dated'. They both
        seem like the same land,
steeling me with a refusal to (a) borrow
on the action of others, (b) imitate those herds
who stampede towards what's prevailing, (c) procure more inade-
        quate words.
    Goodbye Tez: we've a story based on tomorrow starting tomorrow.

MICHAEL DRANSFIELD

Epiderm

Canopy of nerve ends
marvellous tent
airship skying in crowds and blankets
pillowslip of serialised flesh
it wraps us rather neatly in our senses
but will not insulate against externals
does nothing to protect
merely notifies the brain
of conversation with a stimulus
I like to touch your skin
to feel your body against mine
two islets in an atoll of each other
spending all night in new discovery
of what the winds of passion have washed up
and what a jaded tide will find for us
to play with when this game begins to pall

Portrait of the Artist as an Old Man

In my father's house are many cobwebs.
I prefer not to live there – the ghosts
disturb me. I sleep in a loft
over the coach-house, and each morning cross
through a rearguard of hedges to wander in the house.
It looks as though it grew out of the ground

among its oaks and pines, under the great
ark of Moreton Bay figs.
My study is the largest room upstairs;
there, on wet days, I write
archaic poems at a cedar table.
Only portraits and spiders inhabit the hall
of Courland Penders . . . however,
I check the place each day for new arrivals.
Once, in the summerhouse, I found a pair
of diamond sparrows nesting on a sofa
among warped racquets and abandoned things.
Nobody visits Courland Penders; the town
is miles downriver, and few know me there.
Once there were houses nearby. They are gone
wherever houses go when they
fall down or burn down or are taken away on lorries.
It is peaceful enough. Birdsong flutes from the trees
seeking me among memories and clocks.
When night or winter comes, I light a fire
and watch the flames
rise and fall like waves. I regret nothing.

That which We Call a Rose

Black greyed into white a nightmare of bicycling
over childhood roads harried peaceless
tomorrow came a mirage packed in hypodermic
the city we lived in then was not of your making
it was built by sculptors in the narcotic rooms of Stanley Street
we solved time an error in judgment
it was stolen by the bosses and marketed as the eight hour day

Waking under a bridge in Canberra to chill scrawl
seeing the designs we had painted on its concrete like gnawed
    fresco

Venice with princes feasting while Cimabue sank deeper into
  cobweb
as the huns approached in skin boats
back in the world Rick and George on the morgue-lists of
  morning
one dead of hunger the other of overdose their ideals precluded
  them
from the Great Society they are with the angels now

I dremt of satori a sudden crystal wherein civilisation was seen
more truly than with cameras but it was your world not ours
yours is a glut of martyrs money and carbon monoxide
I dremt of next week perhaps then we would eat again sleep
  in a house again
perhaps we would wake to find humanity where at present
freedom is obsolete and honour a heresy. Innocently
I dremt that madness passes like a dream

Writ out of ashes, out of twenty years of ashes
for George Alexandrov and for Rick

Visiting Hour (Repatriation Hospital)

White world after a urine-yellow sundown.
This time is not more crucial,
but there is less of it. An incident.
Chronometers of pity – just
before lunch was brought round
the soldier in the next bed
quietly opted out / not an image / but
ceasing to live as others ate their meat.

350

Day at a Time

For the artist of environments, time too must be flexible.

The great city has a hundred million rooms so any combination
   is possible
one minute the sky is blood and the next is grey
something happens   a building falls   one rises   there are
   wars
nobody wins   shares rise   wages   prices   politicians visit
switzerland   the climate is healthy there and makes
   everything golden

leonardo rides with the borgia   hoping for books   this will
   be held against
him   he rides a white horse   takes no part in the slaughter
   sometimes
designs a siege machine   regrets the ruined towns   will be
   given a castle
historical necessity: *to understand a person one becomes that*
   person

               in the ocean
               in the centre of the sky
               nothing moves
               total purity
               the eye of the hurricane

               and in the desert
               a man burnt dark by the wind
               walks in the night toward rigel

the planet spins   is a treadmill   nobody pauses   nothing
   must be faced
on one side factories make bleeding hearts   on the other red
   stars
these are their totems   the worshipped masochist   the
   sparks of gunfire

after the destruction commences, everything, even regeneration,
   is movement
toward death   the poor build their slums on the earth and
   the rich go hunting

nothing must live   even insects are hunted   a manmade
   bird climbs high
to spray death on the fields

the writer of literature is in his room and has closed the
   window
music from a speaker drowns cries and shellfire   he writes
   busily
he does not hear the door behind him open   nor the red star
   that follows

Endsight

for Union Carbide, A.D. Hope & Sir P. Hasluck, Askin, Clutha etc.

midnights of consciousness, still, and even
silent, for now the jets are grounded, due to
lack of visibility, & only random thought & squads of
landladies' plaster ducks attempt flight. occasionally
an owl thuds into a building. it is always
dark now, the air a factory black
like X-rays of the children's lungs. the coated
earth is brittle, dead horses rot slowly
where they fall. using modified
radar and homing devices, vehicles crowd roads,
sightless, to carry workers from their
shelters to factories. a distant, hardly
safer government issues voluminous
decrees which litter the towns like printed snow.
also the works of the Official Poets, whose genteel
iambics chide industrialists
for making life extinct.

The War of the Roses

for Premier Bjelke-Petersen

they walk around a corner at the back of town,
the high class tramp & his servant, who
pushes the pram with their possessions.
the high class tramp wears a jaunty
homburg hat & longcoat, the servant
some rags or harlequin of patches. for the evening
meal the servant lights a fire in a rubbish tin.
the rubbish burns well & on the spoke of an old
umbrella the servant shishkebabs a
cat & when his master has dined
he eats the leftovers & the head.

Flying

i was flying over sydney
in a giant dog

things looked bad

Self-analysis

you tire of it, this
cleverness
there are too many poems
two walls of shelves a desk
a safe all crammed with poems

your letters turn into poems
your poems into drivel
soon there will be
no one to write to
then you will claim you are misunderstood

A Strange Bird

it is a strange bird
this world

whose habit is
to fight itself

whose left wing
and right wing

tear themselves
bitterly apart

both on the side
of justice and violence

and whose great beak
gobbles the poor

Memoirs of a Velvet Urinal

he turns his back to dress; i've lost him
already. after inevitability took our
hands and made us play, we talked
for hours in the slow
warm dark, touched each other. his body

is red like a fox, i had seen him before,
although he is sandpaper rough, not furry
like his kind. i love all poets; there is
no private self: as, if he needs me,
i go to him. the habit
forms, that we lie together
each time. when he touches me, it is true, a small
space turned in my belly; but
often he starts by brushing his red
fingers through my long, downy hair,
or kisses me. in the next bedroom
our host sleeps in electrified blankets,
wifeless through this and summer when
it comes to his cold province; he guesses
nothing, but would not care.

Minstrel

The road unravels as I go,
walking into the sun, the anaemic
sun that lights Van Diemen's land.
This week I have sung for my supper in seven towns.
I sleep in haysheds and corners
out of the wind, wrapped in a wagga rug.
In the mornings pools of mist fragment the country,
bits of field are visible higher up on ridges,
treetops appear, the mist hangs about for hours.
A drink at a valley river coming down
out of Mount Ossa; climb back to the road,
start walking, a song to warm these lips
white-bitten with cold.
In the hedges live tiny birds
who sing in bright colours you would not hear
in your fast vehicles. They sing for minstrels
and the sheep. The wires sing too, with the wind;
also the leaves, it is not lonely.

PAMELA BROWN

Leaving

so now i have to pack my forests
  and baggages.
so now i have to pack my eagles
  and teardust.
and the way you talked to overflow.
and the way you were so fast to change
  into your many shades of sorrow.
and the way you swept the miracles
  away from your shabby gentility.
and the way you trembled
  as you chose the latest props.

so hello attache case face.
hello briefcase face.
hello screaming suitcase.

I Remember Dexedrine. 1970

one of those days
i'm saying things
i don't usually say
and
verboballistic comets
are shooting
from my mouth
thinking rapidly

like films
run backwards
i race through the rain
like a rocket
to a dance hall
men and women there
are taking off
their shirts
and
they are friendly
but i wonder
what's inside them
ill in the head
by now
but not thinking
'this awful music'
'this stupid rain'
and then
there is something
the saxophone does
and i have to leave.
the taxi driver
looks right through me
and sees
the corroded rubber hose
that is
my bronchial tubes
i cough like a car
and
drop the money
all over the seat.
in the kitchen
i polish the brass taps
for a few hours.
on the table
a scrap of paper
where i have written
'the blank bullet
in the firing squad
is one image
i am sick of'
i tear it up

and later
i feel i KNOW
what REALLY happens
between
dark and daylight
but i've forgotten
by breakfast
which i can't eat.

ANNA COUANI

What a Man, What a Moon

What a man, what a moon, what a fish, what a chip, what a block, what a mind, what a tool, what a drive, what a car, what a tent, what a pitch, what a scream, what a joke, what a suit, what a flash, what a view, what a jump, what a pain, what an arse, what a tree, what a trunk, what a boat, what a sea, what a blue, what a song, what a root, what a jerk, what a pump, what a drink, what a mouth, what a guy, what a doll, what a smash, what a hit, what a fight, what a fuck, what a rock, what a ring, what a stone, what a jar, what a whack, what a jaw, what a cunt, what a sheet, what a mess, what a room, what a crutch, what a limp, what a walk, what a day, what a beach, what a swim, what a bath, what a dog, what a cow, what a pig, what a snort, what a trip, what a shot, what a grape, what a wine, what a glass, what a cut, what a lip, what a hand, what a foot, what a lawn, what a gnome, what a pet, what a fit, what a bum, what a heel, what a nail, what a bash, what a phone, what a dial, what a tooth, what a drill, what a screw, what a ball, what a clinch, what a dick, what a bind, what a scene, what a smoke, what a dive, what a splash, what a height, what a cliff.

The Map of the World

The map of the world is felt from the inside. Rough around the coastlines and smooth over the hills and sand dunes. Warm and moist through the rivers which lead outside to the forests like long hair then sparser like shorter more bristly hair to the touch. Reading a glove of the world with its topography in relief. Reading with the fingers as though blind. Feeling it with the back, down the spine. Making contact with the nipples and the nose only. Moving at a fast rate underwater through the oceans and large lakes. Most of the oceans connect up with each other. Moving so fast that you become aware of the earth's surface being curved. Flying low but fast across the land masses. Make yourself feel like the world. As old but not as troubled.

The Obvious

Suddenly after a few years of abject misery, depression and paralysis, I stumbled upon an explanation of human behaviour which finally explained what had been going on. But this growing realisation of the explanation, the nature of it, was almost as depressing as my previous ignorance and fear. Because it was a realisation about the real nature of people's motives. I began to see people's behaviour in terms of power both attributed and actual, personal and public. Then as I came upon new situations, new people, they also seemed to manoeuvre in relation to each other and to me along these power lines. The stunning thing from then on, was how obvious they are and how blind I'd been to the obvious, before. At the same time I felt as though I'd been a complete fool and that everyone around me had ulterior and unpleasant motives. No one seemed to act out of love, charity, or trust and probably no one would ever do so again, now that I'd realised this.

The Never-Dead

We all know that things look strange in the night. Stranger. They look like they looked today at the beach in full sunlight. It wasn't full sunlight because the sea mist was heavy and dulled the glare. For a few minutes I lay on my stomach with my head under a hat. The others were swimming. I was thinking of you. It was like a nightmare - the idea of your reactions to what I said that night. The looks you gave me, the tricks and deceits you go through now. The way you avoid me. The worst things occur to me first. The more I think the worse I feel. I plunge deeper and deeper into your hatred of me, your lack of understanding and compassion. It's overwhelming. I deal myself blows you could never muster. I kill myself with the idea of your cruelty.

And suddenly I take the hat off and sit up. Everything's okay, I'm exhausted but around me it's all normal again. Like night and then day. But now night. I remember Joanne saying she was at the beach somewhere today too. At the pool where I walked without my glasses. I was wondering if I'd see you, Jo, but instead of not seeing you, I didn't see Joanne. I'm sorry I missed her. Though she was saying today that she's had a hectic rash of coincidences lately. I know how she feels. I knew how she felt. Now. My imagination is running on, now that it's night. Real night, not like a waking nightmare. Just insomnia from smoking too many cigarettes. The thoughts of you rush in again. And as I try to sleep some people arrive in the street below. A man with your cough and a woman with a velvety voice which carries. She's with you. You've come to repeat the episode when we first met again and call my name outside my window. I go out onto the balcony and look down. You're drunk and laughing. You introduce me to your girlfriend. She's pretty and blond, you ask me to admire her but I don't I say she's a creep to be a party to this and that I don't care for you at all. Even though I asked you to marry me, I could forget you in an instant and will.

I come inside and close the door but you're still railing at me. It's embarrassing, the whole street wakes up. I hear your car arrive, the handbrake pulled on, the door slamming. You come and call out my name. I go out and you start this tirade about my desire to marry you. You wave a flagon in one hand and squeeze your pretty blond girlfriend in the other. I quickly assess the situation and say I'll go inside which I do and call the police who question me closely as though I'm the criminal. I think of the dope and all the crimes I could've committed which they'll hit me with as a routine matter. I hear your car door slam and your cough, then a velvety voice I didn't expect to hear. It gives me a shock, it's low and soft but carries so well. I hate it. You call out. I go onto the balcony and you're already completely hysterical and waving a flagon in one hand. You unzip your fly and show me your erection. You start fucking your girlfriend as though she's a doll bobbing up and down on you. You scream at me – You think I can't fuck a woman, what's this? You think I'm impotent?

I'm disgusted and run inside. But they keep going on screaming. It's a nightmare. I get up and go onto the balcony and look at all the quiet cars. Your car isn't there.

JENNIFER MAIDEN

Climbing

This shadow at my shoulder doesn't shed
    The substantial night.
  The rope twists all breath
    From the mountain
      As simple as a bed
  Far above life in heavy wind you might
Fall beyond the common cliff of death.
With all my side and ear adhered to stone
There seems a place like hell to draw the dead
  Down so soft a body wouldn't wither
But hear the desperate lute lament ahead
  To lull the dog across a bloodless river

Taste

    (at the local show, 12 years later)

We eat
bread & stewed sausage,
curdled sauce,
rococo cream,
but the night
smells edible. We watch.

Without taste
the Spider's gears
caricature some general
love of lethal metal.

Horseshoes crunch
blue metal tetchily. Neighbourhood
blue cattle dogs,
lost for years,
return to piss
        in slashes
on the iridescent tar.

Outside the marsupials, an old
woman squats, petulant:
    broken-thonged
& looking
    like Bea Miles or
    the wombats: chubby,
sensitive
    & ponderous
& whole.

New chickens, dyed the pastels
of the fairy floss in packets,
peck her hand's palm in minute
eroticisms long after
all excuse of grain has been consumed.

The horse-stalls smell hotly
of sweat & mulchy porridge.
Behind them, the Freaks
        thrive like history
in tented calm:
                    the lamb
with 6 legs –
none too ample, but there –
still waltzes, as does
the four-pawed goat, the cat
with forked tail. The schizoid
axolotl
meanders from his think-tank
with expert novelty.

> Their
> impassive empathy once soothed
> the boredom of a child. Here
> I shrink from their staid martyrdom
> & Quasimodo charm.

> Satis. Still the night
> is edible. We move
> beyond it, & its tent-flap,
> with toffee apples
>   . . . stroll,
> tasting slowly what was
> on the sharp sticks of pleasure.

Language

I need to learn a language but not english
or at present any further maidenese.
I know some anglo-saxon but it is
a lonely language & like each
loneliness is surfacely
quotable & simple. I've a friend
from Egypt assures me that my knack
with that old language could be workable:
I already do the right things with
my tongue & the roof of my mouth, & so
Egyptian my choice may be, since I
respond to their music, too – it's long
& only ever half-curtailed cry.
I'm reading the Arabian Nights. I will learn
why Burton's wife burned his papers when
he died, if I can only enter now
into the speech which caused them, &
if only that speech does not prove some
secret which the mouth denies the tongue.

Air

Surely the air must still have human warmth
brushing against me in some surprising passing –
now I no longer fear to see my father, whose
ghost I had feared to see? and would
he see me? Blind man dead: the priest
intoned at your funeral once 'He sees
everything now.' And do you, who
protected me and whom I could never
protect enough? Bright wealth of white
hair which I never dared tell you
had turned white, do you see all now
 – the grey at my temples, in my spirit, the love?

    Do you see
the flesh drop from me, is it really you
whose arms I need to hug my shock-cold bones?
You are buried with your mother. Since
your funeral I have never had
the peace to visit your grave, nor did I
see you dead. When you were on display
I mourned most with the dead words that
'I keep thinking of him alone there' –
to be answered 'He isn't alone.'
Today love and terror gust in me
as long, harsh, human rain. I remember
long laughter with my father, and all other
witty passions completing me. The air
is strange.   It would be so
easy to see my father now.

New

Vermeer: Girl Reading a Letter

The morning has its flat first light, its blaze
has not yet flared uneven through the slats.
A pregnant girl reads a letter by the table,
her smock an inverted bluebell. Her face
that flinched with this light has returned
to unyielding sleep but her gaze
averts to the page in her fists. It is
an ageing letter?
Yes.   Her thumbs press ink
without disturbing it. Her eyes
are lowered by certainty, unshy
but still her lips shape: 'new'.

In the Gloaming

The door isn't locked. You walk
through the empty rooms and look for a person –
then for a sick one, then for a dead.
There is only no one home. You aren't relieved.
From the inside, you lock the door.
You shelter in life-surfaces. An electric fire, both
elements wink up slowly. The kettle shivers. You
wish it would whistle, but it cuts out, too
automatic. But the coffee's warm. You pour
the milk from the stout safe glass so that the cream
is the first to fall. You use beige quartz sugar
to thicken your drink. You overfill the cup.
The biscuits aren't rich enough. You search out
cake. Only the icing is stale, and it will
turn tender with hot water in your mouth.
Corpse-air outside makes 'gloaming' tangible.
You shut it out. Venetians snap together.

You sit with your food and beverage until
the capillaries on your calves form a tartan:
red, blue, white, green from electric comfort.
You press your fingers into bruises.
Your shins ache with revival, bright as sex.
The heat in your ankles and throat are the same.
There are too many lights turned on
in the house and you love the guilt.
You are in a house alone and know it, for
you are not home. The furniture cannot
answer you here like dresses or duty.
You make your fingerenails scrape white runs
down and up your arid legs. Your skin
has become the weather again. There is
no key in the door yet, no hope. Sweet coffee
thins within your thorax like a sun.

The Foundations

There are bog-people in the foundations.
Cold and august, the breeze around the highrise
taps out a bony leaf or two on glass.
The skeleton of the weather brings that
skeleton of a tree close by us. A whole tree,
blown like a bog-man, withered, noosed.
There are bog-people in the foundations.
There is the assistant to Mr Crime, who grew
a fraction too political, there is a youngish
heiress who worried too often. Her wrists
were knotted so tight they fell first
from her body, before the tendons
biscuited away. There is a baby
overdressed for the month it was left in,
its bunny-rugged sockets in tulle.
Bog-people – even the baby – seem to have

more teeth than the common cadaver, more
hair to bind the tendrils, many more
juices to feed trees and gardens, but
of course it was the last adrenalin.

Anorexia

Kelly sharpened is powerful, asexual and yawns,
curls up on tartan cushions with pick-me-up arms,
viewed by no one but cat, video, grandmother.
She is cranky with Nan's tabby. He is sleek
and haughtily whores, meanwhile demanding all
the messy food and closeness they can muster.
She ate last night and will not eat this week.
Her body lives off itself like anger.
It was once too dumb, too soft, too tall.
She bites her mouth because it's still a stranger.

The Green Side

Autumn is unquiet everywhere.
Our redhaired Natasha is suing the wind
for sexual harassment. Somewhere
in South America the CIA is plotting
to overthrow the CIA again. We are
re-elected to the Borstal Board. Yes, there's
no such thing as a bad boy here.
We shot them. All the girls
straddle Yamahas, blush, bush-walk
and come down storming. Natasha
wakes up, her molars grinding

together like rough tiles. In barred air
at her window the leaves dance dying.
Half the tree shakes clumsy crimson.
The green side is still with fear.

KATE JENNINGS

Just the Two of Us

Octopus in hot sauce,
games of canasta,
camembert and bread,
Pat Garrett & Billy The Kid,
three bottles of cider,
rain and wind outside,
a hot bath,
an uncertain fuck,
then we sleep and
I dream I am in a mental hospital with Bob Dylan, and
everybody, except me, is forced to sleep four to a bed.

Couples

this is a song an epithalamium it is also
a requiem this is a poem about couples it
is called *racked and ranked*
the title comes from william faulkner
who said

'and thank God you can flee, can escape from that
massy five-foot-thick maggot-cheesy solidarity which
overlays the earths, in which men and women in couples
are racked and ranked like ninepins.'

this is a poem for couples from which i cannot escape
this is a poem for people who are not couples but who
want to be couples from which i cannot escape a poem
for all you out there people who are coupling up or
breaking up just to couple up again and giving me
second prize because

kate jennings, lose him, weep him, couldn't catch a man
much less keep him

couples create obstacle courses to prevent me from doing
all sorts of things easily
couples make sure i'm not comfortable with myself because
i'm only half a potential couple
couples point accusing right index fingers at me
couples make me guilty of loneliness, insecurity, or
worse still, lack of ambition.

what do i do at the end of the day?
lose him, weep him, think of catching a man,
and eating him.

SUSAN HAMPTON

Yugoslav Story

Joze was born in the village of Loski Potok,
in a high-cheek-boned family. I remarked
that he had no freckles, he liked to play cards,
& the women he knew were called Maria, Malcka, Mimi;
& because he was a 'handsome stranger'
I took him for a ride on my Yamaha
along the Great Western Highway
& we ate apples; I had never met someone
who ate apples by the case, whose father
had been shot at by Partisans in World War II,
who'd eaten frogs & turnips in the night,
& knew how to make pastry so thin
it covered the table like a soft cloth.
He knew how to kill & cut up a pig,
& how to quickstep & polka. He lifted me up in the air.
He taught me to say *'Jaz te ljubim, ugasni luc'*
('I love you, turn off the light')
& how to cook *filana paprika, palacinka,*
& *prazena jetra.* One night in winter
Joze & two friends ate 53 of these *palacinke*
(pancakes) & went straight to the factory
from the last rummy game. Then he was my husband,
he called me *'moja zena'* & sang a dirty song
about Terezinka, a girl who sat on the chimney
waiting for her lover, & got a black bum.
He had four brothers & four sisters,
I had five sisters.
His father was a policeman under King Peter,
my father was a builder in bush towns.
Joze grew vegetables and he smoked Marlboros
and he loved me. This was in 1968.

The Crafty Butcher

It's a real old-fashioned butcher's shop
with carcasses on hooks, watch your shoulder,
and sawdust on the floor.
The boy's arms are red-streaked:
he's had his hands inside a cow.
His face has soft white hairs, and while he
tenderly wraps my meat I watch the boss at work.
He reaches to a whole leg on a hook
and slick, neat as an eye in the future,
there's a fingerhold: he tugs the muscle
and begins his craft.

He knows exactly where to put the knife in
and the angle and depth of the cut, and
there's the big knuckle of the knee
and a glistening white thighbone.
A few drops of blood hit the floor,
and away comes the round steak. I reach down
and feel the running muscle
at the back of my thigh, solid as the cow's
which is now hung by the fingerhold
on an empty hook. Don't wince, this
is the craft of the butcher. Look at his face,
those cheekbones, he's perfectly calm
and good at his job.

Then there's just the leg bone with that
glowing knuckle white as the lack of pain
after death, and clean as a finishing line.

Women who Speak with Steak Knives

Hurtling past us in an old Volvo are women who speak with forked tongues. It's a mixture of ancient languages they cast around them, violent languages with no vowels. Their speech is all plosives and screaming. This is not because they have individual traumas but for the sake of art. They are dedicated to art, especially performance works. In the car they're not necessarily practising – they carry on like this anyway. Because of their dedication to art they have developed a lifestyle which incorporates it, so that outsiders can't tell the difference. This act on the freeway going south might be repeated in some form on a stage tonight. There are three of these women and they always undercut each other. Their main mode is interruption. They're like a post-modern Greek chorus. Instead of commenting on the action, they interfere. When the driver holds out her dollar to pay the toll, the others start screaming.

Now there are some curious people who invite these women to dinner. They soon find out that the women speak with steak knives. When you thought a bit of tenderness might be forthcoming, you find they have pierced you between the ribs, just waving their knives to make a point. No damage intended, though when a bloodstain spreads on your shirt they scream laughing. This is the life they lead. No holds barred. No amount of scorn and gossip and bad circumstances are enough for their articulate venom. They always like to be bad. They are bad in bed and bad everywhere else. You get the impression that in life as in art good manners are the enemy. They will go to extremes to prove this. They will open their mouths and cut their forked tongues with steak knives.

In Andrea's Garden

At first nobody could bear the heat, like
   a predator, padding & sweaty
it took over whole glazed conversations
& then familiar as a national event
the southerly buster hit & the trees
were suddenly noticeable, moving like needles
   & cool as the eyes of river fish.
At dark the sky was white from clouds,
it was one of those *white* nights
you remember from childhood,
sitting on the roof of your bedroom
   & the wind in your clothes reminding you
this is the year when your life changes, now
you can have babies

RICHARD KELLY TIPPING

Casino

a drawerful of obscure tools
for a dollar the lot.

a hereford in the butcher's window
carefully crafted in mincemeat & fat

Just after Michael's Death, the Game of Pool

The hot thumb.
That was so plucking subtle:
'I'd just like to accept things
and go for the general good'

Another triple-flutterblast rocks the room.

My father should never
have had children – could have been
a great pathologist – explorer
mapping the mysterious landscapes
of the skin – afterthoughts of body, thin
lines 'distinction' into the latin names, not
having to worry so much about
Mrs Gatchilliano's chilblains, the kids'
runny noses, the cancer
already embedded in sunburnt skin –

The universe is at your feet, Paul.
'I'm just going to put it down that hole'

As history is a language map
thrown backwards

your absence is so fresh
it weaves a gap

My heart hurt too –

you wanted to be with us,
playing drunk pool till 6am

only centimetres from the funeral
pulling you away
in a tremendous gleam.

writing on electrons, entering
the body of the immortals

a shadow of the actual
midnight on the dot, in heaven

living by luck alone
the same things will still exist

we'd gladly be gods
but it would spoil the game.

so death doesn't suit you.
i'm sorry.

sore eyes, sore heart,
so praise the spirit that embarks.

try on these shoes – they fit – you move –
accepting the shadow of original clouds,

all that's tangible
is that you're gone, though the spirit is all
that prevails, this stops you're dead.

Poet at Work

for Nigel Roberts

After the second book
words are a luxury, for a while
it's floorboards, walls & windows first
fixing up the house. Earth holds
wood before paper: measuring, sanding, hammering
nails into a near-perfect join
collaborating craft and art into a livingspace
like a typewriter needs table
& bum somewhere to sit, like you write
where you love eat and shit – it's all this crude
& this much work doing everything yourself
with friends who'd rather language
was the beam and skirting board
than actually helping build a bedroom in the real
world of 'all this for a thousand dollars
and my holidays' – Nigel, you're so *practical*:
construct a new book, against the grain.

ALAN GOULD

Demolisher

By six he's started. I wake to a wince and arrh,
the animal protests of my neighbour's iron roof.
Behind a cypress-dark, the February sky

is blue as gin. The house is nineteen twenties;
he moves along its apex removing it,
and at this hour he's higher than the sun,

flexing a torso of cinnamon brown, his singlet
dangling whitely from his belt. Slav
or Italian, perhaps, he applies that rigid serpent,

the pinch-bar, to open unconsidered caches
of darkness. His work is wholly restoration –
he is recovering horizons, and

with the long arm of Archimedes, bringing
sunlight to gulf the spiders' vertical suburbs,
dense as hairballs in their sudden light.

So ridge-cap, gutter, sheet iron are grimaced free
from battens; sheets of fibro drop-shatter,
nails, clenched in the pinch-bar's single knuckle,

come out with a sigh. By lunchtime the house
is a birdcage of timbers; by evening it's gone,
and the man sits, gleaming like resin,

rolling cigarettes, drinking water,
looking through a gap at new hills,
peering down the shaft he's made in sixty years.

The Observed Observer

From darkness where no stars shine
and the projector is clicking like a stopwatch
you move out from your times to where a time
flickers against an illumined wall,
a time not lost
though its weather is scratchy after sixty years.

This is not occult; you shed no place.
The ducted air crescendos softly,
the further street-noise, sea-noise of vehicles
crescendos softly.

And yet you move into the light that travels
out of former lives, for instance, these five
who strain around their crucial rope,
their vanished bodies rooted to it like molluscs,
their oilskins gleaming like kelp.

They are so close.
Sixty years or sixty centuries –
it is a membrane of time divides you.
Look, here at your shoulder
the sea has spangled in a ruddy beard,
is drooling like a tap from a blonde forelock.

Above them, out of picture,
the drear, monstrous canvas thunders.
But stay with what is shown,
how one has eyes tight-shut
as the atrocious tension draws out his arms,
how one, his head averted, seems ready
to leave his arms behind him,
how their knuckles shine like quartz.

And if you know
the simple vehemence of their effort
will become unfashionable
this knowledge is years off from their dance
of inches and inches and an inch,
remoter than the gull-grey unstable horizons
that shatter to foregrounds of waist-high froth,

remoter than their sun, not seen perhaps for a week,
which only moments ago
broke on them like an epoch,
permitting these pictures, this grainy aureole
where they glitter in their time and yours,
unearthly as stars in daylight.

And as you leave the theatrette
for the animal-quick commerce of streets, you know
you are millions of years from the neighbour creatures
where the dolphin grieving the drowned schoolboy,
the lions grieving the snakebitten lioness,
grieve innocent of ancestry. For it is this,
this widest, this thinnest of loves, astounds you,
this care to catch distinctive light
from the vast shopfloor of former lives
where you also will find your place
below the balconies of hindsight,
the long cables of remembrance,
the historian's desk dishevelled
by diaries, letters, reels of film.

In elation for where light travels
from a myriad vanished origins
you step out beneath your stars
in the light of all predecessors.

LAURIE DUGGAN

from: *Three Found Poems*

3 Hearts (1983)

It is essential that the U.S.A. standard of hygiene and inspection procedures is maintained on the killing floor and throughout subsequent handling of all offals.

The hearts shall be trimmed of protruding veins and arteries making sure the aorta valve is removed. Hearts are to be incised to enable them to be packed flat.

Each heart has to carry a clear impression of the 'Australia Approved' stamp. It is permissible to brand in ink but if a clear impression is not obtained the hearts should be fire-branded. The hearts are to be drained of excess moisture and will be packed flat with care taken to present a neat appearance, into a plain polythene lined regular style solid fibre carton 22″ × 14½″ × 5½″. The hearts are to be bulk packed to 60lb net weight, it being in order to cut one heart to obtain the exact weight.

from: *The Epigrams of Martial*

I xxxvii

You drink from crystal
    and you piss in brass;
it's the vessel between
    that lacks class.

383

III xlvii

Range Rovers carry
the 'mountain-fresh' odour
of aftershave
'up the country'.

VIII xx

Dransfield, who wrote
   200 poems each day,
was wiser than his editor
   who printed them.

X ii

Readers, forgive me
if I sometimes repeat myself.
Look kindly upon my poems,
   old and new.
You, readers, are the greatest gift
   given to me:
through you I escape death.

Ivy cracks marble;
crazed mourners demolish the tomb
   of Jim Morrison;
but these words
   through yourselves
outlast stone.

from: *The Ash Range*

1.1

In a high wind, on a rock in the back paddock
pollen dusts my pants;
180° of the valley before me:
    its scattered dams, sheds,
    fawn and white masses
        of fleeced and shorn sheep;
Mt Elizabeth to the south-east,
and north, the country round Tongio Gap;
the hillside below covered with yellow flowers,
                        green clover,
                            scattered rocks and stumps;
behind me, the electrified fence and low dry scrub
    up the steeper slope to the Angora Ranges,
                            clearings on the spurs;
over to ENE, Ensay township,
the ridge in front of the highway,
cemetery hill on the far side;
behind it the logging country of North Ensay and the
                            Nunniyong tableland.
To the north spirals drop from the clouds;
turbulent convections over Benambra.
In this wind the cockatoos fly unsteadily
but the swallows manage to hang in place.

Nightfall and the wind drops,
                        Crux, due south
                        over the hotel,
lowest in its diurnal course;
west of the cross, Centaurus; further west
Ara, the Altar, Scorpio and red Antares,
Pavo, Indus, Capricorn, Grus, Toucan,
and Bunjil?
                – who made the earth and
                    the people down here; the Classics inverted
overhead –
                        Bunjil

grew tired

385

and told the musk-crow who
kept the winds:
'let some out from your bags'.
And Crow
gave out a blast that ripped trees skywards.
But Bunjil wanted more.
So the knots were all untied
and a gale blew Bunjil and his people off the planet:
flecks of light in a dark sky . . .
. . . looking down on sphagnum bogs
trampled by cattle
to swampy flats
thus, Nunniyong
and the surfaces of the Bogongs,
grey over green, on a yellow field,
slope gently southwards in conformity with the general
inclination, initiated when the Mesozoic paleoplain
was deformed.
At a depth
of four feet, embedded
in solid stratum, Mr Stirling discoverd
bones of forgotten marsupials.
Nargun,
like a rock, all stone
except for his breast,
arms, hands:
no one
knew what these were made of.
The disturbing forces made one course:

that the main range may be fairly considered as a great axis of
perturbation;

that all the elevations, subsidences and inclinations which exist on
both sides of it are posterior, subservient, and perfectly in relation
to the effects of the convulsions of that axis;

that these convulsions, though keeping invariably their north or south
course, did not affect the crust simultaneously;

that the dislocation, fracture and contortion took place at different and
distant periods;

that in these periods the action of different causes greatly and
alternately altered the heaved-up surface; and finally

that the great order of superposition of compound minerals remains
   undisturbed, and in perfect identity to that observed on the rest
   of the globe.

Thus, the eighteenth century displaces the mappemonde,
its special effects of fire, ice and mist,
the Virgogici, the Troglodytes, Mt Purgatory;

the divide shifts to the south,
and the Mitta
   steals the Tambo headwaters
boathooking at Tongio Gap.

Downstream, the Tambo braids;
long strips of rubble;
and at the mouth of the Mitchell
a silt jetty pushes into a lake.
I walked out on that jetty in 1964;
wood huts on the end,
new currents and a shifted entrance
shredding it to islands.

                   5.1

           The Ninety-Mile
           formed by the mills of two oceans
           grinding into meal the rocks
               on the southern coast;
           every tide and gale
           has helped build up the beach;
           the dry sand, spun
           into smooth conical hills
           where low shrub with grey-green leaves
           take root. Strange plants
           with pulpy leaves and brilliant flowers
           send forth long green lines
           having no visible beginning or end,
           binding together the dunes.
           The beach is broken in places
           by narrow channels, through which
           the tide rushes and wanders
           among low mudbanks, studded
           with shellfish, and around

a thousand islands, soil woven together
by the roots of spiky mangrove.
On the muddy flats
black swans build great circular nests
with long grass and roots compacted with slime.
Salt marshes and swamps
stretch away behind the hummocks.

from: *Dogs*

South Coast Haiku

Rain drips through
the tin roof
missing the stereo.

Qantas Bags

Only the truly bourgeois
choose to advertise;
the proletariat wear commercials
like disfigurements.

The Town on the Ten Dollar Note

Too much history
and the place becomes a mausoleum:
the chemist closes for lunch;
the museum stays open all the time.

Nonplussed

we will be passing the telephone booths soon
& then we will be in the suburbs, things that say
'COKE' against the sky.

aerials.

you see the way my foot is nudging yours, underneath
    the dashboard?
boring, isn't it? the way my headache will not leave me
    alone
reminds me of it. I mean to say, if you've got some change
& you want to make that phone call
make it. – I'll
just open the car door   & get a bit of fresh air & stare at
the sky
above the booth, resting. I like the way the red breaks up
the sky, & I can't focus.

JOHN JENKINS & KEN BOLTON

In Ferrara

Sunlight dried the last small patches of moisture
on the table top. Karl wondered if
it was wine,
or dew,
from the night before.
He pushed his cuticles back
with a corner of
the menu. Motor scooters
went by, then a car.
Everything seemed pleasantly European, the
best part of being in Europe, out doors, at
a table. He moved under
the awning. As yet only a few people presented themselves
to the morning glare. His suit,
despite his being a big man, hung loosely on his frame
as Karl bided his time, and made
every effort to keep his mind blank.
Karl had sort of a large round face,
with widely spaced brown eyes,
the sort women found attractive. His
face was slightly red,
though he hadn't walked far to the cafe.
His were the sort of looks
that seemed ripe to fade
though they never had. There
was something vaguely raffish
and un-German about
him, that was not to be
attributed, either, to half a
life in Australia, where
he bought for a chain of bonbonnière.

He made this trip quite often,
visiting glass factories and warehouses
between here and Venice, and
as far north as Southern Germany.
All his life, things had gone
right for Karl. The result
being, strangely enough, a slight
lack of confidence and a self-doubting air.
He had never struggled, and
his success did not surprise him,
but it confirmed nothing. He glanced
at this watch with some abstraction.
He was a handsome man
and when in doubt, as he was so often,
given to pose. The chair beside him
moved. 'Giselle, hello.' Giselle sat
down. 'Good morning Karl.' And
she looked down the plaza,
squinting into the shadows for
the others: 'Have you ordered?'
'No. Well, I think so. The waitress
doesn't seem to have noticed.'
Giselle called to the waitress: 'Prego,
Signora!' And, gaining her attention,
'Per favore, due caffè.' Giselle
scratched her nose and flicked out a
cigarette which she then placed carefully
by the packet, not lighting it.
They were at ease and
Karl chose not to notice, remarking
instead on the Alitalia flight over
the distant conifers, growing on the low
hills that surrounded Ferrara – the contrast
of modernity and ancient towers.
Giselle wore a tight black dress,
and dark glasses which she had removed.
Her nose was finely chiselled,
and fluted, almost pinched, yet beautiful.
Giselle generally was attractive,
and made small flourishes with her hands.
She acknowledged the arrival of
their coffees for herself and Karl

in a way that had become habitual.
She worked as a tour guide, and
her work had bred her
manner and talents. Giselle
worked privately, for well-off tourists.
She was mildly bored with her job
but did not find it irksome.
She looked up as Greg
arrived, and so did Karl. Though they
had spoken on the telephone
this was the first time they had met.
Karl knew Greg from Sydney.
'Giselle, Greg.' 'Hello.' 'Greg, Giselle.'
'Hello, I spoke to you earlier. Yesterday.'
'I know.' Her voice trailed off. 'How's
it going with your arrangements?' Karl asked. 'You've
found a hotel?' Greg put a
map on the table and answered
in the affirmative. 'Which one,' asked Giselle.
Greg looked up from the map. 'The Grand . . .
The Grande,' and went on, 'They're not very helpful.
I was trying to find an all-night farmacia.'
Roberto arrived and called for the waiter.
He gave his order standing up, then sat down.
Giselle introduced Roberto to Greg,
and the others re-ordered. Roberto
exercised an immediate presence,
to which Giselle responded, as did
Greg and Karl. There was about Roberto
an air of some risk,
against which a physical substantiality
gave assurance. Despite the
similarity of size, Roberto seemed
larger, to take up more room, than Karl.
Roberto may have been slightly younger,
though he seemed more mature and far
more active in some indefinable way –
that was something to do with gesture,
the carriage of his head, and even his clothes.
Karl also wore glasses and spoke
with some hesitation. Roberto was dark
where the other was fair. And his business

career had been more volatile. At
present, as the others understood,
he presided over the liquidation
of a marble quarry
from a deceased estate, clearly
at some temporary benefit to himself.
They drank their coffee. Roberto
spoke briefly to Greg. Old friends
from Sydney – though Giselle, who
had been longest away, had
not previously met Greg. With the exception
of Greg all were well-travelled and
at ease with each other. Hitherto,
he had not ventured from Australia.
His presence here was much less
business than the others', though it was
presenting him with the most difficulty.
He spoke vaguely, addressing Karl
and Roberto. 'Is there some way of
going from my hotel to the old
section of town? Is it walking distance?'
At this point there was a confused clatter
and the sounding of a high-pitched horn.
They look around just in time
to see a Vespa scooter describe
an uncertain path across the
cobblestones towards them
and collapse a mere few metres away.
At first none stood. The embarrassed rider,
a young woman, looked to her
slightly buckled machine, and to the bus
that had forced her from her path.
As the girl rubbed dirt
from her knee, Giselle took her
by the arm and led her to
the other three. 'Are
you hurt?' they asked, 'What happened?'
'I think the bus did not see.' 'You
speak English?' responded Karl. 'Mm, Yes.
I go to school in England.' Giselle gave her a chair.
'We are Karl, Robert, and Greg,' indicating
each, 'And I am Giselle.' 'I am

Carla Merighi.' Greg went
to pull the scooter upright
and parked it by the fountain.
As he returned Carla was saying
'I live just near here. Thank
you, you are very kind.' 'You
are alright?' '*You must be very
certain,*' Karl admonished.

'Could I have a glass of water?'

T.V.

dont bother telling me about the programs
describe what your set is like the casing the
curved screen its strip of white stillness like
beach sand at pools where the animals come
down to drink and a native hunter hides his
muscles, poised with a fire sharpened spear
until the sudden whirr of an anthropologist's
hidden camera sends gazelles leaping off in
their delicate slow motion caught on film
despite the impulsive killing of unlucky Doctor
Mathews whose body was found three months later
the film and camera intact save for a faint,
green mould on its hand-made leather casing

Four Heads & How to do Them

The Classical Head

Nature in her wisdom has formed the human head
so it stands at the very top of the body.

The head – or let us say the face – divides into 3,
the seats of wisdom, beauty & goodness respectively.

The eyebrows form a circle around the eyes, as
the semicircles of the ears are the size of the

open mouth & the mouth is one eye length from
the nose, itself the length of the lip & at the top

the nose is as wide as one eye. From the nose
to the ear is the length of the middle finger

and the chin is 2½ times as thick as the finger.
The open hand in turn is as large as the face.

A man is ten faces tall & assuming one leaves out
the head the genitals mark his centre exactly.

The Romantic Head

The Romantic head begins with the hands cupped
under the chin the little fingers resting on the nose
& the thumbs curling up the jaw line towards the ears.

The lips are ripe but pressed together as the eyes
are closed or narrowed, gazing in the direction of
the little fingers. The face as a whole exists to gesture.

The nose while beautiful is like the neck, ignored,
being merely a prop for the brow that is usually
well developed & creased in thought – consider the lines

'the wrinkled sea beneath him crawls' locating the centre
of the Romantic head above the hairline & between the ears;
so the artist must see shapes the normal eye is blind to.

This is achieved at the top of the cranium where the skull
opens to the air, zooms & merges with its own aurora.
Here the whole diurnal round passes through. In this way

the dissolution the quivering chin & supported jaw seemed
to fear, as the head longed for, takes place. The head, at
last one with the world, dissolves. The artist changes genre.

The Symbolist Head

No longer begins with even a mention of anatomy,
the approach in fact leaves one with the whole glittering
universe from which only the head has been removed.
One attempts, in the teeth of an obvious fallacy, to find
the shape, colour, smell, to know the 'feel' of the head

without knowing the head at all. And the quarry is elusive!
If the stomach disappears, butterflies are liberated & while
the head teems with ideas who has ever seen one? Equally,
the sound of a head stroked with sponge rubber or the sound
of a head kicked along the street on Anzac Day could be
the sound of a million other things kicked or stroked.
The head leaves no prints in the air & the shape of an
absence baffles even metaphysics. But the body connects
to the head like a visible idea & so has its uses, for
what feeling is aroused by *The Winged Victory of Samothrace*
but piercing regret for the lost head? And beyond the body,
a landscape is not just our yearning to be a pane of glass
but a web of clues to its centre, the head. And here, like one day
finding a lone wig in the vast rubbish dump devoted to shoes,
the Symbolist head appears, a painting filled with love
for itself, an emotion useless as mirrors without a head.
This art verges on the sentimental. It's called 'Pillow Talk'

The Conceptual Head

1) The breeze moves
   the branches as sleep moves the old man's head:
   neither move the poem.

2) The opening image becomes
   'poetic' only if visualised

3)   but even so
   the head can't really be
                    seen,
                    heard,
                    touched
                    or smelt –
   the Objective Head would be raving nostalgia.

4) Yet the head is not a word
   & the word means 'head'
   only inside the head or its gesture,
                    the mouth.
                    So the poem can't escape,
                    trapped inside its subject
   & longing to be a piece of flesh & blood
   as

Ten Pounds of Ugly Fat
versus
The Immortal Taperecorder
forever.

5) While anatomy is only a map, sketched
from an engaging rumour,
metaphor is the dream
of its shape –
from 'head in the stars'
to 'head of lettuce'

Between the two
the poem of the head is endless.

6) Now the world of the head opens
like the journals of old travellers
& all your past emotions
seem tiny, crude simulacra of its beauty.
& you are totally free

7) Greater than all Magellans
you commence an adventure more huge & intricate
than the complete idea of Mt Everest.
And this academy can teach you no more.
The voyage will branch out,
seem boring & faraway from the head,
but nothing can delay you
for nothing is lost to the head.

8) Goodbye,
send me postcards
and colourful native stamps,
Good luck!

Love Poem

1

This ritzy vista includes the money,
the brain's confused image of its friends
looping into the suburbs. Here blood
draws back like a day in the country
closing its eyes to form a vague penumbra
behind our belief in free speech e.g.
these last words are only seconds away
and every second is a holiday, equal
but insoluble (light, not water, fills
the canals, more blinding than a zinc
tub Dad guessed would last for years.)
The mines of euphemism smoke behind
their facades, that like a big town
ruin the health! The glove-like
voice of its humour is our vote, gossip
rippling inside-out towards the museum.

2

Physique touches the buildings with
its lightning sketch and unreal voices
float in abeyance over the salt air, corroding
the transport system. I don't care.
The city is blessed. Yet just last week
its sky-blue stupidity seemed tungsten
to me. I think those days mimed an accent
I've abandoned for the lovely weather
of you. I'll meet you at 1.30 outside
the museum's fabulous graffiti room. I
know you (plural) will be there. I know
the famous painting leads a double life.

John Forbes

The Age of Plastic

after Ovid

The dictionary definition of change
means your face looks different in the water
& even tho' you'd feel at home down there
each moment spent at one remove, anywhere
between the mammal & the sponge,
you know you'd miss a particular cassette
idle tears or a glass of gin
& be irked by the serious options
a changeless life presents e.g. 'Minor
poet, conspicuously dishonest' would look funny
on a plaque screwed to a tree
while the blue trace of your former life
suggests an exception
generations will end up chanting; for them
the parts of speech will need explaining
          not lakes or sleep or sex,
or the dumb poets of the past
who, being lyrical, missed out on this.

Monkey's Pride

        not the shouted poetry
of well-travelled sandwich fillings
           but the shorter
        more carnal lyric
    that singes the page
like a packet of bungers facing Mecca
with lust in their hearts/hearts that resemble
      Steve Kelen's face
inscribed on a banana, a whole bunch of them
         each with a different face

suitable for various occasions
&,
not bananas either but a bunch of grapes
made of glass –
a tribute to the glass-blower's art.
But while we recognise the faces of the Great,
the big ones at the top
of the bunch/
the ones in the middle are blurred
because the hot glass
was further away
from the artist's controlled breathing
while at the bottom of the bunch
we have to read ourselves
into the vaguely sketched features
– tho' I can see myself ok,
as the light, refracted through the face
of the one I am
shows a glazed somnolence I'd recognise anywhere
& the smashed forepaw
of Elsa the Lioness,
held out towards me
with a reproachful look –
'not me, not my good intentions'
the full rounded lips
on the grape seem to say,
even though digressions appear
like tree lined avenues
because I am a balloon that floats around
bumping into the suburbs
where a cowboy appears from a bookcase
riding on a bottle of pills.
'Soon' the grape goes on
'new technology will detach me
& I'll be employed on a rowing boat
mounted in a park,
the one the avenues lead to
because society has elected me/to decorate
its falling apart
with a useless panache
& I will,
despite my vocation

to become a labour-saving device, opening
        cans by remote control
in the kitchen of your heart/bottling the vegetables
           you grow in your own backyard.'

Speed, a Pastoral

it's fun to take speed
& stay up all night
not writing those reams of poetry
just thinking about is bad for you
             – instead your feelings
follow your career down the drain
& find they like it there
among an anthology of fine ideas, bound together
by a chemical in your blood
that lets you stare the TV in its vacant face
& cheer, consuming yourself like a mortgage
& when Keats comes to dine, or Flaubert,
you can answer their purities
with your own less negative ones – for example
you know Dransfield's line, that once you become a junkie
you'll never want to be anything else?
        well, I think he died too soon,
as if he thought drugs were an old-fashioned teacher
& he was the teacher's pet, who just put up his hand
          & said quietly, 'Sir, sir'
     & heroin let him leave the room.

Death, an Ode

Death, you're more successful than America,
even if we don't choose to join you, we do.
I've just become aware of this conscription
where no one's marble doesn't come up;
no use carving your name on a tree, exchanging vows
or not treading on the cracks for luck
where there's no statistical anomalies at all
& you know not the day nor the hour, or even if you do
timor mortis conturbat me. No doubt we'd
think this in a plunging jet & the black box recorder
would note each individual, unavailing scream
but what gets me is how compulsory it is –
'he never was a joiner' they wrote on his tomb.
At least bingeing becomes heroic & I can see
why the Victorians
so loved drawn out death-bed scenes:
huddled before our beautiful century, they knew
what first night nerves were all about.

PHILIP SALOM

Walking at Night

We roam the streets at night, lovers
heady with perfumes: here are the lushest gardens
where nothing rots or grows still.
We've made each street again and again: precise
as childhood. Streetlights glow overhead
like the teeth of a huge zipper; the universe
steals in when the zipper's open. At the end
is the brilliant villa upon the hill,
where the world ends. I do not know what it is.

After days of love, argument has wrenched the house,
brawling that makes the air spark and the bloodstream
seek its questing. We draw back from the hill.
I walk to the house of my mistress where we pool
attention on our bodies, stick pins in our marital secrets
then wander naked in her desert, looking for answers.
Returning, I feel unspent euphoria. Its place
is the brilliant villa upon the hill
where the world ends. I do not know what it is.

The pleasure of returning is to rebuild.
The same materials never lie in the same way twice.
We are a family sifted by days. Nothing is still.
We cleave together like tender and crazy tapestry
sewing images with deft or indifferent movements
then reaching back, repeating what doesn't suit us
until we get it right. I include my fear, it
is the brilliant villa upon the hill
where the world ends. I do not know what it is.

We are sped against our friends, decide to win.
Make another country and return. She runs off to kill
a weakness, but finds her own and stays until the sun
fades upon her thighs. I get drunk with friends, shout
up revolt in a room filled with publicists. By morning
both of us are famous. By midday our children are grown,
by evening someone has died. My answer
is the brilliant villa upon the hill
where the world ends. I do not know what it is.

Ghazal on Signs of Love and Occupation

for Helena

Someone's licked a finger, touched it to the mirror.
A bleary, innocent fingerprint, but yes, it's me.

Remember gaudiness passing for emotion on TV – yet
spray-can love, in tunnels, questions our art-forms with
flourish.

Imagine at night, the torch hiccupping, the youth bent.
She fucks him so he thinks it's love. But he makes his print.

See the young and rich pressed on their sweet enamel – BMW,
more talk of art seems less and less. Give me the tunnel.

I see aristocratic citizens in the street, columns of faces saying
we don't want your challenges. Out of this make literature.

Racket rises from the block next door – bulldozers
pirouette in the dust, a place in the universe is laid bare.

Bricks all say the same thing. An ambulance makes donkey-
  tones
in traffic. Water-pipes bang from visitation, not you in the
  shower.

When first you struck the keyboard, you found its twin
waiting in your head. Our love goes on. My pen is poised in
  air.

blkfern-jungal

wlk'n down regent street i see
blks hoo display blknez
(i min they sens of blknez)
n they say t' me . . .
                         'ime gonna lif yoo outta
                         yor blk hole n sho yoo
                         how t' wlk n dress n tlk.'
n i sit in th' gutta
of regent street
(outside wair we ol meet)
n i look up n see
arown th'haylo of they hair,
a cosmetic afro ring –
a shiny haze
like it blines me man!!

so mu eyes go down t' thair
smart soot ol prest n cleen,
n'thair hi heel kork shooz
n i turn mu head n look at mu
soiled blknez, n i sezs . . .
                         'ime gonna lif yoo outta
                         yore blk hole n sho yoo
                         how t' walk n dress n tlk.'

CHARLES BUCKMASTER

An End to Myth

Gruyere – is being cleared of its forest – the mountains
become pastures – and carved wastes
and the sub-divisions come – within five miles.
Small farmers die – my mother and father –
cheated – exhausted – There is no dream and death is close
and complete.

Grass-seeds – the paths which once led through the forest
at the foot of great mountains – Light through the gum-tips
on this – holy ground.
The remaining forest – shot through with clearings – which
continue to grow.
The cities will merge.
Gruyere is dying and my dream of change dies with it.
What can be done?
The green walls dissolve.

And there is Satan – who rattles his pockets and laughs   I have
one enemy   And who will die
before me? There is no retreat – you thrust your
obscenities beneath my feet and tell me that I soil *your*
earth!
I scrape at the bitumen of your carnal streets – the soil
in which no thing could grow for a thousand years. So much
destruction!
A re-birth I may never see. A battle
which has yet
to begin.

Wilpena Pound

– Where we had stood
at the peak of the mountain
and had first noticed that we were
inside.

below us, the pass, and about us
a circle of mountains:
red aside orange
the rocks
laced with colour.

and the bushland below
'so dense, in some areas'

  – she had said,

'that one can barely pass through it'

The Pound – originally,
a depressed plateau, the centre
having eroded, leaving a natural enclosure

  – a plain
circled by mountains.

Where we had stood
by the groupings of boulders, inside the Pound

spread on the rocks, exhausted
by the climb

facing west, toward the sun, the miles
of forest against mountain

the isolation!

winding track, below
through the pass

  – the way to the Outside.

Mordor – the mountains –
in the 'other world'.

'This is our home, the place
of our people'
she said
without realising . . .
'to think that we could
climb down that path, into the forest,
to the centre of the Pound

and never
return again'.

(Taking up your axe – the trees
for your home

. . . at some unmarked spring – bathing your child
in the water of the mountains

. . . Gardens about your cabin

. . . Within the voice of the forest . . .)

This circle of mountains! – a natural
and an un-natural
isolation.

'The tribes of the Ranges
were exterminated'. Poisoned flour,
'Aborigine Shoots' –
'near here, a massacre, in the 1880s:'
said John.

    And for this! –

The Pound stretches twelve miles
 – twelve miles of heavily forested plain
thinning on all sides against the mountains.
About and around the centre – the remains of the lost;
where few men have been.
Twelve miles of complete/the final
isolation.

And I had little else to give but love:
now, there is that which we shall take from you,
this land, being
our land:

there is reason for many to be bitter – this land,
your pastures
stained with blood from dark-skinned wounds.

Land of clouds; from the forest and pick up the spear
which fell
from the hand of my brother
as he died
a century past.

Though you refuse our offer; understand, father:
My brothers and I are of the forest
and we are of its nature more fully than you

 – the forest
is our home father:
the battle to be fought is our self-preservation.

. . . And I take up that weapon and return
to the hunt.

Sunset. To the west, etched
in a sky of all colour – a lone tree against light:

and to the north, the Pound: a circle of fire.

Seed

red spattered on an orchard path. Thats all.
I saw nothing.
Perhaps they kicked dust over the blood
allowed you to double
back through the soil.

alone. I manufactured
isolation and found you – and that place
is nothing, less.
For it be
the world of one mind,
we were deceived.

dark sky, cold earth
how you came as such
whispering
the words
of an epitaph still bleeding
within the asylum walls.
Speaking
in a garbled tongue
only one man understands.

this is the place where you came to your end
where our spent worlds turn out
into darkness.

Brother the set paths – the world they have forced
destroyed you.

By this way, how so little
is needed of life, how such demands, to receive life in all seasons
to issue love, so simply and freely

are ordered within themselves.
and yet are betrayed, and counterfeited, and all gestures
are received
only to be abandoned, reverberating

within the skull.
 – And so have shuffled through postures, and cried to be free.
Have lined shotgun
barrel to chest, sounded such
fury
in an instant; your life, mine, standing by you

buried and above you:
I am of these worlds, others, and create my own,
dependant:
                    (And write no epitaph, lay seed).

ANIA WALWICZ

Little Red Riding Hood

I always had such a good time, good time, good time girl. Each and every day from morning to night. Each and every twenty-four hours I wanted to wake up, wake up. I was so lively, so livewire tense, such a highly pitched little. I was red, so red so red. I was a tomato. I was on the lookout for the wolf. Want some sweeties, mister? I bought a red dress myself. I bought the wolf. Want some sweeties, mister? I bought a red dress for myself. I bought a hood for myself. Get me a hood. I bought a knife.

Daredevil

I tried this play one day. My father leaves his medicines open. I take a random bottle. I swig. I'm done for. Walk around so proud to have done something big. I'm John Dare. I'm a devil. I'm Evel Knievel that jumped over twenty buses. On his motorcycle. I'm not scared. Life's good and sharp. Here for the last time I'm not bored. I'm seven and I've read every book in the world. I know everything. I'm an electric girl. World's my oyster. I'm its pearl.

The Tattoo

Beating the drum. I follow the boy with a snake on his arm. This dragon on his back. He is a painted one. I follow this boy with the dragon. He has a heart with a dagger in it. I follow this boy with a heart, with his knife. I follow him around. He has a spiderweb on his leg, a rose on his wrist. I follow him. Can't keep my eyes off him. Can't. I can't stop. Can not. It's written in the cards with the ten of hearts. I follow him. This snake on his arm curling around. Sneaky, sneaky snake. I follow this snake. I try to grab its tail so it won't bite. I follow him. I follow this dragon. Ten miles long. Smelling of fear. But it doesn't matter. Breathing these flames. I follow him. This big red heart, this beating pump. That I can feel his red heart going and gone. I follow him. This big steel knife. This hunter. I know how it feels to hold the handle. I follow him. This rose that opens up. I can remember her. I follow him. In the rose garden, in the park. This spider in his net has me all trapped. Has me all figured.

Big Tease

She's a big teaser. She took him half the way there. Only one half or a quarter, or even less. Than that. She wore these silk stockings. With a black line down the back. Snakeskin pumps. She's a pretty girl. The only thing she was ever good at. She. She didn't have any men friends. My mother flirts with the tailors. They drop their needles. They laugh with pink, distended faces. She's a big teaser. She's this big tease. Big. She knew what they were after. So she was going to give it to them. Notby a half or a quarter or even less. Not at all. You get some sneaky ways if you can't hit. And angry. He couldn't hardly wait. Broke a box, taking me home. Looked ridiculous. And in one big hurry. You can tell when someone just aims. I was talking to Bruce at an opening. Bruce doesn't like me. And he wants to. I'm talking to this Bruce at an opening. I'm talking. Bruce, this he, drinks this red wine. This claret in a cut glass. Hello Bruce I say and more. Bruce hates me. And he wants to. Bruce doesn't love me. Bruce swings his hand around with a full tumbler. Bruce gets too happy with himself. I watch the hand, the glass describe an arc, and spill the red on someone else's white trousers. I'm this big flirt who put a knife in this man's gut. Made him squirt.

The Abattoir

I owe my living to the abattoir. My father, the manager, sat in the office. Red brick, smelling of death. These dumb and frightened sheep that travelled at night. So I could eat them. Each stamp, clip in the office, smelled of slaughter. The purple, indelible pencil left a dot on the pink tongue tip. So very extra mauve like mark. Number or tattoo. Counted the stamp marks on the flesh pink, alive yesterday. And killed. These white paper sheets all written neatly and typed. These tiny pencil marks spelled the ending. The glazed, dumb eyes of the cows waiting. That I ate. That lived inside me. That I became. My vet dad, giving me needles. Like a pig. Earned money for my typewriter in the abattoir. Killing thousands of sheep and eating them all and every one. The blood seeping through the oil paper, these presents he got me. This meat. Red steaks I'd put in my hand. Lovely ladies, each one. Put my hand in the mince. Flesh squelching inside my fist. That's me. In here. Pink and gushing. One little scratch. And I'm one pig. Pigs at the cattle market. Pinks in the abattoir. My father, the artificial inseminator of cows, sits at his desk and kills. With his purple pencil. These healthy butchers. Very happy. Slicing away. Their stomachs taut. Looked at them, excited with their knives. The butcher at home, bending wire in his singlet. I had a cook. Had cooks. Never had the butcher. This butcher cut a piece. Put red meat in his raw mouth. My father stood next to the cow. The pig squealed. The healthy, young, beautiful butchers sang in their silver room. Hosed the floor. Sunshine in their mirrors. Lights in their glass. Glistening pink flesh on their plate. Sausages in my hand. Warm butcher's hands on my breasts.

Wonderful

tips waves up big dipper fires
wings lift me up roll out entry for prince of shiny press into me
furbelows bows on tip toes cartwheels in lovely head lamp glower put
on her dots dot in dot dotter dot dottie lain in finer blades naps cherubs
i'm all wreathed in tulle tulle skirts fly up thighs tight wrap in tunnel
of love need a belt please a chord bang in big peaks up top plaits comes
along so fast to me on my lay press with holds but not against me
at all let flow engaged embraced in carriage of gold to weddings of
mine in ornate halls i'm bride bridely a merry mary she shouts in van
makes me happy prince aloise la belle cadix i'm on my way to become
somebody else relay to longest i'm fiancée of person parson ardent
emperor wilhelm potsdam jesa jesus in yearn honeymoons caress one
doesn't know who one has touch glory goddess of shining gold i can
change places with any move through all orchid pearls arias top speed
epic lushy lush ermines bares my breasts swell forth in my stream of
pours from her in heady welcomen adored faithful prays and pardons
my empress of roses mayerling pulses gives me so much to walk on
flames at top powers it's a telling who says this to me i am given just
let it flow me on ways of does in my furry slipper on ledge sewn arbours
tear my walls for windows build my big spires in my ideal palace in
my breath force i give myself up to my open perfect flow lava wonders
we do every for you a promise on laughey spiky longtimes come on
verge edge urge tingle pops tingles popsy arrow in heal me heart in
my up swing planes upper flyer meet in powder puff rallies plunge
on edge hoppity beam charger from bowsers torch head glory wee wah
glider in air on light beaker mount height am whacko nipper lots
storage steep wheels carousel moves my husbands all flavours in my
roller rinks always young and hairless beloved tilt slides ride scaredy
hop chickens little seats move too fast time flies me go through hoops
sock a bunny buy for my suck pucker tutu girls arc de triomphe on
my prick finger on seventh hour all you pretty hotsie totsie heady rush
up flyer turn head star mary lou my naughtie gizzard racer sweetie
in flannels my biddy buy me buckles hang doily on railings cut into
toppers on gilt edge on my gold plates in my little chairs in flounces
opens my baskets for some don't know what yet but a sure thing toy
clutchey in lea hollow dale dream home beam shiny see a pretty whistle
thistles in boxes fizzy head we'll do most i'll best tie string on laughey
find me a come i'm real queen bow boo tizzy whizzy peaky lovey dovey

peck a dearie rides in main tickles pull up she's on high rip tear me all up lips lucky go far over turn curvy rips seam makes furry balls bounce this is best fluffy pull crisp choco barrel bash what have you got i buy dusky clinger on jiggle dizzy whirl squeeze mincer mince grinds thick slice cutter we go sing cars she jollies wash machine churns my hair clean floater in upsy hothouse with i dine with shah rajah minister of foreign hap ho it's a begin to dream delicious on bites bit o wets swallows long noodles make nest do funs i'm ever have jam petals roses ethel musk spin o bushy on heady clouds thighs pull up tights slicky tapper one hellova fires to wheels churn chopper wispy slides in wades go way greedy marvel burns my in my big flames inflame big fires break out seek a deep little birds sing a ooo let go a teem my little forman of great giddy giddies leap loops alupka aknolinsk my rich regoniff snake trumpet curves there's pinch to bam charge self with wings keep on fires hope a whole spinney dig a hole to in fly man snakes gold nib with thick leap splash darts forth flames a wild swoop shoot shoots sharp knife stalk dagger fish swath curls and ribbons narrow band necklace edmond janvier laure alida drape diaphanous drapes lili pierre fantastiche a torrent take all for my own hare unheimlich uncanny guide hands vibrate dazzling pointsman points arose raw hollow of her neck cowls funnel vase fang strand spiral hale file strike log shore gang my hand obeys bright beads to make my well sifter owner of great flows am impelled guide by force scoop my innerest give into make towers tall spiky do big bigs hoops climbs open siren a rare swing swings me up be my on top make on whirly top spinner flashy every ease in my long thin mirror pulls me to longest wants a every dot lit leaper leap leaps now jump on sharp corners jolt jolts grips me ride on this very yum yum yum oh in on shine look a well upsy go great on fast hopes ho ha ho oo ah on ups shoots pumper pumps romps on upsy my charge commandos my meant for ways on touch pull up backer lounger plunge yahoo rash rush heave ho ah in lift skipper stirrer gushers let out lean on let flow hits i'm maker fed on in oodley baby bounce birds shirtly shortly mary lou juice up feel a coming round corner every come true flow veins fire swings me rightupsy sashay sends me in wonder parks of eagle pounce drums tell fly out heady taut on press mover known all around star strikes flames lobster champ born to bloodbest days i'm happy fire does throats dance in veins giddy up speedstar when you make it on my roller coaster shore winner quiver sleeks a promise in tickey tocks searchlights find my pummel cutter bouncy feel a come on quicks on pourer top powers feel want to break windows feels like hit ball big skies put bounce rod on top joy stick rides on blooms put out gold string from my button belly pulls my can't resist i find all i want shine night climbs up my big chimneys on my lay on on in my open lush in my all of all in my paradise

ROBERT HARRIS

The Call

Still, I lay awake in the dark . . .
I thought pretty lusts had some ugly results
and that the world's bright trash was occult.

And carnage steals us from the eye of summer,
we cannot explain; but sometimes
the cockatoos are upset,
the flock miss one of their number.

And still I lay awake in the dark,
that was where I would have to fall –
out there somewhere in consequences,

in a desert become too hostile for survival;
if by weapons, disease, or auto design,
a cipher subjected to die for enormous grudges.

A cigarette answered that I was alive
though it seemed I had waited for centuries
becoming sure that the dark itself was active.

I was counting too a propensity to misfortune
back to great-grandfather's funny ways.
He worshipped a spurious architect of nothing

and walked on his hands on ordinary Sundays.
But He who drained the cup once for all
and did so under hell's lowest stair,

Christ, called me through from the other side of lightning.
Now I would seek out a comelier praise;
then I felt like one in a room of crimes

as the blind rattles up, and the light crashes in.

The Ambition

Mum, I'll be a fireman!
Did you know they gross around nineteen thousand,
work four days in nine,
quit, if they ever quit, in good faith

& moonlight driving meat trucks?
Aged people sometimes wander in
to look at the fire station,
saying they used to live here,

at this number. They look a long time
at the appliances, till the head shaking
Chief rings the nursing home.

When you're old I'll be a fireman, Mum.
At green upper storey sills, waiting for fires,
I'll lean on my blue arm and look at the sulphurous city.

'Literary Excellence'

finds a tree of unrecorded species
by mule trek
in a rarely trodden valley,
involves peculiar grammars & arts,

then
nets, guns, clubs,
a young goat tethered by a spring
and beaters.
ah, nineteenth century rooms!
ooh, walnut panelling, maps!

and foul water in lost cities
crowned by glowing minarets
before explorers
stagger in wilderness.

years later
in an inglenook
they spill weak tea on themselves and roar,
they pound skinny knees
if it's mentioned.

Riding Over Belmore Park

Riding across the town in a dirty carriage
to read at the library Modern Jewish Poets
I thought of last war's troops in rain at Central,
then the junkies of a decade ago. Men younger

than I am have died for allowing moonlight
to rest on a button. A few have followed
by serum hep., some went ga-ga tripping
& stayed that way, but none of this happened often.

Enough to sense empty chairs on rare occasion,
enough to long for McAuley's baroque sarcasm
to flay alike counsel to rebel, and the nuclear lobby.

What do the Jewish Moderns say
to someone as well dressed as I am?
The vile rooms are not far. I survived them.

PHILIP MEAD

There

Everything was happening for the first time. As we travelled through morning sun and bright tree-shadow flickering like a film. The invitation said noon and the place was easy to find. Birdsong and early light seemed to be leading us there. Where the avenue swung off in a broad arc, like the sweep of generations. The tyres stopping on the gravel drive. The french windows opening with exquisite feminine taste. The curtains like summer dresses and the bare arms.

But that is not the way things happened. We were swerving round the corner, slowing into evening, falling like a healing gauze. The night came, but it came imperceptibly, from behind banked hedges and threading through trees. We were faced with the darkness, falling in the heavy folded drapes of sleep. This was the night and it was much later. At the crossroads there was light but no sign, and the invitation had never arrived in the mail. Like everything, the road was taking us away and down to the house we saw, as the purpose of the night was nowhere sure; and at this darkest point there is fear like the other times. This is not the house we saw from the road.

Melbourne or the Bush

Wouldn't it be great to get away?
From all this I mean. Although the way things are at the moment
it doesn't really look as though we'll be able to.
But perhaps next weekend things will be different,
if there's a high over the Bight
we could take a few days and drive up to the farm.
When it will not be, that Time our troubler is?

We could wake up to the sound of the butcher-bird
splashing about in the runoff from the gutter,
his long, intricate phrases taking up where the rain left off.
In a dank Spring, see how all those yellow soursobs have swept up
    the hill?
If we're really lucky a satin bowerbird
might fly onto the chamfered window ledge and peer in at us
with his violet eyes. Look (half breathless, a hand
not knowing exactly where to find you).
Or we could take the dogs and go for a walk down to the dam
and they can pretend they're sitting for nineteenth-century hunting
    prints.
The clouds closing in then breaking open by mid-morning.

In the afternoon we can lie around on the bed
and browse through the few old books lying around up there:
How to Plant a Native Garden or *The Poetical Works of Matthew
    Arnold*,
its marbled endpapers, each page nearly as thick as a mortgage.
With its tooled leather covers and spine
it might have been bagged on the Serengeti.
Without the slightest urge to read them through.
(I'm not going to take any work are you?)

The screen door might bang shut once or twice
but the unendurable sun is a long way off
through cool rooms and green climbers.
In any case, Bruce and Bronwyn said they might come up later,
because we're a little unsure of too much solitude,
or at least too much too soon and having to share it.
How much experience will it ever take for us to realise?

And the evening, later, drawing us towards it as it withdraws.
We will remember the night as someone
who put his arms softly about our shoulders
and said that life will be like this always. Always.
That now we can let go of that persistent desire
to be at the end of distances, of days.
That none of this, none of this needs to be understood.

Cinema Point

It's been a long day's drive through a landscape
That would mean so much less without you,
But now the road is beginning to slow down,
Dragging our headlights into the cliff-side, turning
Into the opposite of what it has been, a headlong story.
No longer *go where you wanna go, be what you wanna be*
But tardigrade before the night ahead. Way across Eastern View
The Aireys lighthouse has already taken up its
Heavy responsibilities – stalwart fellow!
While further on Roadknight must be curling perfectly
Into the dark like a broken question mark. A ribbon of curving
Ocean road and a lighthouse are haunting in their shape and colour,
But somehow they suggest urgency, destination, heart's desire.
Is it possible our lives could have only surfaces and distances
But no structures, like postcards or the sea?
Behind us the day is reeling slowly backwards along
Shipwreck coast, first an early sunset of high grey washes
And upholstered cloud cover, with lower down, rolls
Of peruked cumulus backlit with pink
Then white shafts of noonday light down through the
Sea gardens of Thunder Cave, then blue, then fugitive blue.

KEVIN HART

The Last Day

When the last day comes
a ploughman in Europe will look over his shoulder
and see the hard furrows of earth
finally behind him, he will watch his shadow
run back into his spine.

It will be morning
for the first time, and the long night
will be seen for what it is,
a black flag trembling in the sunlight.
On the last day

our stories will be rewritten
each from the end,
and each will end the same;
you will hear the fields and rivers clap
and under the trees

old bones
will cover themselves with flesh;
spears, bullets, will pluck themselves
from wounds already healed,
women will clasp their sons as men

and men will look
into their palms and find them empty;
there will be time
for us to say the right things at last,
to look into our enemy's face

and see ourselves,
forgiven now, before the books flower in flames,
the mirrors return our faces,
and everything is stripped from us,
even our names.

The Story

Enter the story here: their battle lost
and foreign soldiers digging as rain falls
or doodles on truck windscreens half the night.

The nearby town hangs weightless from the moon;
its Church's shadow gulps a street, its priest
still looks for God as through a telescope.

Or here: while girls in frothing dresses spin
across the room, caught in the music's arms.
– A year before or after, hard to say.

The border bathes within a river, hangs
between two trees, straight as a bullet's path.
Now watch the hero carefully growing up:

he holds his future as the air holds light,
he dips a pen into his mind and writes.
While dreams italicise his hopes and fears

he sews his name into his country's flag.
And see him here, at forty, at his peak,
the future closer now, but flat and strange

like favourite clothes pegged tight upon a line.
The border must be moved, he tells his men,
it must be pushed right out to meet the sea.

He hammers them into uniforms and guns.
He threads a needle with unravelling thread.
The day begins on time. It knows that much.

Day arches its back, and thunderclouds appear;
a wind goes bragging round dark cornered rooms,
their curtains bulging with the coming change.

DOROTHY PORTER

Lollies Noir

And the telephone comes to mean
    something awesome to us
just like
       those taut stale symbols
          in horror films –

in a kind of heavy-strings suspense
      I ring you
and my heart *hurts*
      as if it were thrilling
          to a beautiful clichéd wound –

I want you
      to creep up on me;
to jam my Sunday School's party line
      with heavy breathing –

and it's that psychopathic step
      on the stair
that makes me sober
      makes me aware –

in *naked terror*
      there's a blurb of stillness
transcending
      bad acting
      cheap sets
      lukewarm love

there's waiting for death
there's shooting someone in the head
there's taking you
      cruelly

by the spines
to find out
what you really said –

but it's the dream
of you
in a black ballet
that really turns me on –

that little *c'est impossible, ma chérie* –

Cobra Lake!

P.M.T.

The moon is out this morning.
Full,
and the yellow
of old dentures.
Nothing like a moon
in a fastidious T'ang poem
it stares through
the mist, the traffic, my windscreen,
like a mesmerising chilblain.

The radio is a box of 'Fantales';
gossip, rubbish
and caramel.
I chew on it
thinking about
my long weekend
my lover's delectable mouth.
But the moonlight
splashes on my driving hands
like freezing water
and I count my jerky heart-beats
backwards.

PETER ROSE

Terminus

The whorl inside my head buzzes,
this cog which no one can replicate.
Somewhere you lie dying,
given till midnight.
You fell down on a tram,
blacked out between terminals,
fit, bright, twenty-one.
Puccini gave Manon an aria
but it hardly seems to matter much.
No doubt they shrank
from your devastating touch,
ricking their necks
in an effort not to look,
just as I, unable to fathom
this ruin, this mystery,
this topical egg,
pause for a moment
before going on with
my reread novel, my *TLS*.

Anglo-Saxon Comedy

Here on Mondays, after the
snaking exodus of toupeed Croesus
and his pompadoured brides
(sullen dance of four-wheel drives),
I have the beach to myself,
except for crazy kelpies,
madly fetching bits of ti-tree
as I toss them in the sea,
a solitary transcendental Japanese,
pertly tattooed by a Mesmer,
the superannuated bank manager
circumnavigating the island
in paisley shorts, and so slowly,
balancing on his Father's Day wind-surfer
like a stroke victim on his frame.
Then a British couple appears,
dressed appropriately for soccer,
even scarved, and vaguely amused
by my compound in the dunes:
grapes, books, dogs, lotions, wind-break.
Had I been quicker I would have
explained that my love went back
to the city last night, how we laughed
as we lay in our last embrace,
some farce about being a working man.
But before I could frame my apology
their Lancashire vowels had dissolved,
confronted with the wonder of . . . Sand . . .
and the new tide yielded a pair
of jazzy sunglasses, turning
everything a vulgar, chancier blue.

The Wind Debates Asian Immigration

Skipping along the footpath
two Asian brothers chatter
on their way to school,
witty, laden, immaculate,
grinning at the possum
splayed on the bitumen,
entrails cemented
by the morning traffic.
Near the junction both
are startled by a tabloid
smacking in the wind,
vortical riot of opinion
choreographed by idiots.

S. K. KELEN

Rabbit Shoeshine

He starts a landslide shooting a
defenceless bear. 'It is impossible
for the redman to perceive honour
as we know it.' But in the wilderness
forced to hunt and scurry for berries
the light moment holds until we cross
that river when we can be enemies again.
Yellow hair is a fool! Fighting
slavery fills you with truth. Incredible
dogs run yapping from the Indian camp,
Custer swims across the river.

The First Circle

A sky of churning cogs and work without weekends
she wears a parramatta into volume 2 of the inferno.

Which circle is this? The one with bad Popes
inverted in buckets of piss by brigadiers who have to drink it

and there's tennis but no net,
Gleneagles and not a ball to be found.

Stockbrokers snort fake cocaine in the lunch hour
while commuters wait for a train forever.

The yellow press can find no fault
but lucky stokers get to shovel coal for eternity

The way out of sin goes through thunder
& lightning factories. Indeed, a veritable hive

of industry, reading books backwards
diving into an all-night movie show.

The Gods Ash Their Cigarettes

Death stepped out of the television
just long enough to catch us off guard
and we mill around a crematorium's lawns.
'I saw her on Friday, now she's gone.'
The women cry and hug men shuddering
at the taste of ashes.
A smile between friends: it could
have been you and me last summer in the accident.
We were suitably dressed, even the sky was grey.
We, bull ants, terrified of sadistic feet
on a footpath curse the gods
look in the other's eyes then look beyond
to the feet. The keepers of the place tell us
to hurry along make space for the incoming cars.
They can't care, it's a living to them.
Our thoughts turn against the black-hearted bastards.
We kick the backs of each other's shoes
and hands in pockets, shuffle back to our cars.
Suddenly her blonde hair, her face.

JUDITH BEVERIDGE

The Domesticity of Giraffes

She languorously swings her tongue
like a black leather strap as she chews
and endlessly licks the wire for salt
blown in from the harbour.
Bruised-apple eyed she ruminates
towards the tall buildings
she mistakes for a herd:
her gaze has the loneliness of smoke.

I think of her graceful on her plain –
one long-legged mile after another.
I see her head framed in a leafy bonnet
or balloon-bobbing in trees.
Her hide's a paved garden of orange
against wild bush. In the distance, running
she could be a big slim bird just before flight.

Here, a wire-cripple –
legs stark as telegraph poles
miles from anywhere.
She circles the pen, licks the wire,
mimics a gum-chewing audience
in the stained underwear of her hide.
This shy Miss Marigold rolls out her tongue

like the neck of a dying bird.
I offer her the fresh salt of my hand
and her tongue rolls over it
in sensual agony, as it must

over the wire, hour after bitter hour.
Now, the bull indolently
lets down his penis like a pink gladiolus
drenching the concrete.

She thrusts her tongue under his rich stream
to get moisture for her thousandth chew.

In the Park

Sitting on the grass
in the park – thinking about
what's going by, about
the pinks and plenary reds

of today's sunset.
Insects rampant as ions
off charged wires nipping,
tingling my legs.

Those buildings are like
bottles of scent fragile
in their lemon spray
mist and cologne light.

The harbour's becoming
dark against the chromocosm
of the moon adrift
under the stars.

A gull squeaks – it's
the sound of a pin
piercing polystyrene – it
carries out to the yachtmasts

moving mechanically
as wiper-bars, out to
the Opera House a cluster
of starched serviettes.

Now, out to the suburbs,
those racks and racks
of tinted light
rising behind the trees.

Dining Out

(after Gilbert Sorrentino)
for Chris

Cochineals and fig colours ripple
into the bedroom. A breeze gets up
from the deckchair of a yacht.
The light's all marshmallow and angel food.
In this moment that is precise
for tasting, we watch the night come on.
You kiss me, drug my taste buds
and the room swirls like the hundred dishes
in a revolving restaurant and we're not here
we're there, at the Summit! where your eyes
rarefy into clear tea, or maybe
maple soup, or Spanish brandy
picayunes and roasted burritos
and, darling, I think I'm getting drunk.
Do enzymes work like contraceptives
I ask as my senses fall mellifluously
as brocade over the foyer
as we're about to hit the fresh air,
stepping over the possibility of tomorrow
as just so much spilt milk. And now,
under the last goose's egg of light
I crave that my heart will brace,
stay clear, unfurred,
know what you are: pure precise taste
of lemonade in the dark field of the fair.

GIG RYAN

In the Purple Bar

She spreads her pale legs
out across the table
and the beer
while he, the last car accident
red and tight across his eyes,
sucks her off, ungracefully.
But is she happy?

The hotel continues,
those expensive drinks. You were late.

He's playing Billie Holiday
unshaven, but careful.
Let's get things straight.
He buys you a cheap gin
and you want / want / want

How resilient you are.

She kisses the man, his mouth smells
of another woman's cunt.
But nothing gets to you.

How well we cope.

Cruising

I dreamt I drank too much lemonade
and it was fatal. Everybody pointed and ran.
The man came into my room in his office clothes.
Go away I said, and I jumped out of my skin.

In the Italian café, I think of the wealthy.
What helicopter must have sunk into the roof
to be used so precariously by the management,
or contrived. (It's common *now*)
I stare at the propeller, it shudders like a failure.
Who can eat under that?

You can see from the street they've added another storey.
The pilot's capsule's been renovated, hired out
for secret occasions, furtive and giddy, so secret
we never heard. I'd find it claustrophobic
and ruin my clothes. (After the bill gets drenched,
the waiter takes it to dry in a microwave oven)
A friend told me it's been rigged without gravity,
looking red and expensive. His mouth sloped down,
about to reveal something xenophobic. I had to leave.

Is there a word which means 'fear of things falling on you'?
I wake up and look at the split in my ceiling.
I jump out of my skin again, glad that I smoke,
glad that I can become historical and calm at the same time,
thinking of how non-smokers taste when you kiss them,
pink and wet and physical like a baby.

If I Had a Gun

I'd shoot the man who pulled up slowly in his hot car this morning
I'd shoot the man who whistled from his balcony
I'd shoot the man with things dangling over his creepy chest
in the park when I was contemplating the universe

I'd shoot the man who can't look me in the eye
who stares at my boobs when we're talking
who rips me off in the milk-bar and smiles his wet purple smile
who comments on my clothes. I'm not a fucking painting
that needs to be told what it looks like.
who tells me where to put my hands, who wrenches me into
    position
like a meccano-set, who drags you round like a war
I'd shoot the man who couldn't live without me
I'd shoot the man who thinks it's his turn to be pretty
flashing his skin passively like something I've got
to step into, the man who says *John's a chemistry PhD*
and an ace cricketer, Jane's got rotten legs
who thinks I'm wearing perfume for him
who says *Baby you can really drive* like it's so complicated,
male, his fucking highway, who says *ah but you're like that*
and pats you on the head, who kisses you at the party because
everybody does it, who shoves it up like a nail
I'd shoot the man who can't look after himself
who comes to me for wisdom
who's witty with his mates about heavy things
that wouldn't interest you, who keeps a little time
to be human and tells me, female, his ridiculous
private thoughts. Who sits up in his moderate bed
and says *Was that good* like a menu
who hangs onto you sloppy and thick as a carpet
I'd shoot the man last night who said *Smile honey*
don't look so glum with money swearing from his jacket
and a 3-course meal he prods lazily
who tells me his problems: his girlfriend, his mother,
his wife, his daughter, his sister, his lover
because women will listen to that sort of rubbish
Women are full of compassion and have soft soggy hearts
you can throw up in and no one'll notice
and they won't complain. I'd shoot the man
who thinks he can look like an excavation-site
but you can't, who thinks what you look like's for him
to appraise, to sit back, to talk his intelligent way.
I've got eyes in my fucking head. who thinks if he's smart
he'll get it in. I'd shoot the man who said
Andrew's dedicated and works hard, Julia's ruthlessly ambitious
who says *I'll introduce you to the ones who know*

with their inert alcoholic eyes
that'll get by, sad, savage, and civilised
who say *you can* like there's a law against it
I'd shoot the man who goes stupid
in his puny abstract how-could-I-refuse-she-needed-me
taking her tatty head in his neutral arms like a pope
I'd shoot the man who pulled up at the lights
who rolled his face articulate as an asylum
and revved the engine, who says *you're paranoid*
with his educated born-to-it calm
who's standing there wasted as a rifle
and explains the world to me. I'd shoot the man who says
Relax honey come and kiss my valium-mouth blue.

Ode to My Car

At least the mechanics are honest.
My poor car, baby, you should be in England,
not here, withering. Though in the sun you can still,
not shine quite, but glow from within like a higher state.
Thin wheel of mine, last forever.
Or is that cliff immortal?

Orbit

What's happened to your beautiful dress
Your haircut disappearing in its concept
Without these things, you're a mess
I mean, the blind walls, the phoney dinner
Don't die on me I used to think you were perfect
And now in the ruined careful conversation

you're just a ghost and your eyes
carry the same green texture from glass to life to table
the same stare with a see-through word in front of it
fizzling like the cone between a film and its projection
Don't you realise I haven't slept for thirty-eight hours
and my face feels like a tight dress
and the room is meaningless and shatters with it
Calm with danger chipping out your 'soul', you thought
     lost,
your last love walking like a moon
and into the late kitchen.

Elegy for 6 So Far

Loneliness comes out of his mattress face
Reading, a nervous habit, a guest, a wig
He looks at his friend in the coffin
for the last time
His face pretty, subversive
His guns of death a whore

. . .

He moves in front of me like a pilot
singing out his high and low
Vine of holiness, his face
like a cathedral corner, complicated, beautiful,
who influenced a generation with moodiness

. . .

His black and white head nods into my arms
when we play. You make a monster
when you kick and sing like a president
as if I can't help
crying. Rocks.
his cube, his cutting head

. . .

Speed loads my head's jamming magazine
with cylinders of mercury
A game. 5 die out of restlessness
out of restlessness his blue slipping hair
the pointed metal drug
We shot

. . .

ANTHONY LAWRENCE

Robert Penn Warren's Book

Robert Penn Warren's book
smells like wet diggings.
I open it and slaters spill
like grey water over my hands;
leaves stick to my fingers.

Having been lifted from recent
delvings into the layered past,
the poems are damp and heavy:
here a rotting beam; here a mattress,
its springs exposed;
here a bottle with its trapped marble
like clamorous language
in the throat of all discarded things.

The book is falling apart
in my hands; the pages go to mud.
The contents page has become a stack
of peat bricks, cut from an acre of bog
and left to dry on the Galtee Road.
I put flame to some of them,
and sit back to read in their light
with The Chieftains on the stereo
and whiskey burning my tongue.

I know nothing of Robert Penn Warren –
the poems refuse me his history.
And yet, sometimes I see him climbing
through headland trees, a purple flower
exploding in his hair.
Sometimes I hear him moaning:
Oh warden, keep that morphine moving.

But it's the smell of his work
that keeps me here, fingering through
the poetry of decay; the poetry
of turned earth and all that issues forth
from its black incarnation.

ARCHIE WELLER

The Story of Frankie . . . My Man

My man, Willard Franklin 'The Bunny' Goodjarrah;
well, he dreams about holding up an armoured car
like his heroes on the flickering TV screen.
But, honestly, he can't even hold up his pride –
or hold his drink neither.
He's given me five years of worry . . . and two kids
and a wicked big scar that cuts across my head.
But I still love that man.
Yes, I feel sorry for my drunken winyarn man.
He never ever wins but still he tries so hard
like a marron that wriggles in an iron trap
always going backwards.
and he makes me laugh when he does the emu dance
he saw once on TV.
He can make you laugh with the stories he will tell
about the wadgulas who try to put him down.
But when his eyes mist over in doubt I could cry
and when that misery shakes his skinny body
I wish I was a cloud to hold him in soft hands
and carry him away.
Hey!! What did *I* ever do wrong? he shouts,
    my man.
One day, you just see, One day I'll be free,
    he says.
One fuckin' day I'll be chief again, no worries,
like my ancestor Munday was, so long ago.
Leader of his people. In his land. On these streets,
fishing from lakes now buried by whiteman's concrete.
Yeah, doll, you want a loverly house of our own?
Best house money can buy.
With a pretty garden too – full of flowers and trees,
like the wild flowers and trees of our destroyed land.
And you can yarn to the neighbours – as good as them –
in your fine house I'll buy.

Then his mates come round – ravaged faces, damaged souls –
with sweet red wine and lucky cards and pretty girls.
Angry words kindle the fire in his restless soul.
A fight tonight . . . I know.
All the shabby warriors fight among themselves
while the white city, with all its white ways, rears back
in disgusted motions.
They know him in the pubs and parks and police cells;
at the race track and in the dole office as well.
There are times when he can hold me so gently
and his body will dance a love dance quiet as dawn.
His eyes will clear from the drink and despair of life
and his deep, hoarse, rusty voice will sing me of his love
. . . I always believe him.
He might go wandering down bush in hot Summer
and, once, he got a job fencing in cold Winter.
It nearly killed him too!!
Why, he come home spluttering like an old wino
almost blue with the flu.
But the money he had was like a bag of pearls
and we could dream once more – him and me and the kids –
until his bludging family came around again.
But . . . he's good for nothing that skinny Goodjarrah.
He couldn't kick a football in a fit – or run.
All he can do is drink and that's no bloody fun.
Oh, yes, my man,
   Billy the kid . . .
      Bunny the boong
gave me a two-inch yellow scar across my head
for a Christmas present one year, when we was drunk.
He gave me two kids and some quiet words and good jokes
a bit of love
   a few laughs
      and that's about all.
Last week, when the wind howled outside our cracked window
and the night was as black as my man's boney bum;
when the moon and stars, thieves of cars . . . and ghosts were out
when the cold air and Bunny wrapped arms around me;
Munadj kicked in the front door and dragged him outside.

They pulled his uncombed hair and tore his dirty clothes.
They broke his sticklike body for firewood
and threw the remains in the van – like a mad dog.
He was only twenty.
   He got life for murder.
For killing a white boy who pushed his pride too far.

LIONEL FOGARTY

Remember Something Like This

Long ago a brown alighted story was told
As a boy, looked up on the hall walls
water flowed to his eyes
for Starlight was carrying snake in his shirt
gut belly
and around the fires a tall man
frightened the mobs that black eyes promised
that night at giant tree, way up
bushes crept in the ant hill
was the wild blackfella
from up north, they said.
Soldier cained him down at the waterhole
but as they bent to dip, sip
behind their backs, old man Waterflow
flew clear, magic
undoing the shackles, without keys
or sounds of saw
saw . . . nah . . . you didn't saw him.
He's old Waterflow, even I'm too young
to remember everything.
Yet clever than pictures them show off
making fun of old Boonah
sitting outside waiting for dreaming
to come to reality.
After that somebody broke into the store.
Oh, the police were everywhere
at every door, roof, in laws
Where's this and that, you know.
So they find out where him came from
by looking at the tracks.
He's headed for the caves

just near milky way.
Happy in strength, we took off
but the hills hid this tribal
bull-roaring feather foot
under Jimmys Scrub
place up deep
where you have to leave smoke
if you want to hunt there
If you don't, you'll get slewed . . .
On earth our people are happy
but we couldn't find that food.
Musta been up the Reservoir
or expecting a life to run over near Yellow Bar cave
    again.
But we bin told, one man got baldy porcupine.
Bring him home and not supposed to.
So him get sick, all life time
like green hands touch murri legs
that's why you don't swim too late
at this creek created.
A spoiled boy one afternoon, went repeating
the bell bird singing.
And he went and went
and sent to Green Swamp, back of the grid. .
Then as eels were caught
Aunties sang out, this the biggest
I've ever seen.
Come boys get more wood, we'll stay
here all night.
So sat waiting, a bit dark, tired light
the lines pulling in slowly
for fish seem to be in message
but two-headed creature appeared
legs chucked back
fires went out
the fish swam back
we raced home.
All cold that night, back of the bend
and rocks.
Just near the bunya tree you can see
this middle age woman, long black hair

walk past our Nana Rosies place
up to the graveyards
but she flows
and many a moons came shone in our minds
watching Dimmydum and Kingy doing corroboree
on stage
in front of the children.
A light story past thru windows
on to you all
never forget
remember more . . .

No Grudge

Let's radio opinions, koorie side effects in death
Commercial educationalists to draw
intwined listeners is what brother about.
Craze sensationalism they scraped
him individual
respective broadcasting.
The overstressed question was impartial
but we demand our radio persuasive
black free editors.
The reason advertising is koori airing
Sponsoring bulletins
informing is what this murri news attracts 'bout.
Don't bias, buy blocked broadcast
on susceptibility, around this murri
for capable brothers and sisters
combining a wave vital vital
to benefit all societies.
Yet we the penniless millionaires
imagine views saving
for time, income wanna infuses
discontent over rich people.

Our educationalist is the yubba
on the koori radio.
Nudge nudge human new one up-man-ship
run by himself.
But community be at each others throats
but we should consider advocating
a hurray wireless playing.
Blackfella media, not political
foot-balling loud-mouth, perturbed.
A happy-go-lucky re-echoing broadcaster
is one tribalism sparkling radio
disc-jockey we seem to criticise
100 psychological conditioning.
Let the yubba mass translate
a mouth communicating
Suppression, hot reply.

PHILIP HODGINS

Death Who

The conversation with cancer
begins equitably enough.
You and he are summing each other up,
trading ripostes and *bons mots*
before the soup.
Everything seems ordinary.
There is interest and boredom,
and you've been drinking all afternoon
which could mean that you're depressed
or that you're in good form.
You get each other's measure
and the conversation settles,
subjects divide and increase like cells.
Gradually you realise
that like the background Mozart
all the emotions are involved,
and that you're no longer saying as much.
Put it down to strength of intent.
He's getting aggressive
and you're getting tired. Someone
says he's a conversational bully
but you're fascinated.
He tells you things about yourself,
forgotten things and those not yet found out,
pieces from childhood and the unhealing wound.
It's all there.
Forgetting food, you drink (too much
red wine will encourage nightmares
but that's not a problem now), you marvel.
Isn't he tireless!
A raconteur like something out of Proust.

He blows cigar smoke into your face
and makes a little joke.
It's actually too much.
You're tired and the more you tire
the more the words are everywhere.
You go and recline on the couch,
but he won't shut up. He follows you there
and makes the cushions uncomfortable for you.
It's so unjust.
Your host is in the kitchen,
all the guests have gone
and cancer's got you like conviction
and he's kneeling on your chest,
glaring over you,
pushing a cushion into your face,
talking quietly and automatically,
the words not clear.
He's got you and he's really pushing,
pushing you to death.

Shooting the Dogs

There wasn't much else we could do
that final day on the farm.
We couldn't take them with us into town,
no one round the district needed them
and the new people had their own.
It was one of those things.

You sometimes hear of dogs
who know they're about to be put down
and who look up along the barrel of the rifle
into responsible eyes that never forget
that look and so on,
but our dogs didn't seem to have a clue.

They only stopped for a short while
to look at the Bedford stacked with furniture
not hay
and then cleared off towards the swamp,
plunging through the thick paspalum
noses up, like speedboats.

They weren't without their faults.
The young one liked to terrorise the chooks
and eat the eggs.
Whenever he started doing this
we'd let him have an egg full of chilli paste
and then the chooks would get some peace.

The old one's weakness was rolling in dead sheep.
Sometimes after this he'd sit outside
the kitchen window at dinner time.
The stink would hit us all at once
and we'd grimace like the young dog
discovering what was in the egg.

But basically they were pretty good.
They worked well and added life to the place.
I called them back enthusiastically
and got the old one as he bounded up
and then the young one as he shot off
for his life.

I buried them behind the tool shed.
It was one of the last things I did before
we left.
Each time the gravel slid off the shovel
it sounded like something
trying to hang on by its nails.

KATE LILLEY

You Have to Strike Back

Now that we move and we breathe apart
you cannot come into my house

Those traces of you I want to keep
are sealed in a wooden box

My fingers are knotted joint to joint
they cannot reach the latch

I've given up those tricks of the heart
alone but not incomplete

Still and loaded down with sleep
I lie with my body easy

Light up your album of beautiful sights
I hunt in my own room tonight

The Sewing Lesson

Assorted needles and coloured threads
    were laid across my desk at school.
I took them home to practise with

to the bunks in the red linoleum bedroom
    where me and Roe stay up all night
with magic radio and books.

Silver scissors cut the shapes
  from her new summer clothes, and then
I started to embroider them
  with every stitch I knew, until

Mum came in and belted me
  and that big man my father pushed
my head down in the bath so I
  would understand what money meant.

JOHN KINSELLA

Orpheus

his head appeared in the hand
of a beach-comber . . .

amongst the netting,
a gathering undetected

by the inspector
of illegal catchings,

they found the head of Orpheus
snow-white and out of place

amongst the stains
of a bark-dyed river,

brown and heavy with mullet.
they pondered its fate:

release it to drift
down to sea,

or dry in the smoking room
with the rest of the catch?

Chess Piece Cornered

Mice in the eaves, and breathe well my dear.
Breathe well my dear, mice in eaves in madhouse.
Breathe well in this   space
                          solitude,
                                    breath never
sweet breath, that lends me not
to the small persistent clutter of mice,
river long, and this, your breath
hard to find. Mice in their short breath
heard only at night. By the vent. By the pillow.

Sick Woman

Don't. Crow and butcher bird
   over garden
   over sand
   over me and sick woman.
Don't.
   Of sick woman, butcher bird
brings crow to ground, crow or
butcher bird fall, brought to ground
by sick woman. What is it we feel?
A draught, maybe as we catch
the falling crow or butcher bird
by sash of light, sash of window.
Sick woman, and me told I look
like a little yellow Valium pill,
rising to the scuffling crow,
butcher bird, sick woman.

INDEX

Abattoir, The 415
Abhorring a Vacuum 187
About this Woman: 209
Action Would Kill It / A Gamble 290
Adamson, Robert 290
Advice 271
Affair of the Heart 163
Age of Plastic, The 400
Air 366
Airliner 141
All-night Taxi Stand, The 6
Alphabet Murders, The 276
Ambition, The 420
Anchor, The 30
And No Help Came 169
And the World was Calm 190
Angels' Weather 149
Angina 49
Anglo-Saxon Comedy 431
Anguish of Ants, The 49
Anniversary 123
Anorexia 369
Around Costessey 140
Art 140
Ash Range, The 385
At Cooloola 62
Australia 16
Automobiles of the Asylum 211
Autumn Supper 119

Back Steps Lookout 321
Backyard 280
Baiame 48
Barn Owl see Father and Child 111
Baroque Exterior 93
Beach Burial 15
Beaver, Bruce 149
Because 82
Being Called For 101
Beveridge, Judith 435
Beyond Phigalia 25

Bicycle 193
Big Tease 414
Bits and Pieces, The see Opener 188
Blight, John 30
Blind Man, The 58
blkfern-jungal 407
Blue Horses, The 72
Blue Paisley Shirt, The 202
Bolton, Ken 389
Bora Ring 47
Boult to Marina 88
Broad Bean Sermon, The 218
Brother and Sisters 52
Brown, Pamela 356
Buckley, Vincent 126
Buckmaster, Charles 408
Bulahdelah-Taree Holiday Song Cycle,
   The 215
Bureau, and Later, The 134
Burns, Joanne 308

Caddy, Caroline 300
Café of Situations, The 326
Calenture, The 195
Call, The 419
Campbell, David 43
Camphor Laurel 54
Carnal Knowledge I 110
Casino 377
Cataldi, Lee 268
Change 65
'Changing Room' 328
Chess Piece Cornered 459
Child, The 53
Child is Revenant to the Man, The 131
Children Go, The 39
Choker's Lane 8
Cinema Point 424
City of Home, The 204
Clair de Lune 107
Classical Head, The 395

Clearing Away 249
Climbing 363
Cloak, The 79
Clockface 320
Clouds 140
Coda (to Colloquy with John Keats) 98
Collective Invention, The 185
Colloquy with John Keats 97
Conceptual Head, The 397
Consolation 116
Copy-writer's Dream, The 177
Corpus, Aileen 407
Couani, Anna 359
Country Dance *see* Blind Man 58
Couples 371
Crafty Butcher, The 374
Cruising 439
Culture as Exhibit 94
Cycle 272

Daredevil 413
Davis, Jack 67
Dawe, Bruce 172
Dawn Wail for the Dead 106
Day at a Time 351
Day 20 154
Death, an Ode 403
Death at Winson Green, A 137
Death of a Whale 31
Death of the Bird, The 19
Death Who 453
Debbie & Co. 281
Déjeuner sur l'Herbe 155
Demolisher 380
Desolation 68
Developing a Wife 248
Dialogue 75
Dining Out 437
Division of O'Dowd, The 345
Dobson, Rosemary 101
Documentary Film 90
Dog Fox Field 226
Dogs 388
Domesticity of Giraffes, The 435
door swung open . . ., The 36
Down from the Country 30
Dransfield, Michael 348
Dreaming Up Mother 298
Drifters 175
Drinking Sappho Brand Ouzo 326
Drugs of War, The 224

Drummer, The 156
Duggan, Laurie 383
Dürer: Innsbruck, 1495 86
Dusk, The 307

Easiest Room in Hell, The 166
Egyptian Register 95
Election Eve, with Cat 340
Elegist, The 245
Elegy for 6 So Far 442
Elegy for Drowned Children 172
Eli, Eli 55
Elise 344
Elm Tree in Paddington, An 299
End of the Picnic 137
End to Myth, An 408
Endsight 352
Envoi 71
Enzensberger at 'Exiles' 277
Epiderm 348
Epigrams of Martial, The 383
Equanimity 221

Fafnir 23
Falcon Drinking 118
Family Man, The 173
Father and Child 111
First-born, The 67
First Circle, The 433
Fitzroy 249
Five Bells 11
Fixed Ideas 3
Flames and Dangling Wire 305
Flight from Manhattan, The 220
Flower Poem 17
Flying 353
Fogarty, Lionel 449
Fool, The 35
For a Pastoral Family 64
For Two Children 194
Forbes, John 395
Forever the Snake 262
Foundations, The 368
Four Heads & How to do Them 395
Four Poems on a Theme 336
(Frank O'Hara) 150
Freedom Fighter 200
Front Window, The 259
Future 339

Garfish 32

Ghazal on Signs of Love and Occupation
405
Ginger-flowers 38
Glow-boys 282
Gnostic Prelude 71
Gods Ash their Cigarettes, The 434
Go on, tell me the season is over 341
Goethe and Brentano 251
Going 177
Going Down. With No Permanence 338
Gorey at the Biennale 327
Gould, Alan 380
Gray, Robert 304
Great Artist Reconsiders the Homeric
Simile, The 279
Green Side, The 369
Grudge, The 119
Gulls' Flight, The 256
Gum-trees Stripping 62
Gunner, The 133
Gutting the Salmon 298

Hammial, Philip 211
Hampton, Susan 373
Hands 48
Hard-luck Story 135
Harris, Robert 419
Harry 143
Harry, J.S. 231
Hart, Kevin 425
Hart-Smith, William 26
Harwood, Gwen 107
Having Completed My Fortieth Year 283
He Mailed the Letters Himself 332
Hearts (1983) 383
Heat 34
Helen Paints a Room (1984) 330
Hemensley, Kris 312
Here, under Pear-trees 45
Hero and the Hydra, The 76
Hewett, Dorothy 121
Hide and Seek 229
High Country 288
Hodgins, Philip 453
Hollow Thesaurus, The 252
Home, The Spare Room, The 297
Homecoming (by Bruce Dawe) 175
Homecoming (by Tim Thorne) 288
Homo Suburbiensis 176
Homosexual 145
Hope, A.D. 16

Hospital-Retrospections, The 41
Hospital Night 139
Hotel Marine 46
how 311
Hunting Rabbits 302
Hut, The 288

I Remember Dexedrine. 1970 356
If I Had a Gun 439
Imperial Adam 20
In a Late Hour 77
In Andrea's Garden 376
In Ferrara 390
In Memoriam (by Martin Johnston)
323
In Memoriam: Anthony Sandys
1806–1883 (by Francis Webb) 140
In the Gloaming 367
'In the New World Happiness is Allowed'
165
In the Park (by Gwen Harwood) 108
In the Park (by Judith Beveridge) 436
In the Purple Bar 438
In Transit: A Sonnet Square 326
Incident in Transylvania 253
Industrial City 199
In-flight Note 207
Inland 140
Inscription for a War 24
Inside of Paradise 336
Into the Ark 33
It's Easy 268
It's Natural 337

Jack Frost 181
James Dean 260
Jane 213
Jenkins, John and Bolton, Ken 390
Jennings, Kate 371
Jerry's Plains, 1848 246
Johnston, Martin 322
Jones, Rae Desmond 258
Journey: the North Coast 304
Judas Touch, The 192
Just after Michael's Death, the Game of
Pool 377
Just the Two of Us 371

Keep the Season 83
Kefala, Antigone 198
Kelen, S.K. 433

Killer, The 56
Kinsella, John 458
Ku-ring-gai Rock Carvings 47

Laid Off 134
Lament for the Country Soldiers 217
Landfall (by Randolph Stow) 196
Landfall, The (by John Blight) 31
Language 365
Last Day, The 425
Last of His Tribe 105
Last Trams 2
Late Night Radio 244
Late Winter 76
Lawrence, Anthony 444
Leaving 356
Legendary 78
Lehmann, Geoffrey 236
Letters to Live Poets 150
Lilley, Kate 456
'Literary Excellence' 420
Little Red Riding Hood 413
Lizards 47
Lollies Noir 428
Louvres 223
Love Affair 36 265
Love Notes 182
Love Poem 399
Lovers, The 47
Lufthansa 285

McAuley, James 71
McDonald, Roger 252
Mackenzie, Kenneth 34
McMaster, Rhyll 320
Mahogany Ship, The 206
Maiden, Jennifer 363
Mailing the Letters 333
'Malley, Ern' 86
Malouf, David 192
Man, a Woman, A 130
Man in the Honeysuckle, The 50
'Man is following me, A' 264
Map of the World, The 359
marble surfaces 309
Marshall-Stoneking, Billy 316
Max Factor Pink 255
Mead, Philip 422
Melbourne or the Bush 423
Memoirs of a Velvet Urinal 354
Men in Green 44

Mental Traveller's Landfall, The 185
Metho Drinker 57
Mid-Channel 113
Mile from Poetry, A 313
Minstrel 355
Mitchells, The 219
Moment of Waking, The 275
Mona Lisa Tea Towel, The 255
Monkey's Pride 400
More than 9 Lives 160
Morning Becomes Electric 178
Mother Who Gave Me Life 113
Mothers and Daughters 46
Mudrooroo 228
Murray, Les 215
My House 294
My Tenth Birthday 295

Nasturtium Scanned 210
Never-Dead, The 360
New 367
New Arrival 41
Nigger & Some Poofters, A 256
Night After Bushfire 55
Night Piece 90
Night-piece (Alternate Version) 92
Nightfall 109
Nightmarkets, The 342
Night-ride, The 10
No Grudge 451
No More Boomerang 104
Nocturne 85
Nonplussed 389
Note 115
Nub 187
Nullarbor 26
Nuremberg 1
Nu-plastik Fanfare Red 208

Observation Car 18
Observed Observer, The 381
Obvious, The 360
Ode to My Car 441
Odes and Days 154
Old Circles 262
Old Currawong 266
Old Friend 117
Old Prison, The 58
Old Timer 144
On the Death of Muriel Rukeyser 318
On the Death of Ronald Ryan 174

On This Day I Complete My Fortieth Year 161
One Day 273
One Hundred and Fifty Years 69
One Tuesday in Summer 81
Oodgeroo, of the tribe Noonuccal 103
Opener 188
Orbit 441
Origins 126
Orpheus 458
Out of Time 4

Page, Geoff 242
Palinode 91
Party, The 199
Passage 316
Passing Through Experiences 291
Peaches and Cream 229
Pelicans 63
Perspective Lovesong 93
Petit Guignol 212
Petit Testament 99
Picture Postcard 317
Pietà 77
Plato's Dog 329
P.M.T. 429
Pneumo-encephalograph 142
Poem Films Itself, The 234
Poet at Work 379
Port Phillip Night 133
Porter, Dorothy 428
Porter, Peter 161
Portrait of the Artist as an Old Man 348
Post Operative 203
Precipice, The 61
Private, The 296
Progressive Man's Indignation, A 115

Qantas Bags 388

Rabbit Shoeshine 433
Rankin, Jennifer 262
reading 310
Receiving the Letters 334
Released on Parole 80
Remember Something Like This 449
Renewal Notice 173
Return of an Ikon 117
Return of Persephone, The 22
revisionism 308
Riding Over Belmore Park 421

Rimbaud Having a Bath 296
River Bend 65
Road Show 242
Robert Penn Warren's Book 444
Roberts, Nigel 255
Rodriguez, Judith 206
Romantic Head, The 396
Rose, Peter 430
Roses 236
Ross's Poems 237
Ryan, Gig 438

Sadie 213
Salom, Philip 404
Scott, John A. 328
Sea Anemones, The 112
Sea-bundle 264
Sea-cucumber, The 322
Searchlights 37
Seed 411
Self-analysis 353
Seven Days of Creation, The 79
Seventh Day, The 79
Sewing Lesson, The 456
Sex and the Over Forties 163
Shadow of War, 1941 201
Shakti 258
Shapcott, Thomas 201
Shooting the Dogs 454
Shot of War, A 232
Sibyl 292
Sick Men Sleeping 37
Sick Woman 459
Silo Treading 157
Singing Bones, The 197
Skins 66
Skovron, Alex 340
Skrzynecki, Peter 302
Sleep 9
Slessor, Kenneth 1
Smalltown Memorials 242
Small-town Gladys 43
Song Cycle of Jacky, The 228
Song Thirty-Four 228
Sonnets for the Novachord 86
Sonnets to be Written from Prison 292
Sonnets to the Left 189
South Coast Haiku 388
South Country 11
Speed, a Pastoral 402
Spiny Ant-eaters 47

Spring 47
Starting from Central Station 48
Stone Dolphin, The 180
Story, The 426
Story of Frankie . . . My Man, The 446
Stow, Randolph 195
Strange Bird, A 354
Strauss, Jennifer 182
Stroke 127
Sulking in the Seventies 312
Summer Solstice 124
Sun 33
Sunday Visit 198
Sweet William 87
Sybilline 89
Sydney Highrise Variations, The 220
Sykes, Bobbi 272
Symbolist Head, The 396

Table-birds 40
Tale 265
Talking to You Afterwards 168
Taste 363
Tattoo, The 414
Taylor, Andrew 248
Tench, 1791 47
Terminus 430
Terri 342
That Which We Call a Rose 349
There 422
13 November 1983 270
This Version of Love 121
Thorne, Tim 287
Three-Inch Reflector 300
Three Fates, The 101
Three Found Poems 383
Three Songs of Love & Hate 180
Tin Wash Dish, The 225
Tip for Saturday, A 132
Tipping, Richard Kelly 377
To a Child 60
To my Brothers 64
To Myself 5
Tomb of Heracles, The 76
Towards the Land of the Composer 135
Town, The 141
Town on the Ten-Dollar Note, The 388
Tranter, John 275
Travelling to Gleis-Binario 251
Treason's Choice 212
Trunkful of Structures, A 336

Tsaloumas, Dimitris 115
Turning Fifty 202
T.V. 395
Typing the Letters 332

Un-American Women, The 278
Under Sedation 24
Up in Mabel's Room 7

Viidikas, Vicki 336
Visiting Hour (Repatriation Hospital) 350

Walking at Night 404
Walking, when the Lake of the Air is Blue with Spring 231
Wallace-Crabbe, Chris 184
Walwicz, Ania 413
War of the Roses, The 353
Ward Two 142
Warru 67
We are Going 103
Wearne, Alan 341
Webb, Francis 132
We Could Have Met 269
Weller, Archie 446
Wet Day 84
What a Man, What a Moon 359
Whatever Happened to Conway Twitty? 287
What I Have Written I Have Written 170
Wild Honey 147
William Street 9
Wilpena Pound 409
Wind Debates Asian Immigration, The 432
Windows, The 184
Winter Drive 85
Woman to Man 53
Women who Speak with Steak Knives 375
Wonderful 416
World on Sunday 84
Wright, Judith 52

You Gave Me Hyacinths First a Year Ago 122
You Have to Strike Back 456
Young Prince of Tyre 96
Yugoslav Story 373

Zwicky, Fay 180

ACKNOWLEDGEMENTS

For permission to reprint the poems in this anthology, acknowledgement is made to the following:

Robert Adamson: 'Action Would Kill It/A Gamble', 'Passing Through Experiences' from *The Rumour* (1971), Prism Books; 'Sibyl', Sonnets 1,2,3,6 from 'Sonnets to be Written From Prison' from *Swamp Riddles*, Island Press; 'My House', 'My Tenth Birthday', 'The Private' from *Where I Come From* (1979), Big Smoke Books; 'Rimbaud Having a Bath', 'The Home, The Spare Room' from *The Law at Heart's Desire* (1982), Prism Books; 'Gutting the Salmon', 'Dreaming up Mother', 'An Elm Tree in Paddington' from *The Clean Dark* (1989), Paperbark to the author.

Bruce Beaver: 'Angels' Weather', Letters I, XIX from 'Letters to Live Poets', Day 20 from 'Odes and Days', 'Déjeuner sur l'Herbe', 'The Drummer' from *Selected Poems* (1979) to Collins/Angus & Robertson Publishers; 'Silo Treading' from *New and Selected Poems 1960–90* (1991), 'More than 9 Lives' from *New and Selected Poems* to University of Queensland Press.

Judith Beveridge: 'The Domesticity of Giraffes', 'In the Park', 'Dining Out' from *The Domesticity of Giraffes* (1987) to Black Lightning Press.

John Blight: 'Down from the Country', 'The Anchor', 'The Landfall', 'Death of a Whale', 'Garfish', 'Into the Ark' from *Selected Poems 1939–75* (1976) to Collins/Angus & Robertson Publishers; 'Sun' from *Holiday Sea Sonnets* (1985) to University of Queensland Press.

Ken Bolton: 'Nonplussed' from *Blonde & French* (1978), Island Press to the author.

Pamela Brown: 'Leaving', 'I Remember Dexedrine, 1970' from *Selected Poems 1971–82* (1984) to Redress/Wild & Woolley.

Vincent Buckley: 'Origins', I,IV,V,VI,VII from 'Stroke' from *Selected Poems* (1981) to Collins/Angus & Robertson Publishers; 'A man, a woman', 'The Child is Revanant to the Man' from *Last Poems* to McPhee Gribble Publishers.

Charles Buckmaster: 'An End to Myth', 'Wilpena Pound', 'Seed' from *Collected Poems* edited by Simon Macdonald (1989) to University of Queensland Press.

Joanne Burns: 'revisionism', 'how' from *on a clear day* (1992), University of Queensland Press; 'marble surfaces' from *Ventriloquy* (1981), Sea Cruise Books; 'reading' from *blowing bubbles in the 7th lane* (1988), Fab Press to the author.

Caroline Caddy: 'Three-inch Reflector' from *Beach Plastic* (1989) to Fremantle Arts Centre Press.

David Campbell: 'Small-town Gladys', 'Men in Green', 'Here, under Pear-trees', 'Mothers and Daughters', 'Hotel Marine', The Lovers, Spring, Spiny Anteaters, Lizards, Bora Ring, Tench 1791, Hands, Baiame from 'Kur-ring-gai Rock Carvings', I, Starting from Central Station, IX, Angina from 'Starting from Central Station', 'The Anguish of Ants', 'The Man in the Honeysuckle' from *Collected Poems* (1989) to Collins/Angus & Robertson Publishers.

Lee Cataldi: 'It's Easy' from *Invitation to a Marxist Lesbian Party* (1978) to Wild & Woolley; 'We Could Have Met', '13 November 1983', 'Advice' from *The Women Who Live on the Ground* (1990) to Penguin Books Australia Ltd.

Aileen Corpus: 'blkfern-jungal' from *The Penguin Book of Australian Women Poets* (1986) to the author.

Anna Couani: 'What a Man, What a Moon' from *Italy* (1977), Rigmarole Books; 'The Map of the World', 'The Obvious', 'The Never-dead' from *The Train* (1983), Sea Cruise Books to the author.

Jack Davis: 'The First-born', 'Warru', 'Desolation' from *The First Born and Other Poems* (1970), Collins/Angus & Robertson Publishers to the author; 'One Hundred and Fifty Years' from *John Pat and Other Poems* (1988) to Houghton Mifflin Australia.

Bruce Dawe: 'Elegy for Drowned Children', 'The Family Man', 'Renewal Notice', 'On the Death of Ronald Ryan', 'Drifters', 'Homecoming', 'Homo Suburbiensis', 'The Copy-writer's Dream', 'Going', 'Morning Becomes Electric' from *Sometimes Gladness* (1988) to Longman Cheshire.

Rosemary Dobson: 'The Three Fates' from *The Three Fates and Other Poems* (1984) to Hale & Iremonger; 'Being Called For' from *Collected Poems* (1991) to Collins/Angus & Robertson Publishers.

Michael Dransfield: 'Epiderm', 'Portrait of the Artist as an Old Man', 'That Which We Call a Rose', 'Visiting Hour (Repatriation Hospital)', 'Day at a Time', 'Endsight', 'The War of the Roses', 'Flying', 'Self-analysis', 'A Strange Bird', 'Memoirs of a Velvet Urinal', 'Minstrel' from *Collected Poems* edited by Rodney Hall (1987) to University of Queensland Press.

Acknowledgements

Laurie Duggan: Hearts (1983) from 'Three Found Poems' from *The Great Divide* (1985) to Hale & Iremonger; I xxxvii, II xlvii, VIII xx, X ii from 'The Epigrams of Martial', *Scripsi* (1989) to the author; 1.1, 5.1 from 'The Ash Range' from *The Ash Range* (1987); South Coast Haiku, Qantas Bags, The Town on the Ten-dollar note from 'Dogs' from *Blue Notes* (1990) to Pan Macmillan.

Lionel Fogarty: 'Remember Something Like This', 'No Grudge' from *Ngutji* (1984) to Cheryl Buchanan.

John Forbes: 'T.V.', 'Four Heads and How to Do Them' from *Tropical Skiing* (1974), Collins/Angus & Robertson Publishers; 'Love Poem' from *Stalin's Holidays* (1980), Transit Poetry to the author; 'The Age of Plastic', 'Monkey's Pride', 'Speed, a pastoral', 'Death, an Ode' from *The Stunned Mullet* (1988) to Hale & Iremonger.

Alan Gould: 'Demolisher', 'The Observed Observer' from *Years Found in Likeness* (1988) to Collins/Angus & Robertson Publishers.

Robert Gray: 'Journey: The North Coast', 'Flames and Dangling Wire', 'The Dusk' from *Selected Poems* (1985) to Collins/Angus & Robertson Publishers.

Philip Hammial: 'Automobiles of the Asylum' from *Chemical Cart* (1977), Island Press; 'Petit Guignol' from *More Bath, Less Water* (1978), Red Press; 'Treason's Choice' from *Swarm* (1979), Island Press; 'Jane' from *Squeeze* (1985), Island Press to the author; 'Sadie' from *The New Australian Poetry* (1979) to Makar Press.

Susan Hampton: 'Yugoslav Story', 'The Crafty Butcher', 'In Andrea's Garden' from *Costumes* (1981), Transit Poetry to the author; 'Women who Speak with Steak Knives' from *Surly Girls* (1989), to Collins/Angus & Robertson Publishers.

Robert Harris: 'The Call', 'The Ambition', 'Literary Excellence', 'Riding over Belmore Park' from *The Cloud Passes Over* (1986) to Collins/Angus & Robertson Publishers.

J S Harry: 'Walking, when the Lake of the Air is Blue with Spring', 'A Shot of War' from *A Dandelion for Van Gogh* (1985), Island Press; 'The Poem Films Itself' from *Hold, for a little while, and turn gently* (1979), Island Press to the author.

Kevin Hart: 'The Last Day' from *Your Shadow* (1984), Collins/Angus & Robertson Publishers; 'The Story' from *Peniel* (1991), Golvan Arts to the author.

William Hart-Smith: 'Nullarbor' from *Selected Poems* (1985) to Collins/Angus & Robertson Publishers.

Gwen Harwood: 'Clair de Lune', 'In the Park', 'Nightfall', 'Carnal Knowledge I', I Barn Owl from 'Father and Child', 'The Sea Anemones', 'Mid-channel', 'Mother Who Gave Me Life' from *Selected Poems* (1990) to Collins/Angus & Robertson Publishers.

Kris Hemensley: 'Sulking in the Seventies', 1,2,47,48 from 'A Mile from Poetry' from *The New Australian Poetry* (1980), Makar Press to the author.

Dorothy Hewett: 'This Version of Love', 'You Gave Me Hyacinths First a Year Ago' from *Rapunzel in Suburbia* (1975), Prism; 'Anniversary', 3 from 'Summer Solstice' from *Greenhouse* (1979), Big Smoke Books to the author.

Philip Hodgins: 'Death Who' from *Blood and Bone* (1986) to Collins/Angus & Robertson Publishers; 'Shooting the Dogs' from *Down the Lake with Half a Chook* (1988), ABC Books to the author.

A D Hope: 'Australia', 'Flower Poem', 'Observation Car', 'The Death of the Bird', 'Imperial Adam', 'The Return of Persephone', 'Fafnir' from *Collected Poems* (1972); 'Under Sedation' from *A Late Picking* (1975); 'Beyond Phigalia' from *Antechinus* (1981) to Collins/Angus & Robertson Publishers; 'Inscription for a War' from *We Took Their Orders and are Dead* (1971), Ure Smith to the author.

John Jenkins and Ken Bolton: 'In Ferrara' from *Airborne Dogs and Other Collaborations* (1988), Brunswick Hills to the authors.

Kate Jennings: 'Just the Two of Us', 'Couples' from *Come to Me My Melancholy Baby* (1979), Outback Press to the author.

Martin Johnston: 'The Sea-Cucumber', 'In Memoriam' from *The Sea-Cucumber* (1978) to University of Queensland Press; 6 The Cafe of Situations, 12 Drinking Sappho Brand Ouzo from 'In Transit: A Sonnet Square' from *The Typewriter Considered as a Bee Trap* (1984) to Hale & Iremonger; 'Gorey at the Biennale' from *Scripsi* to Roseanne Bonney.

Rae Desmond Jones: 'Shakti', 'The Front Window', 'James Dean' from *Shakti* to Makar Press.

Antigone Kefala: 'Sunday Visit' from *Thirsty Weather* (1978), Outback Press to the author; 'Industrial City', 'The Party', 'Freedom Fighter' from *European Notebook* (1988) to Hale & Iremonger.

S K Kelen: 'Rabbit Shoeshine', 'The First Circle', 'The Gods Ash Their Cigarettes' from *Atomic Ballet* (1991) to Hale & Iremonger.

Acknowledgements

John Kinsella: 'Orpheus', 'Chess Piece Cornered', 'Sick Woman' from *Night Parrots* (1989) to Fremantle Arts Centre Press.

Anthony Lawrence: 'Robert Penn Warren's Book' from *Dreaming in Stone* (1989) to Collins/Angus & Robertson Publishers.

Geoffrey Lehmann: I, VI, IX from 'Roses' from *Selected Poems* (1976); 16, 29, 36, 57, 67 from 'Ross's Poems' from *Ross's Poems* (1978) to Collins/Angus & Robertson Publishers.

Kate Lilley: 'You Have to Strive Back', 'The Sewing Lesson' to the author.

James McAuley: 'Envoi', 'Gnostic Prelude', 'The Blue Horses', 'Dialogue', IV The Tomb of Heracles from 'The Hero and the Hydra', 'Late Winter', 'In a Late Hour', 'Pietà', 'Legendary', The Seventh Day from 'The Seven Days of Creation', 'The Cloak', 'Released on Parole', 'One Tuesday in Summer', 'Because', 'Keep the Season', 'Wet Day' from *Collected Poems* (1971); 'World on Sunday', 'Nocturne', 'Winter Drive' from *Music Late at Night* to Collins/Angus & Robertson Publishers.

Roger McDonald: 'The Hollow Thesaurus', 'Incident in Transylvania' from *Airship* (1975) to University of Queensland Press.

Kenneth Mackenzie: 'Heat', 'The Fool', 'The door swung open . . .', 'Searchlights', 'Sick Men Sleeping', 'Ginger-flowers', 'The Children Go', 'Table-birds', New Arrival from 'The Hospital – Retrospections' from *The Poems of Kenneth Mackenzie* (1972) to Collins/Angus & Robertson Publishers.

Rhyll McMaster: 'Clockface', 'Back Steps Lookout' from *Washing the Money* (1986), Collins/Angus & Robertson Publishers to the author.

Jennifer Maiden: 'Climbing', 'Taste' from *The New Australian Poetry* (1980) to the author; 'Language', 'Air', 'New', 'In the Gloaming', 'The Foundations', 'Anorexia', 'The Green Side' from *The Trust* (1988) to Black Lightning Press.

'Ern Malley': 'Dürer: Innsbruck, 1495', 'Sonnets for the Novachord', 'Sweet William', 'Boult to Marina', 'Sybilline', 'Night Piece', 'Documentary Film', 'Night-piece (Alternate Version)', 'Baroque Exterior', 'Perspective Lovesong', 'Culture as Exhibit', 'Egyptian Register', 'Young Prince of Tyre', 'Colloquy with John Keats', 'Coda', 'Petit Testament' from *The Darkening Ecliptic* from *Angry Penguins* magazine (1944) to Max Harris.

David Malouf: 'The Judas Touch', 'Bicycle' from *Selected Poems* (1981) to Collins/Angus & Robertson Publishers; 'For Two Children' from *First Things Last* (1980) to University of Queensland Press.

Billy Marshall-Stoneking: 'Passage', 'Picture Postcard', 'On the Death of Muriel Rukeyser' from *Singing the Snake* (1990) to Collins/Angus & Robertson Publishers.

Philip Mead: 'There' from *This River is in the South* (1984) to University of Queensland Press; 'Melbourne or the Bush', 'Cinema Point' to the author.

Mudrooroo: Song Thirty-four from 'The Song Cycle of Jacky', 'Hide and Seek', 'Peaches and Cream' from *The Song Cycle of Jacky* (1986) to Hyland House.

Les Murray: 1,2,6 from 'The Bulahdelah-Taree Holiday Song Cycle' from *Ethnic Radio* (1977); 'Lament for the Country Soldiers', 'The Broad Bean Sermon', 'The Mitchells', The Flight from Manhattan from 'The Sydney Highrise Variations', 'Equanimity', 'Louvres', 'The Drugs of War' from *Collected Poems* (1991); 'The Tin Wash Dish', 'Dog Fox Field' from *Dog Fox Field* (1990) to Collins/Angus & Robertson Publishers.

Oodgeroo of the tribe Noonuccal, custodian of the land Minjerribah: 'We Are Going', 'No More Boomerang', 'Last of his Tribe', 'Dawn Wail for the Dead' from *My People* (1981) to Jacaranda Wiley Ltd.

Geoff Page: 'Road Show' from *Two Poets* (1971); 'Smalltown Memorials' from *Smalltown Memorials* (1975) to University of Queensland Press; 'Late Night Radio', 'The Elegist' from *Clairvoyant in Autumn* (1983); 'Jerry's Plains, 1848' from *Footwork* (1988) to Collins/Angus & Robertson Publishers.

Dorothy Porter: 'Lollies Noir', 'P.M.T.' from *Driving Too Fast* (1989) to University of Queensland Press.

Peter Porter: 'On This Day I Complete My Fortieth Year', 'Sex and the Over Forties', 'Affair of the Heart', 'In the New World Happiness is Allowed', 'The Easiest Room in Hell', 'Talking to You Afterwards', 'What I Have Written I Have Written' from *Collected Poems* (1983); 'And No Help Came' from *The Automatic Oracle* (1987) to Oxford University Press.

Jennifer Rankin: 'Old Circles', 'Forever the Snake', 'Sea-bundle', 'A Man is Following Me . . .', 'Tale', 'Love Affair 36', 'Old Currawong' from *Collected Poems* edited by Judith Rodriguez (1990) to University of Queensland Press.

Nigel Roberts: 'Max Factor Pink', 'The Mona Lisa Tea Towel' from *In Casablanca for the Waters* (1977) to Wild & Woolley; 'The Gulls' Flight', 'A Nigger & Some Poofters' from *Steps for Astaire* (1983) to Hale & Iremonger.

Acknowledgements

Judith Rodriguez: 'The Mahogany Ship', 'In-flight Note', 'Nu-plastik Fanfare Red', 'About this Woman:', 'Nasturtium scanned' from *New and Selected Poems* (1988) to University of Queensland Press.

Peter Rose: 'Terminus', 'Anglo-Saxon Comedy', 'The Wind Debates Asian Immigration' from *The House of Vitriol* (1990) to Pan Macmillan.

Gig Ryan: 'In the Purple Bar', 'Cruising', 'If I Had a Gun' from *The Division of Anger* (1980), Transit Poetry to the author; 'Ode to My Car', 'Orbit' from *Manners of an Astronaut* (1984) to Hale & Iremonger; 'Elegy for 6 So Far' from *The Last Interior* (1986), *Scripsi* to the author.

Philip Salom: 'Walking at Night' from *Sky Poems* (1987) to Fremantle Arts Centre Press; 'Ghazal on Signs of Love and Occupation' from *The Barbecue of the Primitives* (1989) to University of Queensland Press.

John A Scott: 'Changing Room', 'Plato's Dog', 'Helen Paints a Room (1984)', from *Singles* (1989) to University of Queensland Press; 'He Mailed the Letters Himself' from *Translation* (1990) to Pan Macmillan.

Tom Shapcott: 'Shadow of War, 1941', 'The Blue Paisley Shirt', 'Turning Fifty', 'Post Operative', 'The City of Home' from *Selected Poems 1956–1988* (Revised Edition) (1989) to University of Queensland Press.

Alex Skovron: 'Election Eve, with Cat' from *The Rearrangement* (1988), Melbourne University Press to the author.

Peter Skrzynecki: 'Hunting Rabbits' from *Night Swim* (1989) to Hale & Iremonger.

Kenneth Slessor: 'Nuremberg', 'Last Trams', 'Fixed Ideas', 'Out of Time', 'To Myself', 'William Street', 'Sleep', 'The Night-ride', 'South Country', 'Five Bells', 'Beach Burial' from *Selected Poems* (1976); 'The All-night Taxi Stand', 'Up in Mabel's Room', 'Choker's Lane' from *Darlinghurst Nights* (1981) to Collins/Angus & Robertson Publishers.

Randolph Stow: 'The Calenture', 'Landfall', 'The Singing Bones' from *Selected Poems* (1969) to Collins/Angus & Robertson Publishers.

Jennifer Strauss: 'Love Notes' from *Labour Ward* (1988) to Pariah Press.

Bobbi Sykes: 'Cycle', 'One Day' from *Love Poems and Other Revolutionary Actions* (1988) to University of Queensland Press.

Andrew Taylor: 'Developing a Wife', 'Clearing Away', 'Fitzroy', X Goethe and Brentano from 'Travelling to Gleis-Binario' from *Selected Poems 1960–1985* (1988) to University of Queensland Press.

Tim Thorne: 'Whatever Happened to Conway Twitty?', 'High Country', from *The What of Sane* (1971) to the author.

Richard Kelly Tipping: 'Casino', 'Just After Michael's Death, the Game of Pool', 'Poet at Work' from *Nearer by Far* (1986) to University of Queensland Press.

John Tranter: 'The Moment of Waking' from *Parallax* (1970), South Head Press to the author; 23 from 'The Alphabet Murders', 'Enzensberger at "Exiles" ', 'The Un-American Women', 'The Great Artist Reconsiders the Homeric Simile' from *Selected Poems* (1982) to Hale & Iremonger; 'Backyard', 'Debbie & Co', 'Glow-boys', 'Having Completed my Fortieth Year', 'Lufthansa' from *Under Berlin* (1988) to University of Queensland Press.

Dimitris Tsaloumas: 'Note', 'A Progressive Man's Indignation', 'Consolation', 'Old Friend' from *The Book of Epigrams* (1985); 'Return of an Ikon', 'Falcon Drinking', 'Autumn Supper', 'The Grudge' from *Falcon Drinking* (1988) to University of Queensland Press.

Vicki Viidikas: 'Four Poems on a Theme' from *Condition Red* (1973) to University of Queensland Press; 'Future' from *Wrappings* (1974) to Wild & Woolley.

Chris Wallace-Crabbe: 'The Windows', 'The Collective Invention' from *Selected Poems* (1973), Collins/Angus & Robertson Publishers to the author; 'The Mental Traveller's Landfall' from *The Emotions are Not Skilled Workers* (1980) to Collins/Angus & Robertson Publishers; 'Abhorring a Vacuum', 'Nub', Opener from 'The Bits and Pieces' from *The Amorous Cannibal* (1985); IV from 'Sonnets to the Left' from *I'm Deadly Serious* (1988); 'And the World was Calm' from *For Crying Out Loud* (1990) to Oxford University Press.

Ania Walwicz: 'Little Red Riding Hood', 'Daredevil', 'The Tattoo', 'Big Tease', 'The Abattoir' from *Writing* (1982), Rigmarole Books to the author; 'Wonderful' from *Boat* (1989) to Collins/Angus & Robertson Publishers.

Alan Wearne: 'Go on, tell me the season is over' from *The New Australian Poetry* (1980) (2nd edition) to Makar Press; '5 Terri', '8 Elise', '9 The Division of O'Dowd' from *The Nightmarkets* (1986) to Penguin Books Australia Ltd.

Francis Webb: 'A Tip for Saturday', 'The Gunner', 'Port Phillip Night', 'Laid Off', 'Towards the Land of the Composer', 'End of the Picnic', 'A Death at Winson Green', 'Hospital Night', IV Art from 'Around Costessy', 'Clouds', 1,2,3,5,8 from 'Ward Two' from *Cap and Bells* (1991) to Collins/Angus & Robertson Publishers.

473

Acknowledgements

Archie Weller: 'The Story of Frankie . . . My Man' from *The Tin Wash Dish* (1989), ABC Books to the author.

Judith Wright: 'Brothers and Sisters', 'Woman to Man', 'The Child', 'Camphor Laurel', 'Night After Bushfire', 'Eli Eli', 'The Killer', 'Metho Drinker', 'The Old Prison', II Country Dance from 'The Blind Man', 'To a Child', 'The Precipice', 'Gum-trees Stripping', 'At Cooloola', 'Pelicans' from *Collected Poems* (1971); I To My Brothers, V Change from 'For a Pastoral Family', 'River Bend', 'Skins' from *Phantom Dwelling* (1985) to Collins/Angus & Robertson Publishers.

Fay Zwicky: 1 The Stone Dolphin, 2 Jack Frost from 'Three Songs of Love and Hate' from *Kaddish and Other Poems* (1982) to University of Queensland Press.

474

DOROTHY HEWETT
Alice in Wormland
SELECTED POEMS

EDITED BY EDNA LONGLEY

Dorothy Hewett has been called 'one of Australia's most acclaimed and most important poets' and 'Australia's most daring and controversial playwright'. Her novel *Bobbin Up*, and her autobiography, *Wild Card*, are published by Virago. This selection of her poetry is drawn from her collections *Windmill Country* (1968), *Rapunzel in Suburbia* (1975), *Greenhouse* (1979) and *Alice in Wormland* (1987).

'Many women have been forced into silence, or into disguise and evasion, trying to write poems like these...Dorothy Hewett's *Alice in Wormland* reveals her power as an artist...If the sheer range of grief, ecstasy, pain and love seem incredibly dramatic, that is a good thing. Drama, like poetry, gives us the power to transcend ourselves. A poet who is also a dramatist has given us an enchanting book' – GWEN HARWOOD

'Dorothy Hewett is working in the modern Romantic tradition at the full stretch of her talent, and her poetry gives a feeling of vitality and power under the control of a thoroughly absorbed craft' – JOHN TRANTER, *Melbourne Age*

'A devastating collection of poems written by a poet working at fever pitch...This is a book that could only have been written by an adventurous woman in isolation and at odds with her country' – ROBERT ADAMSON, *The Australian*

'Hewett is a major figure in the history of Australian poetry. She is also a major figure in the history of women's poetry, into which she has introduced a new persona – the "adventurous woman"... When Hewett the adventurous woman poet "speaks her truth", she challenges and disturbs both sexes...Hewett's poems are situated at the pulse of life. They transmit to the reader an extraordinary electric charge' – EDNA LONGLEY

'Passionate, eloquent, and above all, wise' – JOHN PILGER

ISBN 1 85224 125 X   96 pages   £6.95 paperback

AUSTRALIAN POETRY FROM BLOODAXE BOOKS

ALAN WEARNE
Out Here

FOREWORD BY MICHAEL HEYWARD

It was like this. Brett Viney, 17, knifed himself in the school toilets. A botched act, never really suicide.

His teacher speaks first: how Brett stagged into her room, clutching his stomach.

Then there's the family. His grandfather, sounding off about the parents, their *rows*. And Lorraine, the commie aunt. Oh, and Cheryl Browne of course, his father's mistress. Tracey too (the so-called girlfriend), and *her* father, all have their say.

So does Brett.

That's how it was. It happened *out here*, in Melbourne, Australia. In *this* house, *this* room. We hear them talking. It's hot. Passions and tempers flare. Frustrations too. *Out here*, eavesdropping on the break-up of the Viney family.

Ordinary people. Ordinary lives. Extraordinary poetry.

'There is nothing in Australian poetry which might be said to have anticipated *Out Here*, no poem so comprehensively focussed on our domesticity...Strange as it may seem, Alan Wearne has given Australians an authentic (if jazzily refracted) image of the way they speak; and it is Wearne's refusal to narrowly stylise speech, his uncanny ability to dramatise the words we throw away every day, which has ultimately given *him* the freedom to create what Chris Wallace-Crabbe has justly called the most original style in Aust-ralian poetry' – MICHAEL HEYWARD

'Like *Eastenders* down under...with the application of more skilfully contrived emotion and writing' – MARTIN BOOTH, *Tribune*

'In the tradition of Pound, Williams, Zukofsky, Olson and the yellow pages of the telephone directory' – CLIVE JAMES, *TLS*

ISBN 0 906427 72 X   64 pages   £4.95 paperback